BRITAIN'S ENCOUNTER WITH REVOLUTIONARY CHINA, 1949–54

Britain's Encounter with Revolutionary China, 1949–54

James Tuck-Hong Tang

Lecturer in International Relations
University of Hong Kong

M
St. Martin's Press

First published in Great Britain 1992 by
THE MACMILLAN PRESS LTD
Houndmills, Basingstoke, Hampshire RG21 2XS
and London
Companies and representatives
throughout the world

A catalogue record for this book is available
from the British Library.

ISBN 0–333–54896–5

Printed in Great Britain by
Antony Rowe Ltd
Chippenham, Wiltshire

First published in the United States of America 1992 by
Scholarly and Reference Division,
ST. MARTIN'S PRESS, INC.,
175 Fifth Avenue,
New York, N.Y. 10010

ISBN 0–312–07591–X

Library of Congress Cataloging-in-Publication Data
Tang, Tuck-Hong, 1957–
Britain's encounter with revolutionary China, 1949–54 / James Tuck-
Hong Tang
p.   cm.
Includes bibliographical references (p.   ) and index.
ISBN 0–312–07591–X
1. Great Britain—Foreign relations—China. 2. China—Foreign
relations—Great Britain. 3. Great Britain—Foreign
relations—1945– 4. China—Foreign relations—1949–1976.
I. Title.
DA47.9.C6T36 1992
327.41051—dc20   92–9434
                                                    CIP

Contents

Preface   vii

Note on the Romanization of Chinese Names   xi

List of Abbreviations   xiii

INTRODUCTION   1

PART I   POLICY FORMULATION   5

1   **Actors and Stage**   7
    The Setting   7
    The British Perspective   8
    The Chinese Perspective   19
    Conclusions   30

2   **The Decision of Recognition**   31
    The Policy of 'Keeping a Foot in the Door'   32
    Domestic Considerations   42
    International Considerations   52
    The Final Decision   65
    Conclusions   66

PART II   POLICY IMPLEMENTATION   69

3   **From Negotiation to Confrontation**   71
    Anglo-Chinese Negotiations   72
    The Korean War   84
    Esler Dening's Secret China Mission   92
    Conclusions   95

4   **From Confrontation to the Establishment
    of Diplomatic Relations**   97
    China's Intervention in Korea   98
    Branding China as an Aggressor   102
    The Korean Armistice   112
    Geneva and Anglo-Chinese Relations   117
    Conclusions   124

PART III POLICY ISSUES   127

5 **Chinese Representation in the United Nations**   **129**
   Britain and Chinese Representation in the UN   130
   Revolutionary China's Attitude towards the UN   143
   Conclusions   146

6 **British Commercial Interests in China**   **148**
   The Conditions of British Business in China   148
   Sino-British Trade   157
   Conclusions   168

7 **British Colonial Interests in Southeast Asia**   **170**
   Malaya and Britain's China Policy   171
   Hong Kong in Anglo-Chinese Relations   184
   Conclusions   190

CONCLUSION   192

Appendixes:
   1 The PRC's first appointments of diplomats abroad   202
   2 China's Major Trade Partners (1950)   203
   3 Value of Britain's Trade with China, 1946–55   203

Notes   204

Bibliography   236

Index   252

Preface

This book is the product of my interest in Britain's decision to accord diplomatic recognition to a communist regime as the Cold War intensified in the post-Second World War world, and an intellectual curiosity in understanding the interactions between a well established state and a newly formed revolutionary state.

When I began my research on this project at the end of 1983, Sino-British relations entered a most difficult period because of their differences over Hong Kong's future, but as I went through the page proofs of this book in 1991, a diplomatic settlement has been reached: Britain is to withdraw from her last major colonial territory in 1997 when China will resume her sovereign right over Hong Kong. Although the problem of how to ensure the proper implementation of their agreement remains difficult and many people in Hong Kong are still apprehensive about an uncertain future, in the longer run, the two countries can look forward to the development of a better relationship without the burden of history.

The Sino-British talks on Hong Kong's future, in many ways, remind me of their earlier negotiations on the establishment of diplomatic relations in the 1950s which this book examines. In that period Britain would like to maintain a foothold in China, but constrained by limited resources and the wider East-West conflict she was in no position to maintain her once predominant position there. Whereas the new Chinese leaders, attempting to establish their credentials as socialist revolutionaries and nationalists, adopted an uncompromising position in denouncing Britain as an imperial and colonial power. Yet, anxious to demonstrate that they were China's new political masters, the revolutionaries also wanted to be recognized properly by the British government according to established international conventions. Policy-makers both in London and Beijing, therefore, very often found themselves facing competing priorities in formulating and implementing their policies.

Since the establishment of the People's Republic of China in 1949 the international situation has undergone great changes. Revolutionary China has become far more friendly to the capitalist West, and Britain has ceased to be an imperial power. Nevertheless, the ambiguities of both the British and Chinese positions were demonstrated again, when the British government attempted to negotiate an honourable retreat from Hong Kong. Britain's acceptance of her diminished world role has reduced Hong

Kong's importance in British eyes, even though London would still like to see the continuation of British commercial presence in the territory. While policy-makers in London were not entirely unhappy to be relieved of their country's last major colonial burden, they have to find a solution to the Hong Kong question which is politically acceptable both domestically and internationally. The Chinese side, however, found it necessary to promise the people of Hong Kong a 'high degree of autonomy with self administration' for 50 more years after China resumes sovereignty in 1997 under the concept of 'one country two systems'. For political leaders in Beijing, the return of Hong Kong will close the final chapter of Western humiliation of China, yet they also recognize that the continuation of the territory's economic success, and in turn the continuation of its contribution to China's economic well-being, depends on maintaining Hong Kong's existing capitalistic economic system.

Like their predecessors in the 1950s, policy-makers in London and Beijing also have to choose among competing priorities and resolve conflicting considerations when the two sides entered into negotiations regarding Hong Kong's future. In a rapidly changing world, foreign policy-makers have to face new and complex problems all the time, but the dilemma of policy-making that the British and Chinese governments confronted in the 1990s is perhaps not much different from what they encountered in the 1950s.

The opportunity and financial support for undertaking this project was provided by a Commonwealth scholarship for post-graduate research at the London School of Economics and Political Science between 1983 and 1986. I completed my work in London with further financial support from LSE and a grant from the Student Union in 1987. The revision and re-writing of this work took place in 1990–91 at the National University of Singapore where I taught for two and a half years. The project was finally completed at the University of Hong Kong.

At the LSE, I am indebted to Michael Leifer, Christopher Hill, and Michael Yahuda. As my co-supervisors, Michael Leifer and Christopher Hill gave me much encouragement and guidance. They commented on both the substance and style of my work. Professor Leifer guided me through the earliest stage of my research. The subject of this study was defined and crystallised under his supervision. When he was away in Singapore during the final stage of my research and writing in London, he continued to comment on my work and provide support and advice to me with regularity and amazing promptness. He has been an inspiring example that intellectual depth and efficiency can indeed be compatible qualities. Professor Hill also provided much encouragement and comments to my work. I am particularly indebted to him for the theoretical aspect of this study. He and other members of the foreign policy analysis workshop, including Kurt Barling, Carla Garapedian and, Stelios Stazridis, were an important source of intellectual stimulation. Michael Yahuda was another source of encouragement. Although he was in London only during the final stage of my study, he gave me useful advice, discussing with me the general theme of the project as well as commenting on some draft chapters of this work.

In the course of my research, I have been assisted by a number of former British officials and individuals who or whose colleagues were involved in the events covered by this study. A list of the names of those I interviewed and/or with whom I have corresponded is in the bibliography. This study is based primarily on written records, but the reminiscences of those who were involved in the events in question have given me a better understanding of the mood of the time. Sir Denis Allen, Sir Colin Crowe, and Ven. Michael Paton have been particularly helpful by giving detailed written replies to my questions.

I also wish to thank: Lady Younger for permission to consult and use the diaries of the late Sir Kenneth Younger. Professor Geoffrey Warner at the Open University for making arrangements for me to use the diaries and to consult a typed transcript of them in his possession. Mrs Jill Oakeshott for allowing me to read and use her late husband Mr Keith Oakeshott's diaries and his correspondence with her. Professor Paul Evans at York University, Toronto, for making available the typescript of a book on Canada's relations with the People's Republic of China, which he co-edited with B. M. Frolic, just before it went to press.

I am also grateful to the staff of various libraries and institutions which I used for the project, particularly: the British Library of Political and Economic Science at LSE, the British Library, the Royal Institute of International Affairs's Library at Chatham House, the University Library of London University, the School of Oriental and African Studies Library, the Public Record Office (Kew), the British Newspaper Library (Colindale), the University Library (Cambridge), the Churchill College Archive (Cambridge), the Rhodes House Library (Oxford), the Union Research Institute Collection (Baptist College, Hong Kong) and the libraries at both the National University of Singapore and the University of Hong Kong.

Many friends and fellow researchers have given me much encouragement and concrete support in my research. In this connection I am particularly grateful to my good friends Dr Susan Hart, Dr Beatrice Heuser, Ms Sheila Kerr, Ms Tam Yee-wa, and Dr Steve Tsang. I am also thankful for the congenial atmosphere provided by colleagues at the

National University of Singapore and the University of Hong Kong as I revised my work. The revision of this study was greatly facilitated by Ms Susan Trubshaw in London, who typed an earlier version of my work into a format compatible with the computer software that I am using within a very short time. Her assistance and support, provided out of friendship, is very much appreciated. I would also like to thank Ms Carman Tsang for assisting me in preparing the index.

Without the understanding and financial sacrifices of my mother, Lin Pao-hua, I would not have been able to pursue my post-graduate work in the U.K. Lastly, but by no means the least, I would like to express my deep gratitude to my wife, Helen, who painstakingly went through my revisions, helped proofread this book and made many useful editorial suggestions. Her love and care has made my task of completing the project far less difficult than it would have been. Needless to say, all the errors and faults in this book remain my responsibility.

J.T.H.T.

Note on the Romanization of Chinese Names

This book uses the *han yu pin yin* system which has become the standard way of romanizing Chinese names. The only exceptions are the names of the Nationalist Party and its former leaders – Kuomintang, Sun Yat-sen, and Chiang Kai-shek. Throughout the text and notes, when source materials are directly quoted or cited, the names also appear as in the source material.

The following is a list of the *pin yin* Chinese names used in this book; the Wade Giles spellings or names more popularly known in the West are given in a parenthesis:

Names of People

Chen Jiakang (Chen Chia-K'ang)
Chen Yun (Chen Yun)
Dong Biwu (Tung Pi-wu)
Gao Gang (Kao Kang)
Huan Xiang (Huan Hsiang)
Kang Sheng (Kang Shang)
Kang Youwei (Kang Yu-wei)
Lei Renmin (Lei Jen-min)
Li Kenong (Li K'e-nung)
Liang Qichao (Liang Chi-ch'ao)
Liao Chengzhi (Liao Ch'eng-chih)
Liu Shaoqi (Liu Shao-ch'i)
Mao Zedong (Mao Tse-tung)
Nie Rongzhen (Neih Jung-chen)
Peng Dehuai (Peng Te-huai)
Peng Zhen (Peng Chen)
Qiao Guanhua/Qiao Mu (Chiao K'uan-hua/Chiao Mu)
Ren Bishi (Jen Pi-shih)
Shi Chi'ang (Shih Ch'ih-ang)
Wang Renshu (Wang Jen-shu)
Wang Jiaxiang (Wang Chia-hsiang)
Wu Xiuquan (Wu Hsiu-ch'uan)

Yao Chongming (Yao Ch'ung-ming)
Ye Jichuang (Yeh Chi-chuang)
Zhang Hanfu (Chang Han-fu)
Zhou Enlai (Chou En-lai)
Zhou Gengsheng (Chou Keng-sheng)
Zhu De (Chu Te)

Place Names

Beijing (Peking)
Chongqing (Chungking)
Guangzhou (Canton)
Guilin (Kwelin)
Kunming (Kunming)
Langzhou (Lanchow)
Nanjing (Nanking)
Shanghai (Shanghai)
Shantou (Swatow)
Shenyang (Mukden)
Taiwan (Taiwan/Formosa)
Tianjin (Tientsin)
Urumuqi (Tihwa)
Xi'an (Sian)
Xiamen (Amoy)
Xinjiang (Sinkiang)
Yan'an (Yenan)

List of Abbreviations

BT	Board of Trade
CA	China Association
CAB	Cabinet
CATC	Central Air Transport Corporation
CCP	Chinese Communist Party
CDER	*Collection of Documents on the External Relations of the People's Republic of China*
CNAC	China National Aviation Corporation
CNIEC	China National Import and Export Corporation
CO	Colonial Office
COS	Chief of Staff
CP	Cabinet Paper
CM	Cabinet Meetings
CRO	Commonwealth Relations Office
ECAFE	Economic Commission for Asia and the Far East
ECOSOC	Economic and Social Council
FAO	Food and Agriculture Organization
FO	Foreign Office
FRUS	*Foreign Relations of the United States*
HC deb	*House of Commons debates*
JIC	Joint Intelligence Committee
MCP	Malayan Communist Party
MoD	Ministry of Defence
NCNA	New China News Agency (Xinhua)
UNESCO	United Nations Educational, Scientific and Cultural Organization
UNICEF	United Nations Children Fund

Introduction

On a bright cold Thursday morning in London, 15 December 1949, the 54th birthday of King George VI, His Majesty's Government decided to accord diplomatic recognition to the Central Government of the People's Republic of China (PRC), a newly established communist revolutionary regime which had publicly denounced the West. Unfortunately, King George VI did not live to see the formal establishment of diplomatic relations between Britain and revolutionary China, which took place after four years of protracted negotiations. The remarkable decision by the British government to recognize the new Chinese government at a time when the Cold War was intensifying, and the tortuous process leading to the establishment of formal relations between the two countries in 1954, marked an important stage in Anglo-Chinese relations. Their interactions during this period also revealed much about post-war British foreign policy and the international behaviour of the People's Republic in its early years as a revolutionary state.

The end of the Second World War brought great changes both in Britain and China. In Britain the new Labour government which came to power after the war had the unenviable and daunting task of re-constructing the war-torn economy. It was a period of great difficulty for the new leadership: they not only had to face a domestic economic crisis and the crumbling of an empire, but also a new international political order in the form of the Cold War. When the communists won the civil war in China in 1949, policy-makers in London were caught between two competing priorities: maintaining an independent China policy of keeping the door open for better relations, or following the lead of their closest ally, the United States, which was adopting a hostile stance towards the birth of a Communist China.

The problems that China's new political masters had to confront in 1949 were no less daunting than those of their counterparts in Britain. After twelve years of continuing warfare the Chinese economy was in a devastated state. The new leadership had no direct experience in government when they took over. The country was still not entirely under communist control. The Chinese revolutionaries had to consolidate their power and authority, reconstruct the economy, and implement major political, social and economic reform programmes. Furthermore, given the Cold War climate at that time and the division between East and West, the People's Republic as a newly established communist state which had openly declared its allegiance to the Soviet bloc faced a hostile international environment. As revolutionaries, China's new rulers also had to consider carefully whether they should observe the existing rules of international relations.

This study examines Britain's policy towards the newly established revolutionary regime in China between 1949 and 1954, and the new Chinese revolutionary leaders' response to that policy. It focuses on British policy-makers' decision to accord diplomatic recognition to the People's Republic and the lengthy process until official relations eventually established. The purpose of this work is to: first, survey Britain's relations with the newly established revolutionary regime in China; second, examine and explain the formulation and implementation of Britain's China policy in the late 1940s and early 1950s; and third, explore revolutionary China's attitude towards the existing rules and institutions in international relations.

Making full use of internal British documents now available, including official account of Cabinet discussions, records of the Foreign Office and other government departments, supplemented by first-hand accounts of those who were directly involved, this study attempts to provide an in-depth and detailed analysis of the bilateral problems in Anglo-Chinese relation. Until Chinese archives are opened for outside researchers, a parallel study of policy making in China is much more difficult. But through the use of British records and recently available Chinese materials, revolutionary China's response to Britain's recognition can now be explained.

Approach and Structure

The level of analysis in this study is two-fold. First and foremost, the focal point is at the state level; the study analyses the foreign policy of a state in a specific period – Britain's China policy between 1949 and 1954. At a systemic level it attempts to assess the interaction between a well-established member of international society, Britain, and a newly-established revolutionary state, the People's Republic of China.

A decision-making approach will be applied to analyse Britain's policy towards revolutionary China. As Margot Light and Christopher Hill suggested, 'a central part of foreign policy analysis is the study of decision-making'.[1] Shlaim, Jones, and Sainsbury have also argued: 'The great advantage of this approach is that it provides the investigator with some leverage for analysis of the generally elusive process of state behaviour'.[2] The number of different conceptual schemes and models in decision-making is quite considerable. Theoretical ideas such as perception and misperception, psychological analysis, organizational process, bureaucratic politics, and the concept of incrementalism are just some examples.[3]

This study is not an attempt to construct a new model or to provide a case study for testing conceptual schemes. What it intends to do is to apply a decision-making framework in studying Britain's policy towards a newly established revolutionary regime in China from the vantage point of the policy-makers. More specifically, the major factors which will be taken into account are: the personal characteristics of policy-makers; and the domestic and international environment in which policies are made and implemented such as – the decision-making structures and processes, the nature of the regimes, the domestic political and economic situations, international developments, and the particular circumstances at that time. By covering Britain's China policy over a period of six years – between the late 1940s to the mid-1950s, this study also attempts to examine the inter-relations of policy formulation and implementation in the decision-making process.[4]

Using such a framework, this book is divided into three parts. Part I examines the political elites and the policy-making machinery involved in making the decision of recognizing the new government in Beijing, and discuss the domestic and international factors leading the decision of recognition. Part II looks at the policy formulation process and the manners with which British policy-makers attempted to implement their China policy and the difficulties they encountered especially after the outbreak of the Korean War. Finally, to supplement the discussions of the policy formulation and implementation processes, Part III examines in greater depth three specific issues in Anglo-Chinese relations – Chinese representation in the United Nations; British commercial interests in China; and Britain's colonial possessions in Southeast Asia.

At a systemic level, the theme of whether the People's Republic in its formative years was revolutionary in the conduct of its foreign policy is examined. Peter Calvert has suggested that: 'One of the characteristics of revolutionary "style" is frequently the rejection of traditional diplomatic methods and techniques'.[5] This observation is well supported by the experience of the French and Bolshevik Revolutions. The French Foreign Minister Dumouriez at the outbreak of the Revolutionary War in 1792, and Leon Trotsky, the first People's Commissar of the Soviet Republic both declared their contempt for diplomacy.[6]

During the 1960s and early 1970s many studies of the foreign policy of the People's Republic of China had indeed portrayed it as aggressive and belligerent.[7] Revolutionary China's response to Britain's approach for full diplomatic relations only a few months after the inauguration of the new regime provides a fascinating case study of the foreign policy and diplomacy of a revolutionary state during its formative years. In the eyes of many Chinese revolutionaries Britain was a symbol of imperialism and economic exploitation of their nation. Establishing diplomatic relations with Britain would mean not only accepting China's former exploiter, but also the established rules in international relations which had been dominated by Western colonial powers.

In his seminal work, *The Anarchical Society*, Hedley Bull distinguishes between international system and international society in the following terms: (1) An international system 'is formed when two or more states have sufficient contact between them, and have sufficient impact on one another's decisions, to cause them to behave – at least in some measure – as part of a whole'; and (2) An international society 'exists when a group of states, conscious of certain common interests and common values, form a society in the sense that they conceive themselves to be bound by a common set of rules in their relations with one another, and share in the working of common institutions'.[8]

Did the People's Republic make any attempt to join the existing society of states when it was established? Or was revolutionary China merely a member of the international system, with no intention of being bound by the accepted rules of international relations? In this study the international conduct of China's as a revolutionary regime will be assessed through its interactions with Britain in the early 1950s.

Although this book is largely an account of Britain's policy towards the newly established People's Republic of China and the interactions between the two countries in the early 1950s, it is also a bridge-building attempt linking a decision-making framework to a historical study based primarily on archival materials. In addition to covering a crucial episode in Anglo-Chinese relations, hopefully, this work can prove to be useful not only for those who are interested in post-war British foreign policy, but also for specialists in foreign policy analysis and those who are interested in the international dimension of revolutions.

Part I
Policy Formulation

1 Actors and Stage

THE SETTING

'China's foreign relations are largely Anglo-Chinese', remarked a senior Chinese diplomat in 1936.[1] Indeed until the outbreak of the Sino-Japanese War in 1937 Britain was the predominant Western power in China. Anglo-Chinese relations began with the expansion of British commercial interests in Asia. The opening up of China to international mercantile interests following the Opium War by Britain was generally regarded as the beginning of Western domination in China and a starting point in modern Sino-Western relations. As historian Peter Lowe pointed out: 'Britain took the lead in compelling China to open up her leading ports to trade and in erecting the system of extra-territoriality as it functioned until eventually swept by Japanese imperialism'.[2]

Prior to the Japanese invasion Britain had played a dominating role in almost all sectors of the Chinese economy: British investment in China in 1937 was more than one-third of all foreign investment, and more than four times as large as that of any other country, except Japan. Its influence and economic involvement in China were so extensive that some scholars consider it as part of the British 'informal empire'.[3] This privileged status and domination of China's economy was a source of resentment and a symbol of Western domination in the eyes of many Chinese. When the Second World War broke out Britain's leading position in China was brought to an abrupt end. In D. C. Watt's words, 'Britain ended World War II in a state of virtual bankruptcy and with the status and commitments of a superpower'; the 'informal empire' in China could no longer be maintained.[4]

Although British interests in China were considerable, post-war policy makers in London had no intention of asserting their country's former predominance in China, or of intervening in the Communist-Kuomintang rivalry. Preoccupied with post-war domestic economic difficulties, and a fear of Soviet expansionist intention in Europe, British policy-makers paid little attention to China and they observed neutrality in the Chinese civil war. However, the continuation of this stance was clearly impractical when a communist victory in China became apparent. As the Cold War intensified, the 'communisation' of China became a collateral threat. Events in the Far East could no longer be isolated from international politics; Britain's attitude of detachment became unsustainable. British policy-makers were thus forced to turn their attention to developments in China and re-examine their policy there in late 1948.

As for the Chinese Communist leaders, for years their efforts and energy had been directed to the struggle with Chiang Kai-shek's government. They had given very little thought to their relations with the West. However, within only a few years after the Sino-Japanese War, the Kuomintang forces were on the verge of defeat, and the Communists had to assume responsibility for government. As the revolutionaries made preparations for the inauguration of the People's Republic, they also had to formulate the new regime's policy towards the West. Their view towards the British government, however, remained tinted by Britain's past involvement in China. Although Britain ceased to play a central role in shaping developments in the Middle Kingdom, it remained as a symbol of Western imperialism and domination.

The rationale behind the British policy-makers' decision to recognize the new government in Beijing, and the Chinese revolutionaries' response cannot be fully appreciated without an understanding of their perceptions and personal backgrounds. This chapter will examine the personalities and views of those British and Chinese policy-makers who were responsible for formulating the two countries' foreign policies as well as their advisers's role, and the policy-making machineries involved. In addition, it will provide an account of the domestic situations in both Britain and China, and the international environment on the eve of the Communist victory in China.

THE BRITISH PERSPECTIVE

British Foreign Policy-Makers

The Labour leaders elected to power in 1945 were not unprepared or entirely inexperienced in policy-making. They had been directly involved in the coalition government during war-time. In fact there was a remarkable continuity in Britain's foreign policy-makers between 1941 to 1951: there were only two Foreign Secretaries, Anthony Eden and Ernest Bevin, and three Permanent Under-Secretaries, Alexander Cadogan, Orme Sargent and William Strang. There was also one common thread which ran through the minds of the new Labour government led by people who had shared the experience of the hardships of war and fully understood its social, economic and human costs.

The wartime experience of British policy-makers had inspired, however, two different approaches to foreign and defence policies. Post-war strategic planning had proceeded on the assumption that the Soviet Union would be the next enemy. But Clement Attlee, the new Prime Minister in 1945, urged that British interests would be safeguarded best by participating fully in a world organization and not by confronting the Soviet Union as a rival power. After becoming Prime Minister he presented his colleagues with the suggestion that, 'the British Empire can only be defended by its membership of the United Nations Organization'. Later when the Chiefs of Staff recommended that Britain's sea and air communications through the Mediterranean and the Red Sea should be protected against any potential enemy, Attlee put forward an alternative suggestion that the security of the Middles East should rest on the power of the UN. He maintained that Britain's defence should not be based on a strategy rooted in the past. This approach was fiercely opposed by the defence establishment and Foreign Office. They recommended a world-wide offensive against Soviet expansionism. Attlee only backed down after the Foreign Secretary had raised strong opposition to the approach and the Chiefs of Staff threatened to resign.[5]

British policy-makers' belief that the Soviet Union posed the greatest security threat remained a critically important element in Britain's foreign policy after the war. At that time the most urgent task Labour leaders faced was the country's deepening economic and financial problems. They were therefore preoccupied with domestic economic re-construction and with forging a close alliance with the United States to secure financial assistance and to counter Soviet expansionism.

The Labour leaders' participation in the coalition government provided them with useful experience in foreign policy-making. Clement Attlee had a solid background in foreign and defence affairs: he had attended international conferences and allied summit meetings with the wartime leader Winston Churchill, served as Under-Secretary of War in 1924, and as a member of the Simon Commission on India in 1927. As leader of the Parliamentary Labour party throughout the 1930s, issues of foreign and defence affairs had also taken up much of his time.[6]

Foreign Secretary Ernest Bevin had been responsible for the Ministry of Labour in the wartime coalition government, and had experience in international trade union activities. Bevin could not claim an extensive background in foreign affairs, but as his private secretary at the Foreign Office later suggested, his membership in Churchill's Inner War Cabinet 'had given him experience of the problems of handling international affairs at the highest level in most critical times'.[7] Moreover the Ministry

of Labour, as Bevin himself acknowledged, had 'the biggest say, next
to the Foreign Office, in the Peace Treaties and the new economic
arrangements that have got to be made'.[8] He became Foreign Secretary
when economic problems dominated the minds of British political leaders
and economic considerations had become extremely important in Britain's
foreign policy.

At the age of 64 Bevin, a strong domineering personality, was one of
the most influential figures in the Labour movement. After Bevin was
appointed Foreign Secretary, the Permanent Under-Secretary, Alexander
Cadogan, wrote in his diary that, 'He's the heavyweight of the Cabinet
and will get his own way with them, so if he can be put on the right
line, that may be all right'.[9] But Bevin was his own master and there was
no doubt about his dominance in the Foreign Office. His position in the
Labour movement and in the Cabinet also ensured that the Foreign Office
would play a leading role at the centre of policy-making. Moreover he had
a close personal as well as working relationship with the Prime Minister.
In Attlee's words Bevin's relationship with him was 'the deepest of my
political life'. He recalled: 'I was very fond of him and I understand that
he was very fond of me'. Bevin was also a hard-working Foreign Secretary
able to master Foreign Office papers, and that gave him a stronger voice in
the Cabinet. Another important feature of Bevin's foreign policy was his
bi-partisan approach and the fact that he kept in close touch with Anthony
Eden, his predecessor in the Foreign Office. Indeed his relationship with
Eden was sneered by some left-wing Labour backbenchers. The jibe against
him at that time was: 'hasn't Anthony Eden got fat'.[10]

The Foreign Office and Britain's China Policy

During the immediate post-war years, as British political leaders were
preoccupied with more urgent international and domestic problems, the
Attlee Cabinet did not pay too much attention to the Far East. The
formulation of Britain's China policy was largely left in the hands of
senior Foreign Office officials.

Under Bevin, the Foreign Office had an effective and strong voice in the
Cabinet in 1948 when the rapid advance of Chinese communism began to
cause concern in London. The Permanent Under Secretary at that time, Sir
William Strang, was 'greatly respected and liked' by Bevin. As Strang
was a European specialist he relied upon senior Far Eastern officials for
expert advice. His colleague, Colin Crowe, who served in the Far Eastern
Department at that time, recalled that even though Strang did not know
much about the Far East, he was 'wise and moderate and could learn'.[11]

Of the many senior officials who were responsible for Far Eastern and China affairs, Esler Dening has been regarded as particularly influential, especially in formulating Britain's initial policy towards the Communist government in China. As Assistant Under-Secretary in charge of the Far Eastern Department in the Foreign Office, Dening was respected as an expert in Far Eastern affairs. He began his diplomatic career in the Japanese Consular Service and was Lord Mountbatten's political adviser in the South East Asia Command. Physically Dening 'was a vast rock of a man', and his opinion was usually highly regarded. His colleagues recalled that he was a man who valued Eastern culture and enjoyed a very good working relationship with Bevin.[12]

In his analysis of the new Chinese government's foreign policies, Dening had displayed an ability to see things from the other side's perspective, not marred by Cold War rhetoric. He recognized that the People's Republic was a communist state, but he also believed that as a newly established regime, it was anxious to consolidate its rule and willing to establish working relationship with other countries. In a letter to William Strang during an official Far Eastern tour, after Dening's spell as Under-Secretary was over, he wrote, 'there is reason to suppose that the first aim of the Central People's Government was internal consolidation and reconstruction'. Dening's perception of Beijing's priority and his realization of the limitation of Britain's resources were important factors influencing his thinking on the China question. For Dening, the best policy was to establish a working relationship with the new regime and create a split within the communist bloc.[13]

The two Assistant Secretaries who succeeded Dening, Robert Scott and Denis Allen, were also influential figures. But Beijing's policies after 1949 and the outbreak of the Korean War in 1950 had drawn greater ministerial attention to developments in China and the Far East by the time when Scott and Allen took charge. Nevertheless, as Far Eastern affairs experts, their advice continued to be important. Like Dening, Scott enjoyed a good working relationship with Bevin and was 'always warmly greeted' by the Foreign Secretary. Minister of State, Kenneth Younger, who took over the Foreign Office when Bevin was ill in early 1951 had a high regard for Scott and his team. After a trip to San Francisco to sign the Japanese Peace Treaty, he wrote in his diary about his advisers on Far Eastern affairs: 'It was a very strong team. I wish I had as much confidence in other sections of the Office as I have in this bunch who deal with the Far East. I find them as convincing as I find the Middle Eastern people unconvincing'.[14]

Before the war Scott had set up a branch of the Ministry of Information in Singapore. He was captured by the Japanese after the fall of Singapore, and had a traumatic experience as a prisoner of war when he was put in solitary confinement and tortured. After the war, Scott became a principal prosecution witness in the war crimes trials held in Singapore. According to his obituary, 'his testimony was given without rancour and with such fairness that all were astonished, not least the accused'.[15]

Scott, who had been Dening's subordinate as head of the Southeast Asian Department, shared many of his predecessor's views about China. When he took over as under-secretary, Dening, who was away on a Far Eastern tour, had written to the Foreign Office about China. Commenting on Dening's views, Scott noted that, 'from my conversations with Sir E. Dening since his return it is clear that he and we see Chinese policy in much the same light, though the wording may differ when it comes to definition on paper'.[16] Scott's thinking was thus largely along the same lines as his predecessor, but China's recalcitrant response to Britain's recognition and the changes in international situations, particularly in Korea when he took charge of Far Eastern affairs, meant that he had to face a very different set of problems.

Denis Allen became responsible for Far Eastern Affairs after Anthony Eden had resumed as Foreign Secretary following the Conservative Party's return to power in 1951. Eden later praised Allen for having 'a perfect command of his facts on all occasions' and being 'immensely resourceful'. Eden also described Allen as one of the Foreign Office officials who was to play a leading part in the conduct of Britain's diplomacy.[17] Allen's working relationship with Eden was also good. He later wrote, 'during my time concerned with Far Eastern affairs from 1953 onwards I found Eden, though much preoccupied, receptive to official advice and I cannot recall any major differences on China policy'. Allen himself has maintained that the Labour government's decision to recognize the People's Republic was the right one.[18]

Another official whose presence in the Foreign Office may arouse interest was Guy Burgess; the spy who defected to the Soviet Union in 1951. Even though Burgess might have been able to pass on important secret information to the Soviet Union, as a desk officer not highly regarded by many in the Office, he did not appear to have played any direct role in the formulation of Britain's China policy. His colleagues at the Foreign Office at that time believed that he would not have had any significant influence on senior officials like Dening.[19]

Other officials outside of the Foreign Office who played important roles in the formulation of Britain's foreign policies in the post-war years included the Chiefs of Staff and their military advisers and planners; officials in the Colonial Office, the Treasury and the Board of Trade. But until the outbreak of the Korean War, the attention of the Chiefs of Staff and military planners was mainly in Europe, the Middle East and British dependent territories in Southeast Asia. The Treasury and its Overseas Financial Division was a very important group but their efforts were concentrated on Britain's financial problems and their interest in China was minimal. Board of Trade officials were eager to promote British exports but since China was not a hard currency earning area, they had actually considered discouraging too much British exports to that country. Only Colonial Office officials had displayed a strong interest in China, for developments there would have serious repercussions in British colonial territories in Southeast Asia where a communist insurgency was causing great trouble for the local authorities.

Foreign Office officials were able to exercise a strong influence in inter-departmental consultations as the Department responsible for foreign policies and because of their expertise. In fact through the inter-departmental Far Eastern (Official) Committee, which Dening chaired up to 1950, the Foreign Office had a strong voice in Whitehall. The Committee, which was set up in 1947 'for the purpose of formulating policies designed to accomplish the fulfillment by Japan of the terms of surrender', devoted increasing attention to China towards the end of 1948. The terms of reference of the Committee was later revised and it became responsible for reviewing the government's general policy towards the Far East and Southeast Asia. The committee was also responsible for making policy recommendations, but it was an inter-departmental consultative organ rather than a direct policy-formulating organ.[20]

British policy-makers' increasing concern about the rise of Chinese communism resulted in the setting up of a special ministerial committee on China and Southeast Asian affairs in March 1949. The China and Southeast Asia Committee, formed by senior members of the Cabinet, was chaired by the Prime Minister himself. The formation of such a high-powered Committee no doubt indicated that British political leaders had recognized the importance of the Far East by early 1949, but the Committee itself did not supplant the Foreign Office's crucial role in the formulation of Britain's China policy.[21]

Britain's Post-War Conditions

Britain's stance towards Chinese communism cannot be properly under-stood without taking into account the Labour leaders' overall foreign policy objectives and the domestic and international problems that they faced after the end of the war.

After the war had ended Britain faced two grave economic problems. First it had incurred a deficit in its external balance of payments which would take at least three to five years to overcome. Second, Britain's national debts and other overseas liabilities had accumulated to over three thousand million pounds by the end of June 1945. A government survey of Britain's economic position after the war reported that Britain's exports had shrunk to only one-third of their pre-war level; more than half of the pre-war tonnage of British merchant shipping had been lost during the war. Net income from overseas investments had also been reduced to less than half of that in 1938. At the same time the country's reserves had fallen to a level which had become inadequate for British economic needs. The government estimated that the country would require a 75 per cent increase in exports to cover its import needs, repay war and post-war debts, and culminate working capital for post-war economic development.[22]

Britain's post-war economic problems were greatly aggravated when the US ceased the Lend-Lease operation almost immediately after the surrender of Japan. Attlee later recalled: 'Our whole economy had been geared up to the war effort. We had allowed our export trade to decline. We were closely integrated with the United States economy through the operation of Lend-Lease and this had meant that we had not had to worry about our supplies of food and raw materials nor for our overseas payments. Now in a moment, all this was brought to an end'.[23] Washington later agreed to provide financial assistance to Britain, but successive economic crises throughout the late 1940s, continued to trouble British policy-makers. The fuel crisis of 1947, and the devaluation of sterling in 1949 were to create immense problems for the government. Externally there was serious disagreement over the settlement of the German question with the Soviet Union, and in mid-summer 1948 there was the Berlin blockade. With these internal and external problems, British policy-makers turned to their wartime ally, the United States, for assistance. American support came to be essential for Britain's economic and security needs; the Anglo-American alliance became the corner-stone of Britain's post-war foreign policy.

The greatest threat to security, as British policy-makers saw it, came from the Soviet Union. In a Cabinet paper on foreign policy in January 1948, Foreign Secretary Ernest Bevin suggested that the Soviet Union and its communist allies were threatening 'the whole fabric of western civilization'. A few months later in March Bevin again warned his colleagues that the Soviet Union was 'actively preparing to extend its hold over the remaining part of continental Europe, and subsequently, over the Middle East and no doubt the bulk of the Far East as well'. Apparently the Foreign Secretary was convinced of the Soviet expansionist desire. The paper he presented to the Cabinet further said, 'physical control of the Eurasian land mass and eventual control of the whole World Island is what the Politburo is aiming at – no less a thing than that'.[24]

In order to counter the security threat posed by the Soviet Union, and to fulfil Britain's aspiration to remain a world power, Bevin felt that the first aim of British foreign policy was to create a union with Western Europe backed by the United States and the Dominions. His view was: 'provided we can organize a Western Europe system . . . , backed by the power and resources of the Commonwealth and of the Americas, it should be possible to develop our own power and influence to equal that of the United States of America, and the USSR'.[25] This summed up Britain's post-war foreign policy objectives: in order to maintain domestic efforts for economic reconstruction, to counter the Soviet threat and to protect British interests world-wide, great importance was attached to an Anglo-American alliance, to a common front among Commonwealth nations, and to a Western European commitment.

Britain's Post-war China Policy

In the context of Britain's post-war problems and foreign policy objectives, China was not an area of top priority. In early 1945, the Foreign Office's Far Eastern department presented the case for reviving Britain's former position in China. In a draft memorandum, head of the department, J. C. Sterndale-Bennett, suggested that China was a major British interest and the government should 'pursue a more active policy designed to re-establish our interest by a display of greater interest in China and of increased assistance to her'.[26] His enthusiasm, however, was not shared by his colleagues.

The Economic Relations department reacted strongly against Bennett's suggestion. Its Acting head, J. E. Coulson, maintained that the British government's ability to do anything in China was very limited. He minuted, 'I feel some anxiety lest, if we make any sort of splash about our endeavours to help China, we may look as if we are assuming a responsibility which we cannot fulfil, and our position may be made worse than it is now'. This view was supported by other senior officials like assistant under-secretaries, Edmund Hall-Patch and Victor Cavendish-Bentinck, who dismissed the argument for reviving British interests in China as a fallacy. 'China is not vital to the maintenance of our Empire and we can do without our China trade', suggested Cavendish-Bentinck, 'so long as we maintain control of seaways, a direct threat from the direction of China is not serious'. Sterndale-Bennett's

memorandum was pronounced dead before it could reach ministerial
level.[27]

Britain's immediate concern in China was mainly commercial; China
was strategically and politically of lesser importance than Europe, the
Middle East and South and Southeast Asia. Post-war policy planners in
London had accepted that, while Britain's influence in the Pacific area had
diminished, the influence of the US in this area had greatly increased. As
Alan Bullock put it, 'Britain made no attempt to resume the role she once
played in the Far East'.[28]

In early 1946, the Foreign Office's Civil Planning Unit's major concern
was the restoration of British property, and securing protection of rights and
interests which China would accord to other foreign countries. The policy
planners believed that Britain's position after the war would be easier to
maintain, because the British government had renounced its privileges in
China, while the US had replaced Britain as the prominent foreign power.
They also did not expect that the Chinese Communists would win the civil
war decisively within a few years; predicting that, 'the country might
be split into American and Russian spheres of influence, with rival and
contrasting forms of Government'.[29]

In his annual report in 1946, the British Ambassador to China, Ralph
Stevenson suggested that Hong Kong was the only major potential source
of political friction between Britain and China. The report stated that
economic issues had provided some bones of contention. Of these issues,
Stevenson said, 'the most important was the return of British properties to
their owners'. Other questions included the opening of the Yangtze ports to
foreign vessels, and the taking over of the various International Settlements.
Nevertheless, Stevenson was able to report that there had been a steady
improvement in Anglo-Chinese relations throughout 1946.[30] Policy planners in London, however, were more cautious. Apart from Hong Kong, they
were also apprehensive about China's influence on Chinese communities
in British colonial territories in Southeast Asia. While concerned with the
situation in the Far East, the British planners concluded that 'the military
and economic strength of the United Kingdom does not permit us to resume
at once all our pre-war power, influence and responsibilities throughout the
Far East'. They accepted that the United States would play the principal
part in East Asia for the time being.[31]

Britain's post-war position and objectives in East Asia were spelt out
comprehensively in a stock-taking memorandum by Esler Dening in
early 1947. Dening, whose influential views were important in shaping
Britain's policy towards China, wrote, 'Britain's chief assets in China
are her physical properties, experience, good-will and the possession of

Hong Kong'. He believed that these assets could not be exploited to the full until Britain had completed its 'industrial re-conversion' and revived its economy for active competition in the China market. Although the US had replaced Britain's dominant role in China, Dening regarded that it had also relieved Britain's of 'the political and economic anxieties' that the leading western power in China had to bear.[32]

But Dening had not given up hope for the revival of British interests in China. The task was, he proposed, to keep 'a commercial foothold in China until better days come'. While the prospects for conducting successful trade with China were gloomy because of the poor economic and financial situation there, he felt that given Britain's experience in trading with China, 'when conditions improve we shall be able to obtain our fair share of China trade'. He therefore advised a policy by which Britain would 'maintain and strengthen our cultural ties'. Dening, however, did express apprehension at possible Soviet involvement in China. He noted, 'the only serious threat to Great Britain in this area would be if the Soviet Union were to replace the United States as the dominant foreign power in China'.[33]

British traders in China had cherished the idea of continuing their business after the war. In late 1946 a commercial mission of representatives from British industries, trade unions, and the Board of Trade led by Sir Leslie Boyce visited China between October and December. As an exploratory trip the mission did not achieve anything concrete.[34] In fact Britain's financial difficulties and internal economic problems made it impossible to promise significant investments in there. When the commercial mission returned, its members prepared a report which included a forecast of trading opportunities in China. Trade officials, however, remained sceptical about the prospects of Anglo-Chinese trade. They also felt that because of balance-of-payment problems Britain could not afford to encourage exports to China until it had improved its hard currency position.[35]

Thus not only had Britain's position and influence declined in China, but British policy-makers were also not prepared to re-assert their country's pre-war position or become embroiled in developments there. Making this clear in the House of Commons on 28 November 1945, Bevin stated that the civil war in China was an 'internal problem for the Chinese themselves to resolve'.[36] As Christopher Thorne pointed out, the Foreign Office had no admiration for Chiang Kai-shek's Kuomintang. Besides, as the British Ambassador to China, Horace Seymour advised, 'pressure from the Western Powers . . . might be resented by the Communists and the Central government alike'.[37]

Events in China, however, were to present a new problem that British policy-makers could not ignore. The crumbling of the Kuomintang regime under Chiang Kai-shek had become apparent by the end of 1948. The establishment of a communist regime would threaten existing British interests in China. Although British policy-makers had no intention of re-asserting Britain's former position in China, they were not prepared to abandon British interests there altogether either.

British Attitudes towards the Rise of Communism in China

In the early and mid-1940s, most Western journalists represented the Chinese Communists based in Yan'an as 'radical agrarian reformers'. British press comments on the nature of Chinese communism in the mid-1940s mainly dwelt on this theme of agrarian reform and democracy. A leader in *The Times* on 25 January 1945 stated that 'The Yenan [Yan'an] system is not Communism; it resembles an agrarian democracy'. On the other hand, press comments on the Kuomintang regime were largely negative. A few years later *The Times* suggested on 6 January 1948 that while the Kuomintang government was 'still under corrupt influences', some of the programmes and performances of the Chinese Communists had won widespread approval in the US and Britain. This view was later echoed other papers such as the *Manchester Guardian*.[38]

This admiration for the Chinese Communists was not confined to journalists. Britain's ambassador to China until 1942, Archibald Clark Kerr told Anthony Eden that 'mild radicalism' in China was called communism. He had also referred to the Communist leader Mao Zedong as one of the 'agrarian reformers' whom he admired. Even after being transferred to Moscow he continued to argue that the Yan'an regime was 'in no sense communist'. Not everyone in the Foreign Office shared this romanticized view of the Chinese Communists. For example, G. F. Hudson of the Research department believed that the Chinese Communists were 'devoted to the interests of the USSR because it is an essential part of their political faith'. He also maintained that, 'the Communists do not any more than the Kuomintang think of "democracy" as a system which gives a chance to opposition parties'. On the whole the Foreign Office adopted a cautious approach in their assessment of the nature of Chinese communism.[39]

The rapid advance of the Chinese Communist forces in late 1948 posed two major problems for Britain. First, British commercial interests in China as well as its colonial interests in Malaya and Hong Kong were being threatened. Second, in the context of the Cold War, the communisation of China would alter the balance of power in Asia in favour of the communist bloc. The likely repercussions of a communist victory in China were thus most disturbing for British policy-makers.

THE CHINESE PERSPECTIVE

China's Foreign Policy-Makers

The Chinese political leaders who established the People's Republic could not have come from a more different background than that of their British counterparts. Born at the turn of the late nineteenth century and the early twentieth century, and growing up in the 1920s when China was dominated by the Western powers, they were deeply influenced by a strong sense of nationalism in their commitment to revolutionary change to 'save China'. The revolutionary Chinese Communist movement was in many ways also a nationalistic movement.[40]

The Chinese Communist Party (CCP) had come into existence in 1921 when China had been in a state of turmoil for more than half a century. As James Harrison observed: 'It is as if the intellectual, political, economic and social changes that took centuries to occur in the West had been compressed into several decades in China'. The Chinese revolutionary movement was to a large extent a reaction to the impact of Western influences and domination in China. Following the humiliating repeated defeats of imperial China at the hands of Western powers, the imperial government was forced to make concession after concession to the foreign powers. It was not until 1942 and 1943 that Britain and the United States finally gave up their treaty rights in China.[41]

Those Chinese intellectuals who turned to Marxism-Leninism and the example of the Bolshevik revolution for a solution to 'save China' were also motivated by social and economic conditions which were to make the Chinese Communist cause a mass movement. In 1933, China had a population of five hundred million of whom more than three-quarters lived in the rural areas. The support of the rural masses was to prove essential for the Communist movement in China. In Lucien Bianco's words, 'the source of the revolution, the real strength of CCP must be sought in the living conditions that prevailed from one end of rural China to the other, where poverty, abuse, and early death were the only prospect for nearly half a billion people'. Frustrated by the pervasive economic and social problems and the continuation of Western domination in China, which the Kuomintang revolution failed to change, the radicals turned to communism. For the Chinese Communists, Marxism-Leninism served the dual purposes of attacking social inequalities and restoring national pride.[42]

The Communist leaders were therefore both fervent nationalists and revolutionaries at the same time.[43] It was a combination of nationalistic sentiment and frustration because the Kuomintang movement had failed to restore China's national pride and reform the country that eventually converted the Communist leader Mao Zedong to Marxism. Describing his conversion to Marxism to the American journalist Edgar Snow, Mao recalled how he was able to recite books by Kang Youwei and Liang Qichao, two of China's early advocates for reform to save China. When Mao was studying in the Zhangsha Normal School between 1912 and 1918, his mind was, 'a curious mixture of ideas of liberalism, democratic reformism, and utopian socialism'. He told Snow, 'I have somewhat vague passions about "19th century democracy", utopianism, and old-fashion liberalism'. But he also said he was 'definitely anti-militarist and anti-imperialist'. And by 1920, Mao proclaimed himself a Marxist.[44] Other Communist leaders also shared similar experiences. Zhou Enlai, who was to become the Communist government's first Foreign Minister, and Prime Minister for the rest of his life, was also an ardent reader of Kang Youwei's books. When he graduated from his Shenyang School he penned these words to one of his friends: 'keep this in mind everywhere: when China soars over the world I would like us to meet again'. Nine years later, writing for the radical journal Youth, he noted that communism was 'a good strategy for thorough reform'.[45]

The Chinese Communists realized that they could not achieve their goals merely through revolutionary and nationalistic ideas. They were a party of pragmatists: revolutionaries of action. Mao had once told his colleagues, 'I feel that many people talk about reform, but it is only an empty ideal. Where do they eventually want to get to with their reforms? What methods will they use to achieve it? At what point will they themselves or their comrades begin work? There is very little careful research of these problems'.[46] The Chinese Communists were able to come to power only after bitter struggles with Chiang Kai-shek's Kuomintang regime. About half of the first generation of Chinese Communists who remained active after 1921 met violent death. Mao's wife and sister and one brother were executed; another brother died in battle in 1935. As James Harrison noted, Mao 'was fortunate to survive'.[47] The Chinese Communists' path to victory had profound effects on their perceptions and conduct of foreign policies. They were not simply revolutionaries, but also dedicated idealists, tough fighters and pragmatists.

Before 1949 none of the Communist leaders had any direct experience in government or had any extensive experience in international affairs. For most of them, a spell in the Soviet Union was the only foreign experience that they had had. When the new government was formed, a majority of the CCP's politburo members had spend some time either as students or as visitors in the Soviet Union. The thirteen members of the politburo elected at the first meeting of the seventh Central Committee on 19 June 1945 were: Mao Zedong, Zhu De, Liu Shaoqi, Zhou Enlai, Ren Bishi, Chen Yun, Kang Sheng, Gao Gang, Peng Zhen, Dong Biwu, Lin Baiqu, Zhang Wentian and Peng Dehuai. All of them remained in power when the communists won the civil war.[48]

Among those thirteen Politburo members only Mao, the two Pengs, Gao and Zhou had not studied in the Soviet Union. Mao in fact had never been abroad prior to his trip to Moscow in December 1949. Gao had developed close relations with the Soviet Union when he was in charge of the Northeastern military region in Manchuria. Dong and Lin had studied in Japan, and Dong visited the US as CCP representative in China's delegation to the San Francisco Conference in 1945. Zhang spent some time in the US, but he also studied in the Sun Yat-sen University in Moscow. Although Zhu received part of his military training in Germany, the only leading member of the Politburo who studied in Western Europe was Zhou.[49] Therefore a majority of the new Chinese political leaders in 1949 had close connections with the Soviet Union, and their experiences abroad had been confined almost entirely to the Soviet Union. But the CCP had not always enjoyed a happy relationship with Moscow. Stalin had supported Mao's rival Wang Ming in the CCP's internal power struggle and recognized Chiang's Kuomintang regime as the legal Chinese government after the end of the Second World War. In fact the CCP under Mao had been largely independent from Soviet control before it came into power.[50]

The Communist leadership's lack of experience in national economic management, public administration and international affairs created many taxing problems for the new government. Liu Shaoqi, for example, admitted in mid-1949 that economic development was a new problem for the Party. He said, 'we are not well prepared for it'. Lamenting on the fact that Communist cadres were not familiar with economic work, he stated, 'to this day they have no accurate data on China's economic situation'.[51]

Although the new leaders faced many difficulties because they did not have a formal background in running of state affairs, they had acquired political experience and administrative skills during their struggle against the Kuomintang regime. Before they came to power they had their own territories, a huge army, and a large number of party cadres had responsible administrative duties. Mao had developed his political skills, and his understanding of China's problems in the power struggle within the party, and through his exercise of leadership in winning the civil war. Zhu was a formidable military commander who had led the Red Army through many difficult times. Chen had established his reputation as the party's leading expert on economic matters. Liu, the party's major theorist and the leading organizer in party work, had considerable administrative experience. Their training in the Soviet Union and involvement with the Comintern were also important international experiences, if somewhat unbalanced.

Mao as the leader of the Party was obviously the most important policy-maker. The other major foreign policy-makers were those Politburo members with direct responsibility for foreign affairs, defence matters and economic policies, Zhou Enlai, Zhu De, and Chen Yun. Liu Shaoqi as a senior member in charge of party organization work and a potential successor to Mao, also had an interest in foreign affairs.

Zhou Enlai was the only leader with good contacts with Western governments. Before Zhou became Prime Minister and Foreign Minister in the new Chinese government, he had developed connections with many Western journalists and government representatives in his term of office as CCP's chief representative in Chongqing during the war against Japan. As Prime Minister as well as Foreign Minister, he was a key figure in the conduct of revolutionary China's foreign policy.

The relationship between Zhou and Mao was probably not as close as that between Bevin and Attlee, but theirs was also a good working relationship. As Zhou's biographer Dick Wilson put it, 'Zhou accepted that the vitality of Chinese Communism would have to come from a rural leader who knew how peasants lived and thought. Mao, for his part needed a diplomat who could represent the movement to the world'. It was therefore not surprising that their relationship has been described as symbiotic. Zhou was a heavy-weight in the party and the new government, respected and admired by many. He did not lead a formal faction within the leadership, but many Chinese students in France who later filled important posts in the party and the new government were influenced by him in Paris. Having taught most of the Communist generals at the Huangpu Military Academy when he was political commissar there, he had many friends in the People's Liberation Army. Many of Zhou's close subordinates during the Chongqing period were later appointed to senior positions when the new Ministry of Foreign Affairs was formed.[52]

The Ministry of Foreign Affairs

Reflecting the revolutionary characteristics of the CCP, the new government's foreign affairs system included agencies for people to people contact or popular diplomacy such as the People's Association for Friendship with Foreign Countries. There were also frequent exchange of personnel between these agencies and the Foreign Ministry. However the ministry, whose structure resembles similar ministries in other countries and was staffed chiefly by professional officials, remained the major government department responsible for revolutionary China's foreign relations.[53]

Before 1949 the CCP devoted most of its time to the internal struggle against the Kuomintang. Its early external relations were mainly relations with the Soviet Union. It was only after the outbreak of the Sino-Japanese war in 1937 when a liaison office was set up to handle the Party's relations with the Kuomintang and the Western powers that the Party began establishing links with the West. The CCP's permanent mission in Chongqing led by Zhou Enlai was responsible for coordinating the Chinese Communist Party's war effort with the Kuomintang. But 'the early time of wartime cooperation soon gave way to an adversary relationship, and this in turn forced the members of the mission to deal with the Kuomintang more in the fashion of a foreign state than of a coalition government'.[54]

In addition to the normal contacts with the Kuomintang, the office also maintained informal contacts with the Soviet Embassy, and British and American diplomats. It became invaluable in training diplomats and foreign affairs specialists for the new government. Many of Zhou's subordinates in Chongqing, including Wang Bingnan, Chen Jiakang and Zhang Hanfu, later became important figures in the new Foreign Ministry. Wang was appointed director of the general office in the new Foreign Ministry, Chen became deputy director of the Asia division, and Zhang was appointed vice foreign minister. Zhou's office in Chongqing served as nerve centre for two regional centres, one in Guilin headed by Li Kenong, and one in Hong Kong headed by Liao Chengzhi with Qiao Guanhua. The experiences obtained by these groups in the handling of foreign affairs proved important for the conduct of China's foreign policy after 1949.

Of the three Vice Foreign Ministers appointed in 1949, Wang Jiaxiang, Zhang Hanfu, and Li Kenong, only Wang had not worked under Zhou during the Chongqing period. Wang was sent to Moscow almost immediately as ambassador. Li Kenong had been a specialist in intelligence and security affairs. Thus Zhang was the senior foreign affairs expert in the Foreign Ministry. He had been educated at Qinghua University in Beijing and had studied economics and politics in the United States. He was secretary and interpreter for the Chinese Communist Party's delegation to the San Francisco conference in 1945. Before being appointed Vice Foreign Minister he had also headed the Alien Affairs Departments in Tianjin and Shanghai when the Chinese Communists gained control of these areas in 1949. Zhang was made Chairman of the Foreign Ministry's Treaty Committee in 1949. He was the most senior official in the Foreign Ministry whom British diplomatic representatives in China were able to see before the two countries established official diplomatic relations in 1954. Given Zhang's close relationship with Zhou, and his own position as a leading expert in foreign affairs, the British representatives in fact had a direct link to the centre of the Chinese government's foreign policy-making group.

Two other officials who played important parts in China's relations with the West were Huan Xiang and Qiao Guanhua. Huan, director of the Western European and African Department of the Foreign Ministry was educated in an American mission school. He studied political economy at Waseda University in Japan and spent some time at the London School of Economics and Political Science in Britain. Later he became Beijing's first charge d'affaires to London in 1954 and remained there until the early 1960s. Qiao, who was adviser to the new Chinese government's first delegation to Geneva in 1954, was educated at Qinghua University and obtained a doctorate in philosophy from Tubingen University in Germany. He had been a close aide to Zhou Enlai for many years.[55]

Thus a small core group of those responsible for administering the Beijing's relations with Western countries were well-educated and experienced. The Foreign Ministry's legal adviser, Professor Zhou Gengsheng, was in fact a western trained well-known expert on international law.[56] But the Ministry was not filled with Western educated officials; many senior members appointed to the Ministry in 1950 were Soviet educated, and had gained their experience in foreign affairs through their contacts with the Comintern and the Soviet government. Wang Jiaxiang, the People's Republic's first Ambassador to Moscow, and Wu Xiuquan, head of the new government's first delegation to the UN were both educated in the Soviet Union. Wang was in charge of training work during the Yan'an period; Wu had been an interpreter for Otto Braun, Comintern's last representative to China. He was the director of the Lanzhou Eighth Route Army Office during the war when the office was an important liaison post between the CCP and the Soviet government.[57]

The new Chinese government was rather slow in expanding their diplomatic relations with foreign countries in the initial period after its establishment. Apart from the embassy in Moscow which was set up in

November 1949, the People's Republic only began setting up permanent diplomatic missions abroad from July 1950 onward (see Appendix 1). The Chinese government was probably not in a hurry to establish full diplomatic relations with every country if only for the fact that the number of officials who had extensive experiences in foreign affairs was relatively small.

Irrespective of the background of its officials and its administrative structure, the Foreign Ministry's most important function was policy-implementation rather than policy formulation; it did not play a central part in determining the government's foreign-policy decisions. That was the responsibility of the Politburo of the CCP's Central Committee. However, under Zhou, the Foreign Ministry was a key government department. As Ronald Keith pointed out, it was the only ministry not subject to one of the three top-level general offices of the Government Administration Council. Zhou's prestige and position as Premier as well as Foreign Minister had clearly helped to establish the status of the ministry, and enhanced its importance.[58]

China's Condition in 1949

The Communist victory in 1949 was preceded by twelve years of war and turmoil. The Sino-Japanese War which began in 1937 and ended in 1945 was soon followed by a full-scale civil war. China's economy was in a devastated state when the CCP came into power. The country was in ruins after a century of wars, domestic and foreign. In the words of the economist Alexander Eckstein, 'the Chinese economy was inflation-torn, war-disrupted and fragmented'.[59]

The new Chinese government estimated that in 1949 industrial production output was only half of the pre-war level before 1937. Heavy-industry output had dropped by 70 per cent, and light industry's had dropped by 30 per cent. In agriculture, the production of major crops had also fallen far below the pre-1949 period. Compared with the pre-1949 peak, the output of grain had dropped 25 per cent, cotton by 48 per cent, cured tobacco by 76 per cent and peanuts by 60 per cent. Infrastructure was also severely disrupted, only half of the 22,200 kilometres of railways were open to traffic because of war damages. All these problems were further aggravated by the hyper-inflation which the Kuomintang government had failed to control.[60] Thus one of the most urgent tasks for the Chinese leaders was the rehabilitation of the economy.

The new leadership's main aim was the introduction of a socialist programme to China, with the objectives of building up the country's economy, and transforming Chinese society. In 1949 China's industrial output was extremely low for a country of its size. According to official Chinese statistics, the output of steel production that year amounted to less than 0.1 per cent of the world's total; electricity was only 0.5 percent, and coal was only 1.9 per cent. The country also had to import all of its loco- motives, motor vehicles, and most of the machinery needed for industrial production. One major economic objective of the new government was to build up China's industries and increase industrial productivity. The first five-year plan of the new government which began in 1953 was a major effort aimed at industrializing the country.[61]

Economic difficulties, however, were not the only problem that the new leaders had to solve. The collapse of the old regime left behind a country which faced social and political disintegration. The CCP intended to establish a socialist political system, and quickly consolidate its rule. When Mao proclaimed the inauguration of the People's Republic on 1 October, the country was still not completely under Communist control. Communist forces only reached China's Southern border in December; Tibet was not yet under their control. More importantly, Chiang Kai-shek had fled to Taiwan earlier and turned the island into a Kuomintang stronghold.

The priorities of the new leadership in Beijing were therefore the consolidation of the CCP's political position, rehabilitation of China's economy and the unification of all Chinese territories under their rule. To achieve these goals, the Communist leaders needed a peaceful international environment. Yet, as a revolutionary state which had declared its solidarity with the socialist bloc and its support for the Soviet Union's leadership in the socialist movement, the People's Republic became entangled in the Cold War.

The CCP's Post-War Relations with the West

For many years the Chinese Communists had been absorbed in their strug- gle with the Kuomintang. They had not bothered to pay close attention to the Party's relations with the West, or if they had wanted to they could not afford to. Their early external relations were essentially inter-party relations with the Soviet Communist Party. It was only after the outbreak of the Second World War that the Chinese Communists began to develop external relations with Western countries. In the immediate post-war years their foreign policy objective was to obtain support for their struggle against Chiang Kai-shek.

The CCP's external relations with the Western powers began in 1944 following the visit of the US army Observer Section to the base in Yan'an in the summer and the visit of Patrick Hurley, President Roosevelt's representative in November. The Communists had consolidated their power during China's war with Japan and had become an effective rival to Chiang Kai-shek's Kuomintang regime. The US government was anxious to prevent a civil war between the Kuomintang and the Communists which would damage the allied powers' war effort against Japan. American policy-makers also envisaged a post-war China, united and stable, as its prime partner and ally in the Pacific area. The long-term American objective in China, according to the State Department in 1949, was to 'assist in the development of a united, democratically progressive and cooperative China which will be capable of contributing to the security and prosperity in the Far East'.[62]

US efforts to mediate in the Kuomintang-Communist struggle were to prove fruitless. Indeed US relations with the Chinese Communists turned sour after the Americans continued to back the Kuomintang regime when the internal strife in China became a full scale civil war.[63] Nevertheless, the Chinese Communists had accepted American mediation in the Chinese civil war up to mid 1947; official American delegations to Yan'an in 1944 and 1945 were always warmly greeted. Their leaders Mao Zedong and Zhou Enlai had actually offered to go to Washington in 1945.[64]

In the few years immediately preceding the outbreak of a full-scale civil war, Communist leaders had tried to lure foreign support away from the Kuomintang regime in Chongqing towards Yan'an, and especially to improve their relations with the Americans. At the same time they had sought Soviet help in their struggle against their Kuomintang rival. As James Reardon-Anderson has demonstrated in his study of the origins of the CCP's foreign policy, the Party 'followed no master plan; rather it was a series of adjustments to the circumstances that entwined and entangled Yenan'. He suggested that the communists had acted not 'according to some ideology or vision of world order' but, 'in response to the limits and opportunities of the situation they found themselves in'.[65] The background of the communist leadership, their political ideals and practical realities gave rise to a foreign policy which was a product of an interplay of a revolutionary ideology, nationalism, and pragmatism.[66]

Revolutionary China's Foreign Policy Principles

CCP leaders did not formulate a concrete programme for government until early 1949 when a communist victory looked certain. As mentioned earlier foreign policy had not been high on the agenda of the party leadership's major concerns during the civil war. Nevertheless, the foreign policy of the People's Republic was formulated in March 1949 when Mao presented the policy outline for a future CCP government at the second plenary session of the Seventh Central Committee in Pingshan. Mao's recommendation later became the basis of the new government's policy direction in the form of the Common Programme of the Chinese People's Political Consultative Conference. Thus the foreign policy principles which formed the basis of China's conduct with the West in the formative years of revolutionary China had already been set prior to the inauguration of the Republic.[67]

The Central Committee approved Mao's recommendation that the legal status of foreign diplomatic missions and personnel accredited to the Kuomintang regime should not be recognized and existing treaties with foreign governments would not be automatically accepted. Mao also suggested that all 'imperialist propaganda agencies' in China be abolished and the Party should take control of China's foreign trade and reform its customs system. The question of recognition by 'imperialist countries' was brought up by the report which proposed that, 'we should not be in a hurry to solve it now and need not be in a hurry to solve it even for a fairly long period after country-wide victory'. China would be prepared to establish diplomatic relations with all countries on the basis of equality, but as long as the 'imperialists continued their hostile attitude towards the Chinese people', legal status should not be granted to them. Nevertheless the Party accepted that the legitimate interests of foreign nationals were to be protected, and the new government should trade with Western capitalist countries as well as socialist countries. In Mao's own words, 'wherever there is business to do, we shall do it and we have already started; the businessmen of several capitalist countries are competing for such business'.[68]

Therefore half a year before coming into power, the CCP leadership had already decided that China would establish diplomatic relations and trade with non-socialist as well as socialist countries. However, its policy towards the 'Western imperialistic powers' was to be conducted differently. As Zhou Enlai indicated, while the new leadership was willing to co-operate with all countries on an equal basis and would seek foreign diplomatic recognition, it would not compromise its 'independence and self-reliance' and the principle of equality. Revolutionary China's foreign policy was based on three basic principles: 'to make a fresh start, to clean the room before inviting guests, and to side with the socialist camp without reservation'.[69]

The principle of a fresh start in China's external relations was elaborated on at some length by Zhou Enlai in 1952 when he addressed a group of senior foreign service staff. The communist revolutionaries felt very strongly that in the past China had failed to forge diplomatic relations with foreign countries on an equal basis. Thus it was necessary for the new government to repudiate official relations formed between the Kuomintang government and other countries, and to negotiate the establishment of formal diplomatic relations with all these countries on a new basis. The leadership was in no hurry to establish diplomatic relations with 'capitalist, former colonial countries and semi-colonial countries'. Its position was that, 'We have to see if they would accept our principles for the establishment of diplomatic relations. It is necessary not only to listen to their words, but also to see their actual actions.' The Chinese revolutionaries believed that the principal of 'making a fresh start' was essential for China to establish an independence status in international relations.[70]

The second principle of 'cleaning the room before inviting guests' was primarily aimed at former Western imperialistic countries. The revolutionaries were convinced that while imperialistic military presence had been driven away, their economic and cultural influences, which had dominated China for more than one hundred years, were still very strong. Since such influences would affect the independence of China, the Beijing government 'would rather wait for a while, clear the remaining influences of the imperialistic powers, rather than let them continue their activities in China'.[71]

The final principle of 'leaning to one side' had been formally announced by Mao in June 1949. An alliance with the Soviet Union was, to Mao, essential for China's survival as a socialist country in a world which was divided into two camps. He stated that, 'in order to win in victory and to consolidate it we must lean to one side . . . Sitting on the fence will not do, nor is there a third road'.[72] This declaration might have been an attempt to allay Stalin's suspicion that China would follow a Titoist path, by making such an pronouncement public, the Chinese leaders had firmly identified themselves with the socialist camp and as followers of the banner of Marxism-Leninism.[73]

The Communist leadership's three principles on foreign policy were in a sense a reflection of the two major elements of the Chinese Communist movement: nationalism and a revolutionary ideology. However, the fact that the revolutionaries did not rule out establishing diplomatic relations with Western countries, and were prepared to trade with the capitalist West reflected that the new leaders appreciated their country's position and needs. Their repudiation of international obligations was therefore modified by their desire to be recognized internationally and their country's need for continuing economic contacts with the West.

CONCLUSIONS

Revolutionary China's response to Britain's diplomatic recognition in January 1950 was a calculated move based on policy decisions formulated in March 1949. The Chinese revolutionaries were willing to maintain diplomatic and trade relations with the West, but they insisted as a precondition that China's relations with foreign countries had to be established on a new basis, and were not in hurry if these countries were not willing to comply to their terms.

Although the Chinese Communists' attitude towards the West was not entirely antagonistic, by adopting a policy of 'leaning to one side', and declaring it openly, the People's Republic became embroiled in the Cold War even before the formation of the new government was officially announced. The attendant deterioration in Sino-American relations was to have important effects on the new Chinese government's relations with Britain, America's closest ally. The intensification of the Cold War, and the outbreak of the Korean War, further affected the development of Anglo-Chinese relations. But when British policy-makers first turned their attention to China in 1948, their major and immediate concerns were the British interests at stake, and the practical problems faced by British diplomats who had to deal with China's new political masters.

2 The Decision of Recognition

On 1 October 1949 Mao Zedong proclaimed the establishment of the People's Republic of China in Beijing's Tiananmen Square. Some three months later on 6 January 1950 the British government accorded diplomatic recognition to the new Chinese government. The decision of recognition, reached earlier by the Cabinet on 15 December 1949, was a very difficult decision for British policy-makers. Obviously London's stance towards the newly formed Beijing government would directly affect British interests in China, indirectly, but equally important, it would also affect Britain's position in colonial territories in Southeast Asia. For policy-makers in London all these concerns were further complicated by the prevailing Cold War climate; the communisation of China was a serious problem which had to be considered in the light of not only Britain's direct interests in East Asia, but also its wider international repercussions.

The establishment of a communist regime hostile to the West would have far reaching effects on the conflict between the West and the communist bloc. However, newly independent Commonwealth countries in Asia were sympathetic to the Chinese Communist movement, regarding it as a nationalist and an independence movement. The opinions of Britain's allies and foes were essential factors that policy makers in London could not ignore. Domestically, other factors which had influenced the making of Britain's China policy included: Parliamentary politics, public opinion as expressed through the press, and the business lobby.

The Foreign Office and its Far Eastern Department, which had primary responsibility for China policy, played a pivotal role in formulating the decision of recognition. But the organizational process of the decision-making machinery as well as the bureaucratic interests of various government departments which have been discussed in the previous chapter were also important factors which contributed to the decision of 15 December. This chapter examines the policy formulation process leading to Britain's China policy of 'keeping a foot in the door', and subsequently, the recognition of the People's Republic of China.

THE POLICY OF 'KEEPING A FOOT IN THE DOOR'

Cabinet Paper CP(48)299

By the late summer of 1948 a communist victory in China was imminent. The US Embassy in Nanjing's monthly reports to Washington had for several months invariably begun with the sentence: 'During the last month the military, political and economic situation has continued to deteriorate'.[1] In November 1948 the Kuomintang position in Manchuria had collapsed totally after their forces at Shenyang had surrendered to the Communists. By early 1949 north China was firmly in Communist hands. Communist forces entered Tianjin on 15 January; they occupied Beijing two weeks later. In February, after their appeal to the US, Britain, France and the Soviet Union to intervene in the civil war had failed, the Kuomintang government moved their headquarters to Guangzhou. By this time it had become clear that the civil war in China was close to its end.

British officials in charge of Far Eastern affairs had watched developments in China with apprehension since 1947 after the American mediation to end the civil war had failed. In December 1948 the Foreign Secretary presented a Cabinet paper on developments in China. This paper, CP(48)299, contained a brief summary prepared by Foreign Office officials on recent events in China. Its assessment of the situation had great significance in determining Britain's policy towards the Chinese Communists. CP(48)299 recommended that in view of the advance of Communist forces in China the government should co-ordinate its China policy with its allies, and at the same time, strengthen Britain's position in colonial territories in the Far East. The more interesting part of the paper was its annex which argued that the Chinese Communists were orthodox Marxists, and provided a comprehensive account of the economic and political implications of a Communist victory in China for British interest in Asia.[2]

The Foreign Office concluded that Communist rule in China would have adverse effects for the Western position throughout Asia. Foreign Office officials were particularly apprehensive of the political effects on British territories in Southeast Asia, such as Hong Kong and Malaya. In such an eventuality, the retention of Hong Kong would depend on whether the Communists found the existence of a British administered port convenient for their trade with the outside world. Even if the Communists were to use a British Hong Kong for trading purposes, the colony would face a vast refugee problem. They felt that while the colony could continue its life, it would be 'living on the edge of a volcano'. In Malaya, where a communist insurrection had begun in 1948, the Foreign Office warned:

'militant communism would be very close to Malaya's northern frontier, with Siam and French Indo-China as poor buffers; the morale of the Malayan Communists would be bound to improve". One worry was that the Chinese Communist Party agents infiltrating into Malaya might became more active.[3]

Another major problem identified was the economic effects for Britain, one of the major foreign investors in China. There was no accurate up-to-date estimate of British investments in post-war China but the figure for 1941 was three hundred million pounds. Even given allowances for war damage British economic interests would still be considerable. The Foreign Office believed that under Communist rule foreign commerce and business 'would be at a low ebb' for an initial period before a stable administration was established, but it felt that in this initial period conditions would not be very much worse than those under Kuomintang rule with a 'lack of easy and safe internal communications', 'extremely inflated prices', and 'the restrictive attitude' of the government towards foreign business. There was an air of cautious optimism in the Foreign Office's prediction of the prospects for British commerce in China in the short term. The thinking of the Office was that 'the final stage of expropriation or expulsion of foreign commercial and shipping interests and investments, and the undermining of Hong Kong's economic prosperity, may not materialize for some time in view of the extent and essential nature of these interests [for China]'.[4]

British officials realized that there was nothing Britain could do to alter developments in China. They believed that even the United States, the only country with the financial, material, and military resources, would not be able to prevent a Communist victory in China. As far as Britain was concerned, the Foreign Office concluded: 'Our best hope lies in keeping a foot in the door'. That is to say that provided there is no actual danger to life, we should endeavour to stay where we are, to have *de facto* relations with the Chinese Communists in so far as these are unavoidable, and to investigate the possibilities of continued trade in China'. Indeed Britain might have a bargaining counter by virtue of being able to withhold certain essential imports that China would need. The Foreign Office went on to say: 'In order to do this it is essential that we should not abandon our position in China, and we must aim to keep, at an rate, a foot in the door'.[5]

A policy of 'keeping a foot in the door' in China was in the making. CP(48)299 was thus a most important document in the formulation of Britain's policy towards revolutionary China. It was not only the first major policy paper on China to reach Cabinet level since the end of the Second World War, but also served as the cornerstone of a policy which

ultimately led to the decision to accord formal diplomatic recognition to
the People's Central Government of China.

The Foreign Office and the Recognition Question

The Foreign Office began to examine how to pursue a policy of 'keeping
a foot in the door' from early 1949. The most obvious step would be to
recognize the new Chinese government when it came formally to power.
But to recognize a communist regime in a period when the Cold War was
intensifying required consideration not only of British interests in China,
but also of a wide-ranging number of other issues.

British diplomats in China, however, were facing a very difficult situation. The most urgent question was that in areas under Communist control,
foreign consular officials were not able to communicate with their embassies in Nanjing or to continue normal consular functions. Communication
between the British government and their consul-general in Shenyang had
been cut off at the end of November 1948; the same happened in Tianjin
in January 1949. The British Embassy in Nanjing reported that junior
Communist officials in Tianjin were justifying their refusal to recognize
foreign consuls officially on the grounds that diplomatic relations had not
been established. This was seen by Peter Scarlett, head of the Foreign
Office's Far Eastern Department, as a deliberate measure designed to force
foreign governments to recognize the Communist regime.[6]

As an immediate step, recommended Scarlett, British consuls should try
to establish day-to-day working relationships with the local Communist
authorities and tell them that the civil war was of no concern to the
British government. They should request the Communists to allow them
to exercise their consular functions, since 'the question of recognition could
not be decided while the uncertainties of civil war persist[ed]'.[7] But in early
1949 the eventual victory of the Communist forces was only a question of
time.

There were powerful legal arguments in favour of recognizing the Communist regime in China. Britain had a diplomatic tradition of recognizing
governments which exercised effective control over their territories.[8]
The legal adviser at the Foreign Office had stressed that: 'it is both
legally wrong, and in practice leads to every conceivable difficulty,
to refuse to accord any sort of recognition to a Government which in
fact effectively controls a large portion of territory'. Submitting the legal
arguments, Scarlett noted that the as long as the Communist authorities
remained unrecognized, they might have legal grounds for not accepting
the official status of British consuls. More importantly, by accepting the

strong elements of law in the recognition question, the British government 'should be able to justify a politically unpopular step which would really serve our interests'. Scarlett, however, recommended that recognition should be delayed until the Communists had firmly established themselves, and its political implications more carefully considered.[9]

In line with the policy of 'keeping a foot in the door', recognition seemed to be a policy which would serve British interests in China. Yet in the prevailing Cold War climate, it might bring political difficulties for the government. There was no doubt that the Foreign Secretary Ernest Bevin fully realized the political significance and international implications of such an act. He paid personal attention to the problem and discussed Scarlett's submission with Dening. The Foreign Secretary obviously would not want to give Britain's allies the impression that 'when British interests are at stake we are perfectly prepared to swallow our principles.' The Foreign Office's position was that it did not want to oppose recognition in principle, but in early 1949 when the Chinese civil war was still not over, it did not think that the time for recognition had come.[10]

Meanwhile, British officials in Communist-controlled territories in North China were instructed to develop contacts with the local authorities. How to inform the Communist authorities about the British government's willingness to establish a day-to-day working relationship with them was a sensitive and delicate matter. The Governor of Hong Kong, Sir Alexander Grantham, and the British Ambassador in Nanjing, Sir Ralph Stevenson, pointed out that it would be inappropriate for them to contact the Communist authorities directly. Eventually the Foreign Office asked the ambassador to send the message, by open post, to the consular officers at Beijing and Tianjin.[11]

Before this instruction was carried out, HMS Amethyst was shelled by Communist batteries from the north bank of the Yangtze on 20 April. The British frigate was sailing from Shanghai to Nanjing on a routine mission at a time when the Communists were preparing to cross the river to attack the Kuomintang forces on the south bank. It sustained considerable damage and casualties and was eventually grounded; rescue attempts led to further damage and casualties. The Chinese Communists put the blame for the incident on the British. They refused to release the frigate and demanded compensation. The incident created an uproar at home and the government was severely criticized.[12]

Even if the incident had not occurred, whether the Foreign Office's ingenious idea of sending its instruction to British consular officials in Communist-controlled area by open post would have had any significant impact on the attitudes of the Communist authorities is doubtful. The authorities had not responded to the individual and collective approaches made earlier by foreign consular officials in Beijing. A week before the Amethyst incident, foreign consular officials in Beijing had posted a joint letter to the city's mayor declaring their neutral stance in the civil war and requesting that their consular functions be allowed to continue. Five days later, the letter was returned to the French consulate, opened without comment. Commenting on this futile joint effort after the Amethyst incident, the Foreign Office's P. D. Coates remarked that the Amethyst incident might never have occurred had British diplomats been in day-to-day contact with the Communists.[13]

In general, foreign diplomats in Communist-controlled China were not treated badly, but they were only regarded as ordinary foreign nationals. For example, after the Communist forces entered Shanghai in May, it was almost business as usual for the British consulate, but officially the consulate did not exist. When foreign consuls visited the Foreign Affairs Bureau, they were received 'with grave attention and politeness' but only in their private capacities. Mail addressed to the British consulate was not delivered. Writing to his wife, vice-consul at the consulate, Keith Oakeshott, asked her to send letters directly to his home address, but he was hopeful that the situation would improve when the British government recognized the new Chinese government.[14]

The most serious problem for the British community in China was actually not caused by the Communists but by the Kuomintang regime's blockade of Shanghai, where a large number of British residents and businesses were based. As a result of the blockade, according to a Cabinet paper in August 1949, British firms there were in a 'parlous condition'. It noted that the exchange rate in Shanghai was entirely fictitious and was tied to the price of rice. The firms were without funds to pay wages, and the London offices of these firms had to remit huge sums of money to Shanghai in order to avoid labour troubles. Many of these firms could not carry on in the circumstances and would have had to close down if the situation did not improve.[15]

One other important issue was future Chinese representation at the United Nations. Gladwyn Jebb, who had represented Britain in setting up the UN, put it to William Strang that it would be 'greatly preferable' to go on recognizing the Kuomintang government for as long as possible. He wanted to avoid 'a situation in which neither side was recognized by some or all of the permanent members of the Security Council'. Jebb also feared the presence of the Chinese Communists would swing the balance against the West in the Council. But the problem was not acute, as the Chinese Communists had not formed a government at that time. The Foreign Office estimated in August that the Kuomintang government would continue to represent China in the forthcoming session of the UN General Assembly in September. At that time British officials anticipated that the Communist authorities in Beijing would form a central government some time later in autumn.[16]

Meanwhile there were indications that the Chinese Communists might be willing to work with the West. The Governor of Hong Kong received a message in August purportedly from Zhou Enlai to the British government saying that he was in favour of establishing normal relationship with the West, and China would not automatically follow the Soviet Union in the UN Security Council. The message also suggested that there were two groups within the Chinese Communist Party with opposing views on foreign policy and Zhou headed the group which wished to normalize relations with the West.[17] British officials were slightly baffled by this message. The British Ambassador felt that: 'Whether this message is a serious and honest approach or a rhetorical gesture, it does provide an authoritative insight into the inner Councils of the Chinese Communists, and for that reason it is important.'[18] Since the message was not an official communication, the British government clearly would not formulate its policy based on a report whose source would not be confirmed. But it served as an indication that there might be a policy debate within the Chinese Communist leadership and that a well-defined policy towards the West had not yet been firmly established.

More concrete assurances were given in late August by two senior Communist officials in Shanghai. The city's new mayor and its foreign affairs bureau director told British businessmen that the Communist authorities did not intend to squeeze foreign business out of China. The authorities also promised to facilitate the British Ambassador's departure and the consequent movement of British diplomats between posts in China. The message seemed clear: Chinese Communists did not intend to throw foreign businessmen out; and they would be willing to work with them.[19]

The Foreign Office's calculation of long-term British interests and its feeling that the problems confronting British consular officials in China had to be solved presented a strong case for recognizing the Chinese Communists. The Foreign Office, however, was not the only ministry with an interest in China. As Graham Allison and Morton Halperin have pointed out, foreign policy decisions are very often the result of the "pulling and hauling" of competing interests within the bureaucracy.[20] The case of Britain's decision to recognize the People's Republic of China was no exception.

The Battle within Whitehall

Before presenting policy papers on China at the Cabinet level, the Foreign Office usually discussed its views with other departments which had direct interests in the issues involved. Formal inter-departmental consultations on China were mainly conducted through the Far Eastern (Official) Committee, chaired by Dening during the period when the question of recognition was discussed.

Outside of the Foreign Office, British officials in charge of financial and commercial affairs had been watching developments in China closely since the end of the Second World War. The Colonial Office and the Ministry of Defence were also concerned with the government's China policy because it would have serious implications for British colonial territories in Southeast Asia. Other ministries interested in the China problem included the Commonwealth Relations Office and the Ministry of Transport.

On the side of the Foreign Office were the Commonwealth Relations Office and Ministry of Transport. Both supported recognition, agreeing that a British presence in China was important. The Ministry of Transport which was responsible for British shipping interests wanted 'everything possible' to be done 'to enable British shipping interests to resume normal trading relations with China without interference'. In order to pursue British shipping objectives, the ministry urged that it was necessary to accord full *de jure* recognition to the new Chinese government, the sooner the better.[21]

Departments in charge of economic matters, the Treasury and the Board of Trade, were sceptical of the prospect for British business and trade in China. In fact the Treasury had actually advised potential investors against investing in China since the war. As early as 1948 Treasury officials had already expressed concern that the Foreign Office's favourable views on the prospect for foreign business in China would encourage British business interests to remain in China. The Treasury's own assessment was that since the Chinese Communists' priority would be agrarian reform and the development of internal resources, foreign trade would not play any significant role in their long-term economic planning. The department suggested that, 'we should go not further than refraining from discouraging people who on their own decision want to remain in China in the hope of doing business'.[22]

In February 1949 the Foreign Office sought the Treasury's views again on British business interests in a Communist China. The Foreign Office's own assessment was that for an initial period a Communist government would still have to rely on 'the continued operation of foreign interests' to maintain or create a balance of trade and avoid economic chaos. On the basis of this, Foreign Office officials suggested that 'a communist government would not wish to antagonize foreign interests by threats or acts of expropriation or expulsion or by making things difficult for these interests to operate'. The validity of this argument was questioned by the Treasury. As a result, the Foreign Office's revised its policy paper on China to incorporate the Treasury's more cautious assessment.[23] Despite their reservations on business opportunities in China, Treasury officials had no objection to the policy of maintaining a commercial foothold in China. They hoped that, if foreign business were allowed to remain for a period, the Communists might realize their importance for China's economy. In the longer run, they shared the hopes of their colleagues in the Foreign Office that Britain would be able to compete in the China market with the Americans when British production improved.[24]

The Board of Trade's interests in China were two-fold: to restore Britain's traditional trading relationship with China, and to preserve existing British investments and properties in China. Trade officials challenged the Foreign Office's views on the prospect of British trade opportunities in China, and they were sceptical about whether recognition would have any immediate positive effects in these two areas.

Trade officials made it very clear to the Foreign Office that they did not believe that recognition of the Communist government would improve the 'chances of rescuing the British assets'. They felt that recognition might help the companies to resume business, but did not think that it would make any difference to the prospect of Britain's trade. On the basis of these assessments, the Board of Trade was not very enthusiastic about recognition, but it accepted the policy. In a letter to the Foreign Office, the Board put it this way: 'we favour recognition but do not press for it'.[25]

The Ministry of Defence and the armed forces did not have direct interests in China, but they were concerned about the effects of recognizing a Chinese Communist government on Hong Kong and Malaya. In May the British Defence Co-ordination Committee in the Far East informed the Cabinet that, 'there was urgent need for diplomatic, economic and military action to form a containing ring against further communist penetration'. This view was supported by the Chiefs of Staff, who 'considered that the loss of Hong Kong to a communist attack would have such serious effects on our whole position in Asia and elsewhere that we ought to take all necessary steps now to prevent this from happening.' Considered the sensitive political situation of Hong Kong, and the fact that China was not an area of major strategic importance to Britain, the Joint Planning Staff accepted the 'policy of keeping a foot in the door' and did not object to the Foreign Office's argument in favour of recognizing the Communist government.[26]

The acceptance of the Foreign Office's position on recognition within the Whitehall was not unanimous. The Colonial Office, which had direct interests in Southeast Asia, was critical of the Foreign Office's thinking about China. As the colonial authorities in Malaya and Singapore were conducting a campaign against the Malayan Communists, they were anxious to see that the government's policy towards China would not undermine their effort. In August 1949, both the Commissioner-General for the UK in South-East Asia, Malcolm MacDonald, and the Governor of Singapore, Sir Franklin Gimson, expressed their opposition to the policy of recognition.

In a letter directly addressed to William Strang, instead of going through the Colonial Office, MacDonald put his arguments against recognition on record. He made it very clear that the authorities in Malaya and British Borneo were deeply concerned that recognizing a Communist regime in China would have serious implications for their campaign against the Malayan Communists. MacDonald said that because of the large Chinese population in Malaya, Singapore and Borneo, they had 'a powerful influence in local politics and other affairs'. What worried him most was that diplomatic recognition would give the Communist government the right to appoint consul-generals and consuls in Malaya, Singapore and Borneo. His feared that these consular representatives would 'do everything possible to stimulate anti-British Chinese Nationalism.' Thus the colonial authorities suggested that there was a strong case for postponing recognition as long as possible. The letter to Strang said: 'From our local point of view here it looms very large, and is capable of causing very serious trouble for us.' MacDonald also forwarded a letter containing similar arguments from the Governor of Singapore who maintained that recognition would lead the Chinese in Singapore to 'imagine that the British government does not regard the communists in an unfavourable light'.[27]

In reply, the Foreign Office argued that the appointment of Communist consuls could not be avoided indefinitely. Strang wrote: 'If we refuse to have Communist Consuls in our territories, we must expect to be compelled to withdraw all our consulates in China.' To the Foreign Office, an unrecognized China hostile to Britain would present a greater danger to South East Asia for 'there would be no means by which we could hope to induce China to live up to her obligations.' Strang then went on to suggest that any impression that recognition signified the British government's approval of the Chinese government's actions could be countered by 'suitable propaganda'.[28]

In November Foreign Office officials and representatives of the British colonial authorities in Southeast Asia came together at the Bukit Serene Singapore conference to sort out their differences. It was clear from the outset that the Foreign Office was not prepared to shift from its position on recognition. Commenting on MacDonald's suggestion that the recognition question should be put on the agenda, Scarlett agreed that it was a working topic for the conference, but he added that, 'it is surely only a facet of the communist threat and one hopes it won't take up a disproportionate amount of time'.[29]

The Foreign Office had the support of the British Ambassador to China, Sir Ralph Stevenson, and the Governor of Hong Kong, Sir Alexander Grantham. Stevenson was in favour of recognition because of British interests in China. Grantham maintained that because of Hong Kong's proximity and relations with China, recognition was desirable. He recalled the Hong Kong government's anxiety that the colony was in a vulnerable position because 'if any provocative acts against China had their origin in Hong Kong, Hong Kong would be the first to suffer from Chinese retaliation'. Therefore the Hong Kong government had always been sensitive to the political masters in China. The Governor said later, 'On the one hand we did not want to be provocative; on the other we did not want to appease or appear to do so, to give way to unreasonable demands.'[30]

With the support of Grantham and Stevenson, Dening secured agreement for an earliest possible *de jure* recognition of the Chinese Communist government from the British colonial administrations in Southeast Asia at the Bukit Serene Conference. The conference accepted that on political, practical, and legal grounds recognition should not be long delayed. To minimize any adverse effect on the situation in Malaya, an extensive propaganda campaign would be launched to explain that recognition was not inconsistent with an anti-communist policy in Southeast Asia.[31]

As a result of inter-departmental consultations, the Foreign Office refrained from encouraging British business to stay in China, and accepted that recognition could have adverse effects in British colonial territories in Southeast Asia, but its recommendation to recognize the Chinese Communist government prevailed. Except for the Colonial Office, other departments, with varying degrees of reservations, accepted the need of recognition. The Colonial Office's stance was weakened by the conflicting interests of the authorities in Hong Kong and Malaya. For the time being the battle of competing bureaucratic interests ended decisively to the Foreign Office's favour. Over a problem which was not considered of prime importance in Whitehall, as the department primarily responsible for foreign affairs, and with an influential Secretary of State, the Foreign

Office played the most active and direct part in the decision-making process.

DOMESTIC CONSIDERATIONS

Parliament and Party Politics

Post-war developments in China had not attracted much parliamentary attention until early 1949. Left-wing Labour Members of Parliament had occasionally criticized the government's Soviet policy, but they rarely questioned Britain's neutral stance towards the Chinese civil war. The Labour leadership's control of its Parliamentary party was seldom in doubt between 1945 and 1951. After the 1945 election, Labour had 393 MPs in the House of Commons, the Conservatives had only 213, and the other parties combined had only 34. As Churchill put it, 'the verdict of the electorate had been overwhelmingly expressed'. With this decisive victory, the Labour leadership had firm control of the House of Commons, and the Labour government came to power with an unprecedented authority.[32]

The unity of the Labour party under Attlee's leadership has been described as an exception in the history of the British Labour movement. Historian Kenneth Morgan has described the dominant role of the Cabinet in the Labour movement during this period in these words: 'Its leading personalities exercised a sustained and unique ascendancy over the government, the party, and its supporters.'[33]

Within the Labour Party the government's foreign policy was not without critics, but as a popular leader Bevin was widely respected. During the Labour Party's annual conferences in 1947 and 1948, resolutions critical of the Foreign Secretary were easily defeated. In the 1949 annual conference even Bevin's most critical opponents made no attempts to attack his foreign policy. In a debate on foreign affairs during the conference on 9 June, Hugh Dalton was able to say that, 'the most remarkable feature of this debate has been an almost complete absence of criticism of Ernest Bevin'. When the Foreign Secretary spoke to the conference, he had referred to developments in China and stressed that the Labour government would continue to observe neutrality in the Chinese civil war. However, he also indicated that the government would be ready to trade with a new Chinese regime.[34]

The unity of the Party was fully reflected in the Parliamentary party, which again in Morgan's words, 'presented few problems of management for the government down to 1951'.[35] By setting up different policy groups in the House of Commons for MPs, the Leader of the House, Herbert Morrison, was able to provide a bridge between ministers and backbenchers. This created a more harmonious atmosphere among Labour MPs. In Morrison's own words the purpose of the policy groups was 'to make controversy and disagreement constructive'. The Foreign Affairs group which included left-wing MPs such as Konni Zilliacus, and John Platts-Mills, who were critical of Bevin's foreign policies, was perhaps an exception. But this group was not influential at all. Years later in an interview Kenneth Younger, Minister of State in the Foreign Office, concluded that, 'the Foreign Affairs Group was reduced to a very angry and virtually impotent body'. The first serious left-wing challenge to the government's foreign policy in Parliament came in November 1946 when left-wing MPs called for a socialist alternative to the two super-powers. This call was supported by 56 Labour backbenchers, but the government was able to assert its authority easily, and secured the support of the Parliamentary party on almost every occasion up to 1951. In 1948 and 1949 a number of leading far left-wing MPs were expelled by the National Executive of the party.[36]

In the House of Commons the lack of interest about the government's China policy was not confined to Labour MPs; Conservative MPs also paid scant attention to events in China. Developments in the Far East were not high on the agenda in foreign affairs debates in the House. It was only in April 1949, after the Amethyst incident, when British casualties were reported, that the China problem created an uproar in Parliament.[37] The Opposition was quick to seize the opportunity to attack the government's China policy. The government was criticized for both its handling of the Amethyst incident and its China policy in general. Opposition MPs questioned whether it had been necessary to send the frigate to Nanjing on the Yangtze on the eve of a Communist crossing. Another question was whether adequate protection had been provided for HMS Amethyst after the decision to send it to Nanjing had been made. On 5 May, Harold Macmillan asserted that, 'all the trouble springs from certain initial mistakes and confusions, and indeed contradictions, of policy. For this His Majesty's Government alone, are responsible'.[38]

The incident also led MPs to realize that Far East affairs had largely been ignored in Parliament. Summing up the Opposition's position at the end of a Parliamentary debate, Rab Butler suggested that Parliament had not given sufficient attention to Far Eastern affairs. He stated, 'the Government in their policy, to which we have paid tribute and which has been successful in many spheres in the West, have not devoted themselves sufficiently to these vital problems in the Far East which have now been

shown up in a glaring light by this most unfortunate incident'. Turning to
the question of Britain's Far Eastern policy, he cautioned, 'we have to look
at Communism, as one piece, with a concerted guidance from the centre
in Moscow'. The government was urged to bring into force 'a proper Far
Eastern policy'. The debate on Amethyst had turned into, in Attlee's words,
'rather a desultory debate on foreign affairs'.[39]

When the Prime Minister made his first statement on the Amethyst
incident on 26 April he had already declared that the government would
continue to adhere to the 1945 Moscow declaration not to intervene in
the civil war in China. The House was told that British consular officials
had tried unsuccessfully to establish day-to-day contact with Communist
authorities in areas under Communist control. In the debate on 5 May,
the Minister of Defence, A. V. Alexander, stated that, 'as far as we
are aware, there has been no molestation of British subjects in areas
overrun by the Communists, who appear to maintain, in the areas they
have overtaken, effective law and order'. On the question of Hong Kong,
Alexander declared that, 'substantial reinforcements' were being sent to
Hong Kong to bring British land forces up to the strength of two brigades.
The government announced that the Air Force in Hong Kong was being
reinforced with fighter aircraft, an additional cruiser was also being sent
to join the Far Eastern Squadron, and an aircraft carrier would be available
if the need arose.[40]

Despite the action to reinforce British forces in Hong Kong, Parliament
was told that the government's position towards China had remained
unchanged. In his concluding remark on the House debate on 5 May,
Attlee avoided committing himself to any particular policy towards China.
He simply suggested that relations with a future Communist government
would depend on their actions and it was premature to judge what lines a
Communist government would take.[41]

The Amethyst incident highlighted British policy-makers' predicament
in China and prompted them to pay more attention to the situation in the Far
East. After the debate on the Amethyst incident only a few questions were
asked about China throughout May and June. In a House Committee debate
on foreign affairs before the summer recess, only two speakers referred to
the situation in China. The opening speech of the Opposition addressed
problems in Europe, the Soviet threat, and the German question with no
mention of the China question at all.[42]

It was only after the formal establishment of the People's Republic in
October, that MPs once more turned their attention to events in China.
This time it centred on the issue of recognition. Throughout October and
November, many MPs raised the issue in Parliament. Those who spoke

against it were worried about possible adverse effects in Malaya where the authorities were facing a Communist insurgency. However, the majority of those who spoke supported recognition. The most notable figure among those in favour of it was the Opposition leader Winston Churchill. On 17 November he stated in the House: 'when a large and powerful mass of people are organized together and are masters of an immense area and of great populations, it may be necessary to have relations with them. One may say that when relations are most difficult, that is the time when diplomacy is most needed'.[43] A bi-partisan approach in Parliament favouring a policy of recognition was evident.

The Press

During the late 1940s, British journalists, like British politicians, were very much preoccupied with their country's economic problems and the situation in Europe. It was the time of sterling devaluation, the fuel crisis, the Marshall plan, the Berlin blockade, and the formation of the North Atlantic Alliance. China was not considered to be a matter of great public interest by the press. Newspaper headlines about economic crises and the German problems were a good indication of the focus of public and press attention.

In the early post-war years, British newspapers had often called the Chinese Communists 'agrarian reformers'; but by 1948, when a Communist victory in China was becoming more and more likely, the newspapers gradually changed their attitudes. Cold War rhetoric and official concern about the communist threat in Asia were increasingly reflected in the press throughout 1948.[44] Reflecting official concern about developments in the Far East, the British press began to link the Chinese Communists with Moscow in mid-1948. Articles on the threat of communist expansion in Asia and its the implications for British interests there appeared. In June the *Manchester Guardian* warned of possible Soviet ambition in Asia. More specifically, *The News Chronicle* reported that, 'the growth of communism in South East Asia, slowly in British possessions and quickly in territories that have gained independence, is causing concern in London'. Similarly a *Scotsman* article commented that events in Southeast Asia had 'awakened Whitehall and some private observers to the fact that a Soviet pattern for the conquest of Asia is being followed out ruthlessly'. Reports along the same line appeared in other newspapers.[45]

The changing mood of the press clearly reflected Foreign Office's views about China. The Office's news department had regular briefings for diplomatic correspondents which were a major source of information for the press.[46] The deepening of the Cold War and the Chinese Communist leadership's indication that they were part of the Soviet camp were also important factors influencing press opinion. From late 1948 onward, Chinese Communist leaders had displayed a clear pro-Soviet line in their official pronouncements and policy declarations. The Chinese Communists' stance did not go unnoticed. By early 1949 it seemed that illusions about the nature of the Chinese communism in the British press were gradually being replaced by apprehensions about the consequences of a communist-dominated China for British interests.

But there were still different opinions about what should be done in China. British journalists were undecided about the nature of the future Communist regime in China. The *Manchester Guardian* argued in January 1949 that the Chinese Communists had to 'swallow a large number of allies and collaborators. Through them communism in China may well become not pink in colour but distinctly yellow'. By February the paper changed its position and asserted that, 'if the communists win in China the iron curtain would probably fall across it, at least after the first period. There is no evidence that the Chinese Communists are independent of the Kremlin'. One month later the newspaper's editorial changed its opinion again. It stated: 'while there was no doubt that at its centre Chinese Communism was Marxist Leninist, on its perimeter it was considerably watered down'. It then suggested that the 'Chineseness' of the Chinese would assert itself over whatever ideology.[47]

These inconsistent remarks reflected a sense of uncertainty as to where the Communist movement would lead China to. The press, however, were less uncertain as to what Britain should do in China. There was a feeling that whether the Chinese Communists were orthodox Marxist or not, they probably would not be completely subservient to Moscow. The newspapers also believed that there would still be opportunities for British trade in China. An editorial in *The Times* on 21 January 1949 maintained that it would be a mistake to assume that Communist China had to be a mere pawn of the Soviet Union unless world events forced them into a desperate coalition. It believed that the priority of a new Chinese Communist government had to be domestic problems and they would need Western capital goods and technical resources. The newspaper advised: 'the opportunity of trading with all parts of China should not be ruled out'. Echoing this view a few months later in April the *Manchester Guardian* suggested that after the Communists had won the civil war they would need several years to restore the country's industries. Therefore, it maintained, the West should 'take advantage of the market offered during the period of China's industrial expansion'.[48]

Thus by early 1949, the British press had already been urging the government to respond more actively to developments in China. But it was only in April when HMS Amethyst was shelled by Communist forces, that China stole the headlines in British newspapers. The press not only lamented the damage to British vessels and the loss of British lives; questions concerning Britain's position in the Far East were also raised. *The Times* asked: 'why no British contact could be made beforehand with the Communists'? But as the *Glasgow Herald* suggested, the incident raised not just personal or departmental responsibilities, it raised the question of Britain's Far Eastern policy. The newspaper concluded that, 'in that area Britain no longer stands where she did'.[49]

In the two months following the Amethyst incident numerous newspaper articles and editorial comments on the government's China policy appeared. They almost unanimously agreed that while the priority of British foreign policy was Europe, it was time to do something about China. The incident served as a catalyst for more public debates and discussions on the government's policy towards China and came as a reminder of how much was at stake for Britain in China.

The attack on HMS Amethyst led the British press to come to the conclusion that in order to safeguard British interests in China, it was necessary, at least, to establish contact with the Chinese Communists. The *Daily Telegraph* maintained that, 'some sort of official contact will obviously have to be made with the Chinese Communist authorities, if only to prevent unnecessary loss of British lives and property'. Another line of argument in favour of building contacts with the Chinese Communists was put forward by Patrick O'Donovan in the *Observer*. While asserting that by nature the Communist government in China would be 'no friends of the West', he argued that there was a handful of 'painfully honest men' trying to do something for China with whom the West could work.[50]

Newspaper leader writers and political commentators all accepted the need to establish a working relationship with the Communist authorities, but they disagreed with each other as to whether Communism or Chineseness would prevail in China, and were divided on whether the government should take more decisive action in response to developments in China. The *Manchester Guardian* urged that given the substantial British interests involved the government ought to act decisively immediately. It warned that, 'there may be little time in which we can wait and see'. The government was criticized by the newspaper for 'a lack of preliminary planning for a situation which involves many major issues'. For the paper, 'the position is now much too dangerous for us to go on drifting; it is too easy to muddle into a disaster because we imagine that we can muddle through it; an agreed policy must be reached before the communists get any further'. On the contrary, *The Times* believed that while the conflict was still continuing, there was nothing much the government could do. Although the paper rejected that 'unrealistic speculations' about the immediate prospect of British commercial interests, it argued in favour of establishing 'some working relations with the communist authorities in those parts of China where they are in effective control'.[51]

After the People's Republic was formally established, the question of recognition became not whether but how and when. The view of the press was almost identical with that of the business lobby and the Foreign Office. *The Times* commented that, 'the British government must soon make up their minds when and under what conditions they will recognize the new rulers of a country in which Britain, of all the Western Powers, had the largest financial and industrial investments'. This view was widely shared by other newspapers.[52] The British press were thus generally in favour of recognizing the new Chinese government, but there was no strong pressure on the government over how and when to accord it. Throughout September and October newspaper headlines were dominated by economic issues particularly the devaluation of Sterling and the Anglo-American negotiations. British investments in China were considered to be substantial and significant, but problems in that country were not a very controversial political issue and it was by no means the most important item in the minds of newspaper editors.

The Minister of State at the Foreign Office, Kenneth Younger, later wrote that during his career in public office he could think of no occasion when he or his superiors 'had been greatly affected by public opinion in reaching important decisions', though he also admitted that policy-makers tend to be influenced by their perceived sense of general will. Indeed many studies on the role of public opinion indicate that the general public exert little influence on foreign policy decisions. Nevertheless, public opinion can be an important constraint limiting the options of policy-makers by 'creating the imagery and rhetoric' within which policy-makers act.[53] The British press, an important medium of public opinion, did not play a direct role in the British government's decision to accord recognition to the Chinese Communist government. But it had helped clear the way for the policy-makers by reports and commentaries which were in general supportive of the decision of recognition.

The Business Lobby

Britain did not have a pressure group comparable to the China lobby in the US. The most active and influential pressure group with a direct interest in China was the China Association, which represented all the major British commercial interests in China. It was a powerful lobbying group with direct access to the government. In 1949 the President of the Association was Lord Iverchapel, former Ambassador to China, and he was succeeded a year later by another former Ambassador to China, Sir Horace Seymour. The chairman of the Association at that time, William Keswick and his brother John, directors of Jardine Matheson, also had good connections in official circles. Other influential business groups of the Association included the Hong Kong and Shanghai Banking Corporation, and the British American Tobacco Company.[54]

Unlike the right-wing China lobby in the US, the British business lobby pressed for a policy in favour of the Chinese Communists. British business communities in China were reluctant to abandon their investments and properties. After the Chinese Communist forces had established firm control in North China, the China Association was anxious to see the British government establish a working relationship with the Communist authorities. This, the Association believed, would facilitate British business activities in China. When the People's Republic was formally proclaimed, the Association again pressed the British government to establish diplomatic relations with the new regime in Beijing as soon as possible.

In their lobbying efforts, the China Association stressed that the importance of British business interests in China were far greater than that revealed in trade statistics because of the large number of British industrial enterprises in China. Therefore the British commercial stake and investments in China were exceedingly valuable and would bring substantial dividends to Britain as 'invisible' exports. Moreover, many British businessmen who were rather unhappy about the policies of the Kuomintang regime were prepared to continue their businesses under a Communist government. The British commercial communities in China, the most important being Shanghai, were determined to remain there. The business community was so disillusioned with the Kuomintang government that, 'whatever alternative replaces it, it is unlikely to be any worse'. British merchants in China were optimistic that, ' it will be possible to carry on business, even under a communist regime, once the wave of Civil War has passed by'.[55]

Early experiences of British businessmen in areas under Communist control indicated that conditions would be difficult for private business but they also gave some reasons for hope. Foreign businessmen found new regulations introduced on taxation, wages and prices extremely restrictive, but the Communist authorities in North China made no attempt to close down foreign businesses or to seize their properties. One of the early messages from the joint chief manager of the Kailan Mining Administration in North China was: 'Our situation deplorable, prognosis bad, but not entirely hopeless'.[56]

The foreign business community were actually impressed when the Communists took over Shanghai in an orderly manner at the end of May. Keith Oakeshott, Vice-Consul at the British Consulate, described the discipline of the Communist soldiers as 'incredibly good' in a letter to his wife. He wrote: 'Conditions here are very satisfactory now. The Communists seem to be a great improvement on the Nationalists'.[57] The American Consul-General John Cabot recalled that the mood at that time 'bordered on euphoria'. He remembered that, 'The rejoicing couldn't have been greater if the city had been liberated by American forces. American and British businessmen were convinced – I can't think why – that they would do better under the Communists'. The attitudes of the foreign business community were not too difficult to comprehend. David Middleditch of Jardine Matheson, who believed that China needed a foreign outlet, noted in his diary that: 'The idea of doing business with the Communists may seem a bit cynical to people at home, specially after they have just shot up three of our ships. We have, however, a tremendous amount of capital sunk [sic] in Shanghai'.[58]

Meanwhile, the Communists had also made encouraging gestures directly to foreign businessmen. In August the chairman of the Shanghai British Chamber of Commerce was able to meet senior officials of the local Communist authorities. The Chinese officials expressed a willingness to keep in contact with the foreign community and stressed that they did not intend to 'squeeze the foreigners out'. Later in September the British consul-general in Tianjin, S. L. Burdett, learnt of a similar message from a Chinese businessman connected to the Communist authorities who just returned from a trip to Beijing. Burdett was told that the authorities were 'anxious to promote commercial relations with the British in particular'.[59]

Despite the optimism, conditions for British business in China continued to deteriorate steadily in 1949. The Kuomintang blockade of the port of Shanghai made the situation even worse. British businessmen believed that one major problem was that they did not have access to the Communist authorities when they had complaints or suggestions for better arrangements. Thus, they turned to their government for assistance.

In July 1949, representatives of the British American Tobacco Company went to the Foreign Office and presented their problems to Peter Scarlett. In the meeting Scarlett was shown an internal company memorandum which recommended that the government should be asked to enter into negotiations with the Communist authorities to secure better arrangements for British business. The memorandum suggested that the government should send a British diplomatic representative, not necessarily in an official capacity to take up residence in Beijing and develop relations with the new Chinese authorities there. It was clear that British businessmen in China would very much like to see government intervention on their behalf to secure better arrangements for British business.[60]

Two days later it was the China Association's turn. This time the problems for British traders in China were brought to ministerial level. The Minister of State, Hector McNeil was told that the situation in China was such that many British firms in China were living on remittances from London of three hundred and fifty thousand pounds every month. McNeil gave a non-committal answer to the request for official assistance, promising that the government would consider its members' problems.[61] It was clear that British businessmen were trying to put as much pressure on the government as possible.

After McNeil's meeting with representatives from the China Association, Sir William Strang felt that the situation was becoming very serious. In a lengthy submission to the Prime Minister, he noted that, 'we have always contemplated that the Communists would eventually introduce a pattern of state trading which would eliminate British mercantile concerns and lead to the expropriation of their properties'. Nevertheless, with the belief that the Communists had a real need to trade with the West, the Foreign Office had assumed that the Communists would tolerate British interests in continuing trading for a least a year or two. Unfortunately, the Shanghai blockade, and the fact that the Communist authorities had not taken any steps to assist foreign business, were making the situation very difficult for British businessmen. Strang concluded that, 'we may expect therefore that pressure will increase for the Government to do something to help our merchants'.[62]

The pressure from the British merchants did increase. In October, the China Association forwarded a telegram from the British Chamber of Commerce in Shanghai to the Foreign Office which urged the government to accord 'the quickest possible recognition' to the newly formed Chinese government in Beijing. They believed that the two major problems they faced – heavy taxation and a recalcitrant labour force – would not be resolved without assistance from the local authorities, and they could only expect any sympathy from the authorities in Shanghai if London recognized the Beijing government. This view was fully supported by the China Association which informed their members in Shanghai that: 'You can be assured that majority opinion here, including we believe the Foreign Office, agrees with you that early recognition is much to be desired'. The Association, however, also realistically told the Shanghai business community not to build hopes on any early outcome because further consultation with the US was necessary before the government could act.[63]

The business lobby accepted that the government had to take into account other political considerations, especially the attitude of the US government, but they had become increasingly impatient when the Communists formally established a central government in Beijing. They had expressed their views in favour of recognition, loud, strong and in unequivocal terms. Interest groups are generally found to have limited impact on foreign decision-making because they usually cannot compete effectively with governmental groups,[64] the British business lobby in 1949 seemed to be an exception. As a well connected and relatively cohesive group with influential friends in government and access to information direct from China, the business lobby was quite effective. Since the group's interests in China converged with the broader official intention of 'keeping a foot in the door of China', British businessmen were able to assert considerable influence on the government's decision of recognizing the People's Republic.

INTERNATIONAL CONSIDERATIONS

International Politics and China

Britain's attitude towards developments in China could not be seen in isolation from wider international politics. For economic and security reasons, the Attlee government had come to the conclusion that it was crucial that Britain had to maintain a close relationship with the US. To fulfil Britain's ambition of maintaining its major power position, however, British policy-makers also attached great importance to the Commonwealth, and to a Western European union. It was hardly surprising that the US, Western Europe and the Commonwealth, with divergent strategic, political and economic interests, would have very different views on international issues. Thus in 1949 when the Chinese Communists claimed victory, British policy-makers not only had to consider their country's direct interests there, they were also caught in the differing interests and perceptions of their allies whose views towards the Chinese Communists were far from identical.

One major problem arising from the establishment of a major communist regime was its effects on the East-West balance in Cold War terms. For the West, the China question was thus connected to its wider concern of global communist expansion directed by Moscow. The problem was further complicated by American past involvement in China. Washington was deeply disturbed by the prospect of 'losing China' to the communists. The Americans felt that in return for their friendship and assistance to the Chinese nation, they were being treated with hostility by the Chinese Communists.

On the other hand the newly independent members of the Commonwealth, especially India, held very different views about the Communist regime in China. They believed that they could not afford to maintain a hostile relationship with a neighbour like China, which had a vast population and territory. Being newly independent themselves, they were also sympathetic to the Communist movement in China because it had a strong nationalistic character. The Foreign Office was well aware that the British government could get into trouble with its allies over the recognition question because there was a diversity of views among them over this question. In early 1949, Esler Dening remarked: 'Both the US and France, not to mention other powers including the Commonwealth would be outraged if we were to make up our minds about recognition without consulting them'. Realizing the wider international significance of the China problem, Bevin agreed that it was essential that other friendly governments should be consulted about Britain's China policy.[65]

The United States

Anglo-American policy differences in the Far East have been regarded as a major point of divergence in the two countries' postwar co-operation.[66] In the eyes of one British businessman in 1949: 'The situation in a nutshell is that Washington and London are poles apart about what to do about China'. The major reason for their different position was that, he suggested, while the British had always traded 'in' China, the Americans had always traded 'with' China.[67] Before the war, Japanese and American competition had threatened Britain's commercial position in China. British traditional importance and influence in China had also been greatly reduced after the war. Nonetheless, Britain still had far more economic interests at stake than the US when the Chinese Communists came to power.

In March 1949, the Americans suggested that trade and shipping should be used as a lever to induce the Chinese Communist authorities to allow foreign consulates in China to function. Responding to this suggestion, the British Ambassador Stevenson noted that Britain and the US 'seem to approach this matter from different angles'. The Americans were thinking of using their commercial interests to strengthen the position of their consulates while the British considered the maintenance of their consulates as being important primarily to assist trade interests. The Ambassador concluded that on the basis of these two different angles 'a common policy seems therefore difficult of attainment'.[68]

Anglo-American divergence over the China problem stemmed not simply from different economic considerations. Although American commercial interests in China were less substantial than those of Britain, the US had become the leading Western power in the region after the Second World War with far greater overall interest in the Far East than Britain's. Furthermore, US policies towards China incorporated an emotional dimension rooted in American historical involvement in China which were also closely connected to American domestic politics.[69]

After General Marshall's failure to mediate in the Chinese civil war in January 1947, the US government continued to back Chiang Kai-shek with economic and military aid. By early 1949, it was clear to the Truman administration that the Communists were going to win the civil war. The American government, which had become disenchanted with the Kuomintang regime, was not prepared to become embroiled in China. With the publication of the document *United States Relations with China with Special Reference to the Period 1944–1949*, more commonly known as *The China White Paper*, in August 1949, the Truman administration declared that it would not attempt to intervene in the Chinese civil war. Secretary of State Dean Acheson wanted to adopt a flexible approach and suggested that the US should 'wait until the dust settles'.[70]

Cold War politics and the role of the China lobby in the US, however, exerted great pressure on the administration to adopt a tougher stance towards the Chinese Communists. By 1948, the American government had already become engaged in a bitter Cold War with the Soviet Union. The Truman doctrine, as embodied in Truman's speech to congress on 12 March 1947, had asserted openly that the United States intended to stop the advance of communism in all parts of the world.[71] Cold War rhetoric provided a most powerful argument for Chiang and his supporters in the US to attack the administration's China policy. By linking such rhetoric to developments in China, the Republican Party also found a most useful weapon to repudiate the Democratic leadership. The Chinese Communists' arrest of US consulate officials and the seizure of the compound of the

American consulate in Beijing made the situation even more difficult for the US administration. Truman and Acheson suddenly found that they had in their hands an explosive issue called China which had to be handled with great care.[72]

In May 1949, the American Ambassador to China, Leighton Stuart, recommended that the US should not take the first move to recognize a Chinese Communist government. He suggested that the administration should secure the support of Western powers and for tactical reason should wait for the new regime to make the first approach. This was fully supported by Acheson back in Washington. The US Embassy in London was quickly instructed to stress to the Foreign Office the importance of a common front.[73] The Truman administration did not want to see Britain, among other Western powers, fall out of step with the US over the China question.

Given Britain's substantial interests in China, Washington was particularly concerned that the British government might, under pressure from business circles, accord 'premature' recognition to the Communists. In July 1949 Acheson told the US Ambassador in London, Lewis Douglas that, 'we are somewhat disturbed by reports of British business interests approaching Commie officials and suggesting cooperation'.[74] There was little doubt that Bevin was anxious not to let the China question affect Anglo-American relations; his officials were instructed to secure the agreement of Britain's allies on the China question. Nonetheless, during a meeting in August with Douglas, Bevin made clear that Britain's policy was: 'to stay where we were in China and try to avoid having to withdraw or being pushed out'.[75]

In September Esler Dening accompanied Bevin to Washington to consult the Americans about Britain's position on the recognition question. He told the Americans that Britain was finding it increasingly difficult to resist the combined pressure of the Left and commercial interests for the recognition of the Communist government. State Department officials reacted strongly to this, arguing that hasty recognition of the Chinese Communist regime would be 'tantamount to acceding to blackmail'.[76]

Bevin and Acheson, together with their senior advisers, met in the State Department on 13 September to resolve their differences over the China question. The American and British versions of the meeting reflected the fact that the two sides come to the meeting with different purposes: the Americans were anxious to persuade the British not to accord premature recognition, and to broaden export restrictions on military goods to China; the British saw it as an opportunity to explain their position and secure American agreement for their China policy.

According to American records, Acheson reiterated the US position that there should not be any hasty recognition, and that nobody would gain anything from the Chinese Communists by it. The American stance remained that the Atlantic countries should concert their policies, and not extend 'any extra facilities to a Chinese Communist regime'. Acheson felt that as a prerequisite to recognition the Chinese Communists should accept international obligations in full, and should already be in full control of China. Acheson also expressed reservations on the use of recognition as a means of 'keeping China out of Russian hands', adding that, 'they will be there anyway'.[77]

The British records stressed that even though Acheson felt that premature recognition would discourage the anti-communist forces in China, he agreed with the British view that the objective was to encourage a Sino-Soviet split. These records also noted that Acheson had stated that the American government understood that the British government had to behave differently from the US because of the much more extensive British commercial interests in China. Acheson's attitude, according to these British records, was: 'It was a difference in situation rather than a difference in policy, and as long as the objective of the two governments remained the same he did not think it mattered greatly if there was some divergence on tactics'.[78]

It was not too clear whether Acheson shared Bevin's views that recognition was merely a matter of tactic. What emerges clearly from the records is that the American position was not completely rigid. At this stage it was premature recognition that they objected to, not the principle of according it. The US government had doubts about recognition as a tactic with which to split the Soviet Union and the Chinese Communists, but they did not dispute the need to encourage such a split. They had also accepted that the British government had to pursue different 'tactics' in China because British interests there were more extensive.

The American position remained unchanged after Zhou Enlai made the first move by inviting all foreign countries to establish diplomatic relations with the new government. In a press conference on 19 October, Truman did not rule out the possibility of recognition, but he declared that, 'I hope we will not have to recognize it'. He accepted the possibility that the government might have to recognize a Communist China, but he did not relish the prospect and the administration certainly did not feel that time had come for such a decision. Accordingly the American government was extremely upset when they obtained through the French a text of the British government's reply to Zhou's invitation which addressed the Beijing government as the 'People's Central Government' and expressed the hope that Anglo-Chinese political and commercial relations would be continued.[79]

The text of the British government's note to the Communist authority was considered to amount to *de facto* recognition. This, as well as the fact that the Americans had to learn about it through a third party greatly disturbed Truman and Acheson. They felt that they should have been consulted before the British delivered the note.[80] Acheson sent a personal message to Bevin on 14 October suggesting that the note appeared to imply *de facto* recognition and urged that any future British action on this question be 'preceded by the full consultation envisaged in our earlier discussions'. Truman remarked that, 'the British had not played very squarely with us on this matter'.[81] Later British officials explained to the Americans that it was a procedural error. Dening told the US Ambassador Douglas that instructions to the British Embassy 'had been sent by airgram instead of cable'. The question was later settled when Dening apologized again and admitted that the Far Eastern department had not checked with the Legal Adviser on the implication of the note.[82]

The Truman administration were upset probably more because of the fact that they had not been consulted in advance than because of the content of the text. Indeed a State Department memorandum in November stated that, 'US recognition of the Chinese Communists is not to be regarded as a major instrument for showing our interest in the Chinese people or for winning concessions from the Communist regime. Our attitude on this question should not be an eager one, but should be realistic'. Given the domestic political situation in the US, the State Department was anxious that the legal status of the Communist government not be raised in November as the UN General Assembly was in session at that time. Washington was willing to consider recognition at a later date when the Communists softened their hostile attitude, and when domestic opinion as well as Congressional sentiment towards the Chinese Communist regime became less unfavourable.[83]

The Truman administration's position was made very clear when the British Ambassador in Washington, Sir Oliver Franks, met Acheson in early December. Acheson was well aware that the British Cabinet were likely to approve recognition, yet he made no attempt to dissuade the British from taking the decision. He told Franks, 'I appreciated that the arrangements had been made to consult but that no commitment had been made necessarily to act unitedly, it being recognized that the interests of states differed and that in matters of recognition they would, in the final analysis, be governed by their views of immediate and long term self-interest'. The US government seemed prepared to accept

Britain's unilateral act to recognize the Beijing government. Acheson's only request was: 'if this decision were taken, I hope we would at least be given as much advance notice as possible so as to minimize the effects that misunderstanding might well create and cause repercussions on other Anglo-American concerns'.[84] Even though Washington had registered disapproval and misgivings about recognition, Acheson's response after the British Cabinet reached the decision of recognition in December was one of understanding rather than resentment. In a personal message to Bevin, the US Secretary of State said although the two governments were adopting different courses in this instance, he hoped they could follow a common course in all other important matters of mutual interest in the Far East.[85]

India and other Commonwealth Countries

Most Commonwealth countries only had minimal interests in China compared with those of Britain or the US. They had adopted a non-interventionist stance towards the civil war. Even by early 1949, when it was obvious that the Kuomintang regime would soon collapse, their China policies were still uncertain. However, the newly independent members and the old members had different views about this question.

The newly independent Commonwealth states in Asia, especially India, were more sympathetic to the Chinese Communists. The tide of nationalism which had led India and other former British colonial territories to become independent was still riding high in Asia. These Asian states regarded the Chinese Communist movement as a revolutionary and nationalistic movement with which they could identify. The Indian Prime Minister Jawaharlal Nehru wrote as early as 1939 on the solidarity between India and China after visiting Chongqing.[86] Indian leaders also felt strongly that it was not in their country's interests to have a large and populous neighbour as its enemy. Although developments in Tibet later soured India's relations with China after the establishment of People's Republic, on the whole Indian opinion was in favour of developing close relations with the Chinese Communist government. Some Indian politicians even harboured hopes that India and China together could become joint leaders of Asia. In March 1949 Nehru told the Indian Parliament that his government's policy towards the Communist regime in China was 'trying to make friendly co-operation possible.' These sentiments were expressed clearly by Nehru's sister Vijaya Lakshmi Pandit. Mrs Pandit, who had held important diplomatic posts in post-independent India, wrote in her memoirs that, 'We in India, with more than two thousand years of contact with China, felt that it was not possible to ignore the claims of the Chinese millions or the revolutionary changes that had taken place there'.[87]

Thus at an early stage the Indian government was in favour of keeping in contact with the Chinese Communists. In early 1949, the Indian High Commissioner in London, Krishna Menon, told Attlee that, 'Any hostility towards a communist-controlled China by other countries will tend to throw it more in the Soviet orbit'. He concluded that, 'A realistic policy should therefore lead to contacts being maintained with the new Government without any commitment'. This Indian position was similar to the Foreign Office's.[88] In fact at this stage the Indian government did not want to pursue a China policy in isolation. The Foreign Ministry's Secretary-General Girja Shankar Bajpal made it clear to the Americans in May 1949 that the Indian government would consult other Western countries before taking any step to accord either *de facto* or *de jure* recognition to the Chinese Communist government. Later in June, Bajpai again reaffirmed that the Indian government did not intend to act unilaterally on the question of recognition.[89]

But when Zhou formally invited all other countries to establish diplomatic relations with the People's Republic, the Indian government felt that it could no longer delay recognizing Beijing. In November, the Indian High Commissioner in London told Bevin that the Indian government intended to recognize the new Chinese government. There was no doubt that the new regime was 'well established, stable, and likely to endure', and there was no real alternative to it. For Indian policy-makers the question was thus not whether but when recognition should be accorded. They told Bevin that, 'We are strongly advised that delay in direct action may well be injurious both politically and economically and may encourage wrong tendencies in China'. They urged early recognition and proposed that it should be accorded between 15 and 25 December, after the conclusion of the UN General Assembly.[90]

While feeling that an early recognition by India might break the ice as far as US opinion was concerned, the Foreign Office thought that if India acted unilaterally then US-Commonwealth relations and Commonwealth solidarity might be affected. Thus the British government was under pressure to act more quickly on the question of recognition. When Bevin met Nehru on 12 November, he still tried to persuade New Delhi to wait for a collective decision. He told Nehru that, 'It might be that the USA would change her view if we arrived at an orderly and proper decision'.[91]

The Commonwealth High Commissioners' meeting in 15 November in London demonstrated that a collective decision could not be achieved; Countries like Canada, Australia, New Zealand were reluctant to break ranks with the US, while Asian states like Pakistan and Ceylon were willing to follow Britain's lead. While the Canadian government agreed that recognition was inevitable, they were in no hurry to do so. The Canadian High Commissioner listed three factors in Canada's cautious approach: First, the repercussions of recognition on Chinese living in Canada; second, Canadian interests still remained largely in territories controlled by the Kuomintang in Western China, third, Canada was reluctant to march out of step with the US. Both Australia and New Zealand were to hold general elections soon, and the two governments did not want to make any decision on the issue or recognition before them. The Asian states in the Commonwealth were more prepared to recognize the People's Republic. India made clear its position that it was prepared to act independently, if the others were still not decided. Both Pakistan and Ceylon agreed to wait until early in the New Year.[92]

At this stage the British government was still reluctant to take the plunge. Apart from the fact that there was a UN general assembly in session, and elections were soon to be held in Australia and New Zealand, Bevin was still anxious to be in step with the United States and France as far as possible. The Commonwealth High Commissioners' meeting served to clear the air of Commonwealth opinion. There was a division on the timing of recognition, but all had accepted the principle of it. Thus, the British government was under no pressure to refrain from recognizing Beijing from the Commonwealth. If there was any such pressure, it would have been pressure to accord recognition sooner rather than later because of India's position.

Western European Countries

Two different approaches were adopted by Western European countries towards the China question. For countries such as France and the Netherlands, China was of importance because developments there would affect the situation in their colonial territories in Southeast Asia. Those without colonial possessions in Asia did not want to take the lead in a question of international importance in an area of no major concern to them. The principle of recognition, however, was widely accepted.

Thus the British government found a sympathetic audience when it approached friendly European governments on its China policy. In general European governments had doubts about the prospects of developing friendly relations with the new Chinese government, but to a varying degree, they all accepted the British government's opinion that they would have to live with a Communist China. In November 1949 the Scandinavian countries, Belgium and Luxembourg told London that they were prepared to follow Britain's lead to recognize Beijing.[93]

For those countries with colonial territories in Southeast Asia, the question was more complicated; the painful de-colonization process was underway. Their policies towards the establishment of a nationalistic Communist regime in China might affect their colonial interests. The Dutch were beginning to retreat from Indonesia after failing to create a post-colonial order that they wanted. The Dutch government did not want to accord recognition to Beijing prior to the transfer of sovereignty in Indonesia which was to take place at the end of December. Nevertheless, they supported Britain's position as a 'realistic approach' and were prepared to recognize the new Chinese government themselves. Portugal and Italy were more hesitant, but they did not raise any objection when the Foreign Office informed them of Britain's intention.[94]

France's reaction to developments in China was the strongest amongst Britain's European allies. Engaged in a difficult fight against Vietnamese Communists in Indo-China, the French government's attitude towards the Chinese Communist regime was ambivalent subject to developments in Indo-China. Thus although the French realistically assessed that the Chinese Communists were to stay, their policy towards recognition had not been always consistent. In January 1949, the French Foreign Minister, Robert Schuman, had suggested that it was possible that the Chinese Communists might be more independent of the Soviet Union than the East European states. A French aide memoire in February also shared the British government's views that the West must preserve its position in China as far as possible, for any position abandoned would be lost for good. While the French Foreign Ministry wanted to see an 'active' and energetic policy of defence against the 'repercussion of the Chinese Communist movement' in Southeast Asia, it admitted that in China itself 'the only possible course seems to be to bow to circumstances'.[95]

When the Foreign Office informed the French of Britain's intention to recognize the new Chinese government, the French Foreign Ministry changed its tone. The French argued that it was not necessary to take any political step which might further diminish the resistance of Kuomintang forces against Mao's army in Southern China. This consideration was linked directly to the situation in Indo-China because the French government was apprehensive of 'the world-wide consequences which the arrival of Communist troops in the immediate vicinity of Vietnam might have'. The French concluded that it was in the interest of the Atlantic Pact allies, and the Commonwealth that the advance of the Communist forces towards the Vietnam-Chinese border should be 'postponed as long as possible'.[96]

The French government also suggested that once Britain had accorded recognition to Beijing, all other countries which did not follow suit within a short time would be considered by the new government as hostile. This, the French felt, would damage the future relations of these countries with the People's Republic and would make contacts between their diplomatic representatives and the new government more difficult. As the French had to safeguard their interests in Indo-China, they were not prepared to recognize the Communist regime in Beijing, and they urged the British government to re-consider their policy.[97] Foreign Office officials rejected the French arguments as unconvincing. Scarlett dismissed the suggestion that recognition of the Communists would weaken the Kuomintang's will to resist. He stated bluntly that, 'resistance ceased north of the Yangtze many months ago'. Dening believed that 'the French probably in their hearts accepted the fact that we will recognize, but will tend to reproach us'.[98]

Despite the French government's misgivings, most Western European countries shared the British government's analysis of the situation in China. For a variety of reasons, some of them disagreed with the timing of recognition, but they all agreed that it was necessary to recognize the new government in Beijing. A number of them were in fact willing to follow suit.

The Soviet Union

By the end of 1948, British officials in charge of Far Eastern affairs had come to the conclusion that the Chinese Communists were orthodox Marxists. Yet they believed that it might be possible to drive a wedge between them and the Soviet Union. There seemed to be grounds for such a hope. On the one hand, the Soviet Union had not shown too much enthusiasm for a Communist victory until the final stage of the Chinese civil war. On the other hand, the strong nationalistic fervour in the Chinese Communist movement also suggested that they would not be willing to became subservient to the Soviet Union.

The first group of Chinese Communists had gone to Moscow for formal training in the early 1920s. The Soviet Union had actually set up a university, the Sun Yat-sen University, specially for Chinese students in 1925. These students were mostly communist activists and for a short period included some senior Kuomintang officials. As shown in Chapter 1, many Moscow-trained Chinese Communists later took up important positions in the new Chinese government formed in 1949. Chinese Communist forces had been greatly strengthened when Soviet troops in Manchuria turned over captured Japanese military equipment to them at the end of the Second World War after the Japanese had surrendered.

However, the Soviet government's relationship with the Chinese Communists was not without strains. Stalin had been in favour of a Kuomintang-Communist alliance before the Chinese Communist victory had become apparent. Stalin had admitted that he had asked the Chinese Communists to reach a vivendi with Chiang Kai-shek, but they would not listen to him.[99] Another Soviet action which had earlier upset the Chinese Communists was the treaty which the Soviet Union signed with the Kuomintang government in 1945 to secure Chiang Kai-shek's acquiescence to the Yalta agreement granting the Soviet Union special rights in Manchuria. By signing the treaty with Chiang, the Soviet Union had recognized the Kuomintang regime as the sole legal government of China. Some of the Chinese Communists had expressed their bitterness at the signing of the treaty to members of the American Embassy.[100] In February 1949, when the Kuomintang moved their headquarters from Nanjing to Guangzhou, the Soviet Union was the only major country which followed the Kuomintang and moved its embassy.

But as the Chinese civil war was coming to an end, the Chinese Communist leadership made it clear that they looked to Moscow for leadership. As John Gittings put it, 'The Soviet Union was for better or worse the leader of the world communist bloc, and therefore the only realistic major ally for a Communist China'.[101] In late 1948 Mao pronounced that a 'middle road' did not exist between the revolutionary and the imperialist camps. In March 1949, a New China News Agency editorial declared that the Chinese people regarded 'the leaders of the world anti-imperialist front, the great socialist state, the Soviet Union, as their comrades in arms, from first to last'. The Chinese Communist leadership were also very critical of the North Atlantic Pact. Mao denounced the Pact when its negotiations concluded. More significantly, Radio Beijing also commented that if the Nato Pact provoked 'an aggressive war', 'the Chinese Communists will unite the people and march forward hand in hand with China's ally, the Soviet Union'. Later on Mao openly proclaimed the Communist leadership's policy of 'leaning to one side' in the *People's Daily*.[102]

From mid-1949 onwards, the Soviet Union had also displayed greater interest in the success of the Chinese Communists. The Communist crossing of the Yangtze in April was prominently covered by the Soviet press. In response to Mao's request Soviet economic advisers also went to China to assist the Communist leadership on how to solve the economic chaos in China well before the formal establishment of diplomatic relations between the two sides in October 1949.[103] By the end of that year the Chinese Communists were moving closer and closer to the Soviet Union. When the British Cabinet met in December 1948 to discuss CP(48)299 on China, it was acknowledged that a Communist victory would represent 'a grave threat to the position of non-communist governments throughout Asia', and that economic and military arrangements against the communist threat similar to those in Europe should be considered. However, British policy-makers also harboured the hope that, 'Far Eastern communism might develop on Chinese rather than Slav lines'. They reasoned that Chinese communism might be forced by economic necessity to modify its position because of economic considerations. While feeling uncertain about long term British interests in China, they were optimistic that in the initial stage the Beijing government might be prepared to allow foreign commercial activities. On the basis of this assessment, the Cabinet accepted that, 'It would be unwise to pursue a policy which might have the effect of driving a Chinese Communist Government into the arms of the Soviet Union'. This calculation later became an important element leading to the British government's decision to recognize the Communist regime.[104]

In early 1949 British officials had gathered evidence to support their claim that the Chinese Communists were orthodox Marxists.[105] Later on, however, arguing in favour of recognition, the Foreign Office suggested that there was the possibility that the relationship between Communist China and the West might 'develop along the lines of our present relationship with Yugoslavia'. The Foreign Office concluded that, 'the Western Powers should be careful not to prejudice future possibilities by developing an openly hostile attitude towards a Communist regime from the outset'.[106]

British policy-makers saw the USSR as a menace to British security and a threat to the Western position on a global scale in the post-war world, but the main focus of British foreign policy was Europe. Communist or not, China was relatively unimportant politically, economically and strategically. The formation of a Chinese Communist government would undermine British colonial interests in Southeast Asia, but it would not be a direct security threat to Britain. Moreover, the British government was in no position to avert a Communist victory in China. It is not clear whether policy-makers in London were convinced that recognition would unsettle Sino-Soviet relationship at that time, but there is no doubt that they wanted to pursue a policy which would serve British interests in China and might also encourage a Sino-Soviet split in the long run.

THE FINAL DECISION

The question of recognition was first brought up directly at full Cabinet level discussion at the end of October 1949 after the new Chinese government had been formed and extended invitations for diplomatic relations with the rest of the world. During the meeting Bevin told his colleagues that the first step 'must be to consult other Commonwealth Governments and the Governments of the US and other friendly Powers'. In fact, the Foreign Office, after more than one year's efforts of consulting Britain's allies as well as sorting out internal differences among the bureaucracy, had already come to the conclusion that now the time for recognition had come.[107]

In replying to Zhou's invitation to establish diplomatic relations, the British government which had addressed the Beijing regime as 'the Central People's Government', expressed the hope that the 'friendly and mutually advantageous' commercial and political relations which had existed between Britain and China for years would continue. The reply further proposed informal links should be established between British consular officials in China and the local Chinese authorities before the establishment of proper relations between the two governments.[108] The note of reply in effect amounted to *de facto* recognition of the Beijing government. To the British Ambassador Stevenson, the reply was the right thing to do 'both from a short term and a long term point of view' and 'it was done at the right moment'. He believed that the reply would ease the position not only for British communities in China but also for those of other non-communist countries during the period when their countries did not have official diplomatic relations with the new Chinese government.[109]

Although Bevin was in favour of recognition when the Communist government was formed in Beijing, he still preferred to act in concert with other friendly governments and he also wanted to wait for the outcome of the Bukit Serene Conference of UK representative in South East Asia which was being held in Singapore at that moment. Britain's consultation with the US and other friendly governments eventually dispelled the Foreign Secretary's worries about the international reaction to recognition. When Dening returned to London after securing the support of senior British officials in Southeast Asia, he told Bevin that recognition should not be delayed any longer. On 8 December Dening informed colleagues in other ministries that: 'Having shivered on the brink of recognition for so long, we were now recommending that the plunge be taken and *de jure* recognition be accorded to the Central Government of China'.[110]

The Foreign Office subsequently submitted a Cabinet paper on 26

November recommending recognition. After reiterating the legal arguments, the Foreign Office maintained that not to recognize the Communist government while there was no further effective authority in China, 'would imply a deliberate policy of boycotting China'. The paper concluded: 'the effects of such a negative policy on Britain's long-term relations with China as well as on our trading interests in China need no elaboration'.[111]

The Cabinet was urged that a decision had to be taken quickly because if recognition were delayed too long, the new Chinese government would put pressure upon British interests in China or demand the withdrawal of British Officials. In that case the British government would be 'compelled either to accord recognition under duress or to withhold it indefinitely as a gesture against coercion'. This would, in the eyes of the Foreign Office, create a dilemma for the government because to adopt the first alternative would weaken British prestige and position in the Far East, and to adopt the second would sacrifice British interests in China that the government had wanted to maintain.[112]

Bevin's recommendation was approved by the Cabinet on 15 December. After months of indecisiveness during which painstaking internal discussions and extensive international consultations were carried out, British policy-makers finally took the decision to accord *de jure* recognition to the new Chinese government.[113]

CONCLUSIONS

Both external and internal factors had influenced London's decision to recognize the new Chinese government. The international environment, and Britain's post-war foreign policy objectives: to maintain a close alliance relationship with the US, to create a Western European union, and to forge a common front with the Commonwealth, provided the external contest within which the decision-making process operated. British policy makers faced a very difficult international situation after World War Two: their country's global interests and commitments were extensive, but its resources were limited. Further, the international scene was becoming dominated by the US and the USSR in opposing camps. In formulating their China policy, British policy-makers not only had to take into account their country's direct interests in China, but also their overall foreign policy objectives, and interests in other parts of the world. There was no doubt that British policy-makers were fully aware of the fact that their China policy could not be isolated from their other policies. The recognition decision was thus made only after several months of consultations with other friendly governments.

Detailed calculations of British interests in China were made by the bureaucratic machinery in Whitehall. The Foreign Office was the major bureaucratic force in the decision-making process. Although, as suggested in Chapter 1, ministerial attention to events in China had increased in 1949, China was not a priority for them. Thus, Foreign Office officials played a central part in the formulation of Britain's China policy. Officials from other ministries also took part in the policy formulation process, but different bureaucratic interests were resolved without too much difficulty, partly because China was considered relatively unimportant. Equally important was the fact that the Foreign Office as the primary organ of foreign policy formulation had the backing of an influential Secretary of State, who was highly respected within his own party and trusted by the Prime Minister. However, the views of the Treasury, the Board of Trade, the Ministry of Defence, and the Colonial Office, which had different interests in China, were not ignored. The Foreign Office's assessments of the situation in China, and the implications of a communist dominated China for British interests were revised as a result of inter-departmental consultation. Both organizational processes and bureaucratic politics played their parts in the policy formulation process.

The British government's decision to recognize the Beijing government was in fact less daring than it appeared to be. Despite the Cold War, the international and domestic environments at that time were not that unfavourable to their decision. Most Western European countries shared the British government's assessment of the situation in China. Many Asian members of the Commonwealth were all in favour of recognition. India even exerted strong pressure on Britain for an early recognition. Other Commonwealth nations which favoured a concerted action with the US made no objections to the British decision.

The different responses of Britain and the US towards the establishment of the People's Republic have been interpreted as an example of post-war Anglo-American divergence. A closer look at the Anglo-American consultation process reveals a very different picture: the two allies' views about the Chinese Communist regime differed, but as far as recognition was concerned, the Truman administration was against according it prematurely, rather than the principle *per se*. When Dean Acheson was informed of the British Cabinet's intention in December 1949, he put his objection on the record, but made no attempts to pressure the British government to reverse their decision.

Domestically, British policy-makers were actually under intense pressure from British business interests to maintain relations with Communist China. The business lobby formed a most powerful pressure group in the form of the China Association, arguing in favour of recognition. The government's Far Eastern policy was severely criticized in Parliament and by the press after the Amethyst incident, but it only highlighted the need to maintain relations with the Communists. In the House of Commons, with the leader of the Opposition in support of the government over this issue, the debate on recognition centred largely on its timing rather than on its merits. Thus, one year and a week after the policy of 'keeping a foot in the door' appeared in CP(48)299, the government was able to turn it into the more concrete act of recognition.

One important factor that British policy-makers had not taken into account was the likely response of the new Chinese leadership to recognition. After coming to the conclusion that the Chinese leaders were orthodox Marxists, they were understandably apprehensive that the emergence of a Communist China hostile to the West – isolated diplomatically – would have serious consequences for British interests in Asia. At a time when the most dangerous threat to Britain was perceived as the Soviet Union in Europe, British policy-makers formulated a China policy with the aim of establishing a working relationship with a Chinese Communist government, and splitting the communist bloc as far as possible. In formulating this policy, they had given very little thought to whether a newly established revolutionary regime would have different views about existing diplomatic practices, and the international order. This was perhaps inevitable. As a well-established member of the existing international society, Britain pursued its foreign policies within the framework of the accepted code of international diplomatic practice. The British policy-makers proceeded on the premise that the new Chinese government would respond to *de jure* recognition swiftly in accordance to usual diplomatic practice, by establishing diplomatic relations with Britain. This proved to be a miscalculation. In December 1949 British policy-makers could have hardly foreseen that recognition would be only the beginning of many other problems ahead. The implementation of their China policy, following Britain's recognition of Beijing, proved to be equally difficult, if not more so.

Part II
Policy Implementation

3 From Negotiation to Confrontation

After Britain's recognition of the Beijing government, policy-makers in London expected that formal diplomatic contact and channels would be set up smoothly. They were to be disappointed as their expectation failed to materialize. Beijing's immediate response was not entirely negative; the new leaders in China expressed a willingness to establish diplomatic relations. The problem for Britain was that recognition was considered by the new Chinese leadership merely as a first step towards normal diplomatic relations which required negotiations. The Chinese side's insistence for negotiations proved to be only the first of many hurdles that the British government had to cross in implementing their China policy of 'keeping a foot in the door'.

Direct Anglo-Chinese negotiations over diplomatic relations began shortly after Britain's recognition of the People's Republic but were discontinued when the Korean War broke out in June 1950. These talks lasted for about six months but the two sides were not able to come to an agreement. The negotiations were in fact not proper negotiations in the sense of both sides appointing a team to sit around the same table for a number of agreed meetings and discussions. Instead, they took the form of a number of unscheduled meetings between the British charge d'affaires in Beijing and the Chinese Vice-Foreign Minister, during which written and oral communications were passed to each side.

Meanwhile the diplomatic status of British officials in China was not even recognized. The importance of these meetings, however, should not be underestimated. They were the first major negotiations between revolutionary China and a Western country. Through these preliminary negotiations the two sides made their positions clear to the other and extended feelers to test each other's intentions and policies.

The preliminary negotiations coincided with a difficult period for the Chinese government. Revolutionary China was only in its infancy with urgent social and economic reform programmes to undertake. When the Chinese Communists declared victory they had yet unified the whole country and their Kuomintang rivals were still challenging their rule from Taiwan. The new government had to prove their legitimacy to represent

71

China and demonstrate that they were able to govern a huge country in an unfavourable international atmosphere.

For the British government, implementing its China policy during this period was probably no less difficult. London had to deal with a revolutionary state which was deeply suspicious of the West and hostile at times. To complicate things further British policy-makers not only had to face the recalcitrance of the Chinese revolutionaries, but also an increasingly critical opposition to their policy from Washington as Sino-US estrangement deepened. Their task was thus a balancing act in trying to achieve what they wanted in China on the one hand, and to avoid antagonizing US opinion on the other.

Twice, the British government took the initiative to break the deadlock in the Anglo-Chinese talks, the first time by preparing to support Beijing's claim in the UN, and the second time by seeking to upgrade the level of the negotiations with secret diplomacy. Both attempts were overtaken by events: the outbreak of the Korean war in June 1950 and China's subsequent military intervention in November made the continuation of the Anglo-Chinese 'negotiations' on diplomatic relations impossible. It was only after the 1953 Korean armistice when the international climate became more favourable that relations between the two countries could improve. Ernest Bevin did not live to see the establishment of formal diplomatic relations between Britain and China; he stepped down as Foreign Secretary in March 1951 and died one month later.

This chapter will provide an account of the negotiations between Britain and revolutionary China. The problems which British policy-makers had to face in trying to establish diplomatic relations with the Beijing government, and the measures employed to solve these problems, will be discussed.

ANGLO-CHINESE NEGOTIATIONS

The Preliminary Stage

The British government expected that once recognition was accorded, the only remaining problem would be the technical details for the formal exchange of Ambassadors. There were some forewarnings of problems to come when the Chinese government did not respond positively to the recognition by Burma and India; both countries had recognized Beijing ahead of Britain in December 1949. In reply to their messages of recognition, the Chinese government insisted that as a precondition for the establishment of diplomatic relations they had to sever their relations with the Kuomintang and send a representative to begin negotiations on this issue.[1]

Beijing's response to Burma's approach caused some concern in the Foreign Office. John Hutchison, who was to be appointed charge d'affaires in China suggested from Nanjing that what the Chinese had in mind was 'merely such questions as rank and identity of "envoys" referred to in the Burmese statement, the dates of their appointment, the location and setting up of embassies or legations and other business of that kind'.[2] Nevertheless, the Foreign Office instructed the British Consul in Beijing, Walter Graham, who was to pass the note of recognition to the Chinese Foreign Ministry, to make it clear that he was only 'authorised to discuss procedural questions'. If the Beijing Government insisted on making the establishment of diplomatic relations conditional on the outcome of negotiations even though recognition had been accorded, Graham should report immediately, and ask the Chinese to clarify the nature of the negotiations.[3]

Hutchison, however, remained confident in awaiting the Chinese reply. On the day after recognition had been accorded, he noted that Britain's case was different from that of the India and Burma because at the time of recognition it already had a representative in Beijing and had nominated a charge d'affaires who could take up his post as soon as possible.[4] It transpired that the Chinese government's reply (which came on 9 January) not only attached the severance of relations with the Kuomintang as a precondition of diplomatic relations, but it also asked Hutchison to go to Beijing as the British representative for negotiations.[5]

On the same day the official Chinese news agency, New China News Agency (NCNA) issued a commentary highly critical of the manner of Britain's recognition. In it, NCNA expressed resentment that at the time of recognition, the Central Information Office in London had suggested in a press release that recognition did not necessarily mean approval and illustrated this using the example of the Franco regime in Spain. NCNA commented that, 'Thus the British imperialist elements do not in the least conceal their instinctive enmity towards the Chinese People's Republic'. The commentary then turned to the continuing presence of a British Consul in Taiwan who was stationed in Tamsui. NCNA also announced 'the Central People's Government will decide what actions it will take towards the British Government in the light of the actual actions of the British towards China and not in the light of its statements'.[6]

The British Government was very disturbed by this Chinese response. On 13 January the Foreign Office asked Graham 'to seek elucidation of the Chinese government'. The Foreign Office decided that Hutchison would only go to Beijing 'in the capacity of Charge d'Affaires which itself would

imply that diplomatic relations have been established'. At the same time
the British government approached other countries facing a similar problem
to arrive at concerted action not to send their charge d'affaires to Beijing
unless their status were also clarified.[7]

Hutchison telegraphed London on 13 and 25 January arguing that the
Chinese wanted diplomatic relations; he was anxious to go to Beijing.[8] The
Chinese reply came shortly afterwards. On 28 January, Huan Xiang, Head
of the Foreign Ministry's Western Europe and African Division informed
Graham that Hutchison might come to Beijing 'in the capacity of Charge
d'Affaires of the British government to discuss preliminary and procedural
matters of the establishment of diplomatic relations'. Although the Chinese
government had not spelt out clearly whether or not they considered that
diplomatic relations had been established, Hutchison was greatly encouraged and believed that the statement 'now provides a sufficiently clear
basis of agreement for me to proceed to Peking without further delay'. On
31 January, the Foreign Secretary agreed that Hutchison should proceed.[9]

On the same day when the British government made the decision to let
Hutchison go to Beijing, the Foreign Office learnt that the new Chinese
government had made the question of China's representation at the UN
an issue in its diplomatic relations with Norway. Earlier the Norwegian
government had failed to vote for the Beijing government when the
question was put to a vote in the Security Council on 13 January. The
British government too had failed to support Beijing's claim in the UN.[10]

Meanwhile Hutchison did not have any time to think about such problems. After more than three weeks of uncertainty, Beijing had now made
clear that him would be accepted as the charge d'affaires representing the
British government. While his main task was to secure normal diplomatic
relations with the new Chinese government, he was also under strict
instructions to limit discussions to procedural questions. The instructions
stated, 'What we must guard against is an attempt to impose conditions
unfavourable to us as the price for the establishment of normal relations'.
The Foreign Office insisted that any formal official discussions on matters
other than procedural questions must await the establishment of diplomatic
relations.[11]

Direct Negotiations: the first stage

On 13 February 1950, four days before the Chinese New Year, Hutchison
arrived in Beijing together with the Indian representative. They were welcomed by a senior Foreign Ministry official from the protocol department.
In a brief news report by NCNA Hutchison and the Indian representative

were described as 'appointed Charge d'Affaires of India and Britain sent to conduct talks on the establishment of diplomatic relations with the Chinese Government'.[12] It was perhaps not an opportune moment to arrive to conduct official business, just before the Chinese New Year. More importantly, many top Chinese leaders, including Mao Zedong and Zhou Enlai, had still not returned from Moscow where they had just concluded a friendship treaty with the Soviet government. In the event, this did not make any major difference to Hutchison: never during his one year stay in Beijing was he to have the chance to meet these Chinese leaders.

On 17 February, Chinese New Year day, Hutchison made his courtesy call. He was received by Huan Xiang, director of the Western Europe division, but there was no substantive discussion. Ten days later Hutchison had the first of his meetings with Vice Foreign Minister Zhang Hanfu, who turned out to be the only Chinese official of ministerial rank he could see in Beijing. Zhang told him that the Chinese government was not ready for discussions and no time was set for another meeting. All that the British side could do was to sit and wait.[13] Then on 3 March, almost three weeks after Hutchison's arrival in Beijing, the Foreign Ministry summoned Hutchison again and Zhang spelt out the questions that they wanted to discuss prior to the establishment of diplomatic relations.

British officials were thus kept in the dark for almost two months before they know what conditions the Chinese government wanted to see fulfilled prior to the establishment of diplomatic relations. There was also another question on the minds of Foreign Office officials. A general election was being held in February and a change of government might mean a change in Britain's China policy.[14] This consideration was soon swept aside when the Labour Party was returned to office. The government's China policy would go ahead. With Hutchison already in Beijing as charge d'affaires, the British government was not in a position to retreat easily. Yet the Foreign Office was determined that any conditions not favourable to Britain would not be accepted.

The meeting with Zhang on 3 March at least enabled the Foreign Office to know what the Chinese government wanted. During this meeting Zhang demanded that the British government must sever its relations with Kuomintang. Specifically he raised three issues: the British government's policy over Chinese representation in the UN, its attitude to Kuomintang organizations, and Chinese national property in British territories. Britain had abstained from voting in the Security Council of the UN on 13 January when the Soviet delegate proposed that the Kuomintang representative should be replaced with Beijing's representatives. The Chinese government regarded this abstention as Britain's continued recognition of the Kuomintang's legality. The Soviet delegate later walked out of the Security Council when his demand to expel the Kuomintang representatives was not accepted. Zhang made clear that the Chinese government regarded Britain's support for their representation in the UN as crucial for the formal establishment of Sino-British diplomatic relations.[15]

The two other questions concerned Kuomintang organization, and Chinese national property in Hong Kong. What the Chinese referred to as Chinese national property were seventy aircraft in Hong Kong which belonged to two former Kuomintang government agencies, the China National Aviation Corporation (CNAC) and the Central Air Transport Corporation (CATC). Zhang demanded an early statement of the British government's attitude on these two questions. Reporting this interview Hutchison said the tone of the meeting had been 'courteous and friendly'.[16]

Friendly and courteous it might well have been, but the message was clear: the Chinese government was taking up substantial political questions rather than procedural problems in the negotiations. It had also become clear to the Foreign Office that, 'the Chinese regard Mr Hutchison purely as someone authorised to negotiate on behalf of the British government and not as the head of the British Diplomatic Mission in China'. The British Embassy's existence was not even acknowledged by the Chinese government.[17] At this point the British side, however, did not have too many choices, except to answer the questions raised by the Chinese; the alternative would be to give up the policy of 'keeping a foot in the door' in China.

The Foreign Office thus decided to explain Britain's attitude towards the severance of relations with the Kuomintang government in Taiwan, and the three specific issues raised by the Chinese government. Observing the progress of other countries' negotiations with the Chinese government closely, Foreign Office officials found that the Chinese government had raised similar questions with the governments of India and Scandinavian countries.[18] However India's position was different from Britain's as the Indian delegate in the UN had supported Beijing's claim in the Security Council on 13 January. As far as the Scandinavian countries were concerned, the problem of Chinese property was almost non-existent. On Chinese representation at the UN, the Swedish government told the Chinese government that if the question could not be settled in the Security Council, it would vote in favour of the Beijing in the General Assembly.[19]

On 17 March Hutchison delivered the British government's official reply to the Chinese Foreign Ministry. He reaffirmed that diplomatic relations with the Kuomintang government had been severed and explained that Britain's abstention from voting for the expulsion of the Kuomintang representative in the UN was not against Beijing's representative. 'The decision to abstain was taken', Hutchison told Zhang Hanfu, 'because there was at that time no likelihood of a majority decision and it was consequently premature for the question to be raised.' The reply assured the Chinese that Britain would vote for the new Chinese government in UN organs as soon as a majority of members of those organs also decided to vote in favour of them. On Kuomintang organizations and activities in Hong Kong, the British reply made clear that these organizations and individuals did not have any political status because in Hong Kong all group political activities were banned by law. Regarding Chinese state properties in Hong Kong, Britain's position was that Beijing's rights over China's state properties were recognized, but if the Chinese government was not in actual possession of such properties, and those holding them refused to give them up, the disputes had to be settled through the Courts.[20]

After listening to the explanations Zhang did not have any direct reaction. He only said that the Chinese government had to study these explanations and a reply would be given as soon as their study had been completed.[21] The British government had no illusion that their explanations would satisfy the Chinese. In early March they began to manoeuvre behind the scenes to secure majority support for Beijing's representation in the Security Council and approached other members of the Council to vote in favour of the new government. This attempt eventually failed, largely because it did not have the support of the US and France.[22]

While British officials were waiting for the Chinese government's response, encouraging signs emerged from China's negotiations with India. On 16 March the Chinese government made it clear that they were satisfied with the Indian reply and agreed to the establishment of diplomatic relations. Observing this development in London, John Shattock, head of the Foreign Office's Far Eastern department, was hopeful that the Chinese were ready to establish relations with Britain as well. Meanwhile Hutchison, who had remained optimistic in Beijing, also anticipated that Anglo-Chinese negotiations might soon be concluded along the same lines as the Indian case. He telegraphed London suggesting possible procedural steps to take for the establishment of diplomatic relations. The Foreign Office duly gave him guidelines for action. Thus, both Hutchison and the Foreign Office were preparing for a step forward.[23]

This optimism, however, was to prove unfounded and the Chinese government remained silent for more than a month. At the same time when Britain was facing a wall of silence, China concluded negotiations with Sweden and Denmark and established diplomatic relations with them in April.

Direct Negotiations: the interlude

The interlude between 17 March, when Hutchison delivered Britain's reply, and 7 May, when the Chinese gave their response, was to prove a most difficult period for the British side. Contrary to the hopes of the British business communities in China, recognition did not improve their situation. By March it had become apparent that instead of improving, the situation of British firms in China had deteriorated.[24]

During a meeting with China Association representative on 16 March, the Foreign Secretary admitted that 'he now had some doubts of the Government's decision to recognise the Central People's Government'. He also added that it was not easy to deal with a revolution, and suggested that the situation might have been worse if the government had not recognized the Beijing government. The Foreign Secretary was told that because of the worsening financial situation some British firms were almost 'on the brink of collapse'. Association representatives urged Bevin to appoint an Ambassador to China for negotiations with the Chinese government. Bevin assured them that he recognized the stake of British interests in China and suggested that the businessmen would have to 'hold on a little longer'.[25] Unfortunately, it soon became clear that the firms had to hold on not just for a little longer; their position continued to deteriorate throughout April.

The problem of British business interests in China was not simply an economic problem for the government. It had also become a serious political question and there was mounting pressure for a change in the government's China policy. The deteriorating financial position of the British firms, despite recognition, was seen as an indication that the government's policy was not working. The announcement of the recognition of the People's Republic was made when Parliament had been in recess and the delay in the establishment of diplomatic relations had attracted the attention of many MPs after the House of Commons had resumed business in March. The Labour government, which was narrowly returned to office after the general election, had only a small overall majority. The government's diplomatic problem with the new Chinese government was seized on by opposition MPs and many embarrassing questions were raised in the House.

On the very first day of the new Parliamentary session, Air Commodore Harvey maintained that what the Chinese government had done 'has been a virtual snub for Britain', and that, 'British prestige has never been lower in China than it is at the present time'.[26] The Minister of State at the Foreign Office, Kenneth Younger had to concede that after recognition, 'British nationals continued to encounter difficulties of all kinds'. Younger blamed it partly on the Kuomintang blockade of Shanghai, and partly on the 'situation prevailing in China'.[27] By April, when there was no apparent progress in the Anglo-Chinese talks, the wisdom of recognizing the Communist government was being questioned again. One MP went as far as demanding that recognition be withdrawn.[28]

Opinion critical of the government's China policy was not confined to Westminster. There were voices against the policy of 'keeping a foot in the door' in China even within Whitehall. British colonial officials in Malaya, who had kept a wary eye on the policy of recognition, were apprehensive that the Beijing government would send diplomats to Malaya after the establishment of Anglo-Chinese diplomatic relations. They feared that the presence of Communist Chinese consuls might undermine their drive against the Malayan Communists. With the support of the Colonial Office they demanded that China should not be allowed to appoint consuls to Malaya because admitting them would 'amount to a major setback in the anti-communist campaign'. The Malayan authorities felt that the situation in Malaya was so critical that it would be justified in refusing the appointment of Chinese consuls even at the expense of a rupture in Anglo-Chinese diplomatic relations.[29] The Foreign Office had to back down and acquiesced in the Colonial Office's recommendation. This decision to exclude Chinese consuls from Malaya, however, was never implemented. Britain and the people's Republic failed to reach an agreement in their talks and the question of appointing Chinese consuls to Malaya never arose.

The British government's failure to resolve the deadlock in Anglo-Chinese relations also had international implications. The fact that the British government was not able to make any headway in its negotiations with the Chinese government several months after recognition hardened American opposition to Britain's China policy. Apart from the Scandinavian countries and some Asian countries, by early May Britain remained the only major Western country which had recognized the new Chinese government.

In a preparatory meeting between British and American officials prior to the tripartite foreign ministers Conference between Britain, the US and France in London, the two sides disagreed on all the major issues concerning China: on recognition, Chinese representation in the UN, and Taiwan. On all these issues the only thing they could agree upon was that they would continue to disagree. The memorandum that emerged after this meeting stated that both sides had the same objective, which was to prevent the alienation of China from the west and her domination by the Soviet Union. In pursuit of such an objective, the two sides agreed to concert tactics and information policy 'so as to advance our common aim and to reduce any risk of mutual recrimination'. The two sides, however, agreed to 'continue to pursue our respective and somewhat divergent policies'.[30]

The British government's China policy had encountered a broadside, but it stayed on course. In a memorandum presented to the Cabinet on 10 April, Bevin asserted that, 'however dark the immediate prospect may be, the policy which we have pursued of entering into diplomatic relations with the Chinese People's Government is the correct one'.[31] The immediate prospect looked very gloomy however, and the future of Anglo-Chinese relations remained uncertain. The Chinese government had yet to respond to the last communication on the question of diplomatic relations.

Direct Negotiations: the final stage

The Chinese government's reply which was delivered on 7 May came as a great disappointment to British policy-makers, for it maintained that Britain's explanation was unsatisfactory and demanded further clarification. The Chinese government rejected as unacceptable Britain's explanation that their abstention from voting in the UN in favour of Beijing was not an expression of support for the Kuomintang. Zhang informed Hutchison that the British government had to demonstrate in action that they had indeed severed relations with the Kuomintang and were ready to take a friendly attitude towards the new Chinese government by supporting Beijing's claim in the UN. The Chinese side also brought up the Hong Kong administration's handling of the CNAC and CATC, aircraft dispute. The fact that the Hong Kong government had impounded the aircraft pending legal settlement was considered an example that Beijing's rights over Chinese state property were not respected by London. The Chinese government thus requested further clarifications and by implication declined the establishment of diplomatic relations until these two issues had been settled.[32]

The Chinese Foreign Ministry's response dealt a double blow to the British government. On the one hand, it had made clear that an early settlement of Anglo-Chinese diplomatic relations was not possible. On the other hand, it provided fresh ammunition for those opposing the policy of 'keeping a foot in the door'. Even inside the Foreign Office's Far Eastern department scepticism began to gain ground. Andrew Franklin suggested that it was reasonably clear that during the negotiations in Beijing 'the Chinese have been largely insincere'.[33]

Shortly after receiving the Chinese reply, Hutchison felt that the negotiations would not make any progress unless Britain could support Chinese

People's Government in the UN and that Beijing could take possession of the aircraft in Hong Kong. His reports from Beijing, however, were not entirely pessimistic. They continued to say that the Chinese were not holding back or trying to demand a price for establishing formal diplomatic relations. This view was not accepted unanimously by his colleagues in London. Franklin found Hutchison 'too readily inclined to give the Chinese Communist Government the benefit of the doubt'.[34] Even Assistant Under-Secretary, Dening, who had supported the policy of recognition strongly, found the Chinese response difficult to swallow. He was still anxious to establish diplomatic relations with the Beijing government, but he felt that a different approach was required.

Following the Chinese response Dening proposed a tactic of trying the patience of the Chinese and recommended that the government should not reply in a hurry. In proposing this as negotiation tactic, however, he had other considerations in mind as well. The American Secretary of State, Dean Acheson, was in London holding meetings with the Foreign Secretary. Dening was anxious to avoid sending a reply while the Americans were in London as it might give an impression that the British government was 'acting at American instance or dictation'. He felt strongly that all the contentions of the Chinese should be rejected and that 'our contribution to the exchange of correspondence is such that it will vindicate us if subsequently relations break down and explanations have to be given in Parliament'. The Foreign Office were prepared for the worst, but not entirely frustrated by the Chinese reply. Dening proposed to put it bluntly to the Chinese whether the Chinese government was prepared to exchange ambassadors. This proposal for an exchange of ambassador represented a tactical change in the government's effort to break the stalemate in the Anglo-Chinese talks.[35]

The crux of the matter, however, remained that not much had been achieved since January after Britain had recognized the new Chinese Government. The latest Chinese reply provided another chance for Opposition MPs to attack the government's policy in the House of Commons. In a foreign affairs debate in the House on 24 May, Anthony Eden concluded that, 'recognition has in fact brought out no advantage at all today'. Bevin came to the defence of the government but could offer no comfort except that the decision of recognition had been a correct one and that, 'one cannot judge the outcome of an action in international affairs immediately'.[36]

Not long after the Chinese government had requested further clarification from the British government, China's official media began to give their version of the Anglo-Chinese talks. On 19 May an editorial in *Shijie Zhishi* (*World Knowledge*), which was reported by NCNA, reiterated

China's resentment against Britain's 'two-faced' policy. More importantly the editorial took up the situation of Chinese nationals in Hong Kong and Malaya. It concluded by warning that, 'We must remind the British government that the agreement of the Chinese People's Republic to establish relations with Britain is not unqualified'. Then just two days before the 24 May Parliamentary debate on foreign affairs, the Chinese Foreign Ministry released a detailed account of Anglo-Chinese negotiations, putting the blame for the lack of progress in the Anglo-Chinese negotiations squarely on the British government.[37]

Even though this version was an accurate factual account of the negotiations from a Chinese perspective, the fact that it was given publicity prompted British officials to suggest that the Chinese were prepared to delay establishing diplomatic relations and were building up their case in the event of a complete break at a later stage.[38] Following Bevin's remark during the 24 May Parliamentary debate that 'it was an unpleasant decision that we must recognise the Communists',[39] criticism of Britain's position appeared in the Chinese media again. The *People's Daily* maintained that the statement was 'extremely unfriendly towards China'. A few days later, an editorial in the *People's China* expressed resentment of remarks made by British officials that recognition was a recognition of fact and not necessary a gesture of approval, saying that they 'implied an attitude of hostility'. It also added that events in the past few months had shown that even Britain's 'acknowledgement of fact' was confined to words alone. The editorial said that British government's 'deeds distort and contradict its words', and accused it of 'indulging in duplicity'.[40]

A deadlock had arisen, and unless either side was prepared to make concessions, the prospect for normal diplomatic relations between Britain and China looked bleak. On 26 May Bevin discussed the China problem with his Permanent Under-Secretary William Strang. In line with Dening's recommendation, the Foreign Secretary believed that the government's response to Beijing's request for clarification of British policies should not be apologetic as the points raised by the Chinese were not justified as preconditions for full diplomatic relations. But the British side was prepared to move one step forward and do something about Chinese representation at the UN. Although Bevin found it very difficult to meet China's demand since it would be 'interpreted as appeasement of Russia', he was willing to vote for the Beijing government in specialized UN agencies.[41]

The earliest opportunity for so doing was in the UNICEF meeting on 19 June, but the Foreign Office was obliged to withdraw its instruction to the British UN delegates as a result of American pressure. The British government, however, decided to stick to their guns and gave the Americans clear notice of their intention to vote for the Beijing government when the UN ECOSOC met on 3 July.[42]

On 17 June, Hutchison was instructed to deliver a further explanation of Britain's policy. The British government reiterated their opinion that the question of Chinese representation at the UN had to be settled by members of the Security Council and the question of the ownership of the CNAC and CATC aircraft had to be decided by the Law Courts. The British government, however, was willing to support Beijing's claim in the UN at an appropriate moment; the reply also mentioned Britain's effort in March to secure majority support for the Beijing government in the Security Council. The British government made clear that they were 'perfectly prepared to discuss' these issues when effective diplomatic relations were established and put forward offer for an exchange of ambassadors. After delivering the official statement Hutchison maintained that the failure of the Chinese government to establish normal diplomatic relations with Britain was the reason why the other member states of the UN had refrained from recognizing them or supporting their claim in the UN. He suggested that the way to settle the disagreement between the two sides was to establish 'the normal machinery of diplomacy to deal with such questions'.[43]

Thus the British side was making a genuine attempt to secure normal diplomatic relations with the Chinese government. An explicit offer of an exchange of ambassadors with the Chinese government was put on the table. In unequivocal terms, the British government had stated that it was willing to vote for the Beijing government in specialized UN agencies at an opportune moment and it had actually tried to persuade other members of the Security Council to do so. Indeed at the same time when Hutchison was trying to make the British position clear in Beijing and to offer an exchange of ambassadors, Britain's delegates to UNICEF were preparing to cast a vote in favour of Beijing to show that the British government's deeds matched their words.

Developments in China also provided some grounds for hope. Earlier, in late May, Hutchison had approached the Foreign Ministry over the plight of British business interests in China and made a representation on the matter. The Chinese did not reply, but soon afterwards, British officials both in Beijing and Shanghai were able to report that there 'has been a lessening of difficulties' for British firms. At the beginning of June, the Chinese government also produced a set of foreign trade regulations which allowed both export and import trade. British businessmen in China were able to report that relations between management and the work force had improved.[44] These developments did not represent a genuine improvement for British firms in China, and the fact that 'lessening of difficulties' had been used to describe the situation was indicative. Such developments, however, did indicate a change for the better, and provided a more favourable background for an agreement between Britain and China.

In other words, there was real prospect for an improvement in Anglo-Chinese relations in June. The fact that the talks had dragged on for so many months might be attributed to the limited foreign policy options of both countries. As both governments were conducting their foreign policies in the context of the Cold War, it was not possible for them to see the establishment of formal relations as a simple bilateral diplomatic process. When implementing its China policy, the British government had to consider American sensitivity, and at the same time, prove its sincerity to the Chinese side and impress them of the necessity for establishing formal diplomatic relations. For the new Chinese leaders, national pride and an anxiousness to be recognized as the sole legal government of China were very much in their minds. The Chinese revolutionaries' communist ideology and memory of the years of Western domination and humiliation, however, also shaped their thinking. Then there was the need for Soviet support to consider. All these considerations had made it almost impossible for the new Chinese leaders to be too conciliatory. By June both sides seemed to be making efforts to improve their bilateral relationship. It appeared that the difficulties in the Anglo-Chinese negotiations were soon to be resolved.

Events beyond the control of both the British and Chinese governments, however, were to thwart London's new initiative to end the deadlock in Anglo-Chinese relations. On 25 June North Korean troops marched into South Korea and the international situation was changed drastically. The war was to have an enormous impact on Anglo-Chinese relations.

THE KOREAN WAR

Initial British and Chinese Reactions

The outbreak of the Korean War presented both the British and Chinese policy-makers with a major problem far more important than their bilateral relations. Korea did not have any direct political or military significance for the United Kingdom, and there were no direct British interests involved. The conflict between the North and South Koreans could indeed be seen as a civil war. The Cold War, however, added a complex dimension to a conflict, whose outcome could significantly alter East-West balance of power in the region. For Beijing leaders developments in Korea were even more ominous: a direct military confrontation between the rival Eastern bloc and the Western alliance so close to China would threaten the security of the newly formed People's Republic. As a result of the outbreak of the war, not only was Britain's decision to vote for the People's government in UNICEF immediately withdrawn, but its offer of an exchange of ambassadors was also never answered. The twenty-fifth of June 1950 marked the suspension of direct Anglo-Chinese negotiations on diplomatic relations.

Two days after North Korean troops had marched across the 38th parallel, Washington informed their British ally that President Truman was preparing a public condemnation of 'centrally directed Communist imperialism'. Truman's statement was also to include a declaration that the US Seventh Fleet had been deployed to the Taiwan Strait to prevent a mainland Chinese attack on Taiwan or an attack by Taiwan on the mainland.[45] The Western response to the War was presented as a counter-action to Communist expansion; the defence of a link in a global chain of containment against the Communist bloc. The Cold War had become a very hot war.

London was obliged to consider the outbreak of the War in an international context, not merely that of immediate British interests at stake. The initial military assessment was that the only effective action would be direct US military involvement supported by other UN members. The Chiefs of Staff unanimously agreed: 'it is only by showing that we mean business to the point of (bringing?) [sic] matters to the brink of war with them that the Russians can be driven to withdraw from a course on which they have embarked'. Nevertheless they were reluctant to commit military forces to Korea because British resources were already severely stretched, particularly in Malaya and in Hong Kong. They feared that 'the Russians might stage a diversion elsewhere and we must continually guard against this eventuality', and concluded that, 'By deploying an undue proportion of our resources in Korea we would be playing into the Russian hands'.[46]

The British Cabinet met on 27 June to consider the Korean problem. The Foreign Secretary was ill and could not attend this crucial meeting. He was represented by the Minister of State, Kenneth Younger, and the Permanent Under-Secretary of State, William Strang. The Cabinet agreed at once that the British government should give full backing to the US government's proposed UN resolution, which was to be introduced in the Security Council urging all members of the UN to assist the South Koreans to repel the invasion.

British policy-makers, however, were divided on whether to treat the invasion as 'centrally-directed Communist imperialism'. One view was that there was no proof that the North Koreans had acted on Soviet instructions and there were advantages in isolating the incident by regarding it as an act of aggression committed on the North Koreans' own initiative. This would enable 'the Soviet Government to withdraw, without loss of prestige, any encouragement or support which they may be giving to the North Koreans'. Another consideration was that by linking the Korean incident with communist threats in other parts of Asia, other controversial issues might be brought up in the Security Council. British policy-makers were also concerned with the implications of the US action on Anglo-Chinese relations, for US policy towards Taiwan might make Britain's relations with the People's Republic more difficult and even provoke the Beijing government to attack or to ferment disorder in Hong Kong.[47]

The Foreign Secretary, who had been consulted the day before, advised against making any public statement isolating the incident from other matters mentioned in the US announcement. His opinion was that the British government 'would not wish to discourage' the US from giving help to Britain and France in their campaigns against communist activities in Malaya and Indo-China. This view was accepted by his Cabinet colleagues who also decided to urge the US government not to include in the UN resolution any reference to communist encroachment in other parts of Asia, and not to issue a public statement explicitly attributing the North Korean action to 'centrally-directed Communist imperialism'. Truman's statement later simply used 'communism' instead of 'centrally-directed Communist imperialism'. The order to the Seventh Fleet, however, was not rescinded.[48]

Washington's decision to dispatch the Seventh Fleet to the Taiwan Strait provoked a strong response from Beijing. The Chinese government expressed far more concern over American policy towards Taiwan than developments in Korea. This concern of the new leadership in Beijing over Taiwan was easy to appreciate. The island was the last refuge for their rival, the Kuomintang; one remaining major Chinese territory not under their direct rule. American action now threatened the new Chinese leadership's final step to unify the country. The Beijing leadership's priority was directly reflected in their official media. The Chinese press coverage of events in Korea was belated and not very prominent. The number of anti-American articles did not increase significantly until late August and only reached its height after the Chinese had intervened directly in Korea.[49] Contrasting with their reaction to events in Korea, Zhou Enlai's reaction to the stationing of the Seventh Fleet in Taiwan Strait was quick and strong. Two days after Truman's statement, he rebuked the US action as 'armed aggression against the territory of China', and enunciated that it was 'a gross violation of the United Nations Charter'.[50] The estrangement of the People's Republic and the US had turned into open confrontation.

This development put the British government in a difficult position. Their attempt to seek better relations with revolutionary China had been criticized by the US government before the outbreak of the Korean War. As a result of the Korean conflict, a reassessment of Britain's China policy had become necessary. The main aim, as a China specialist in the Foreign Office noted, 'should be to reduce the points of conflict and divergence' between Britain and the US 'to the minimum'.[51]

Anglo-American Disagreement in the Far East

Anglo-American policy differences in East Asia came to a head as a result of the Korean War. In early July, Younger, who had been virtually in charge of the Foreign Office since the end of May when Bevin was taken ill, predicted a difficult period in Anglo-American relations. He noted in his diary on 6 July that, 'the divergence between US and British policies in the Far East must now become acute'. He feared that the Soviet Union had a good chance to 'drive a wedge' between Britain and the US or to 'force [the] UK into open hostility with the new China.[52]

As the British government saw it, one major question was a possible Soviet threat in other parts of the world which would directly threaten the security of Europe. The British government did not want to see American attention and commitment in Europe diverted by events in Korea. In a message to the US President, Attlee maintained that the implications of the war 'will concern not only the way in which we should like to see the situation in Korea develop but also the likely reactions which may be expected not only in the Far East.' His concern was: 'the Russians have involved the Western Powers in a heavy commitment without themselves playing an overt part', and warned Truman that Moscow might use the same tactic in other parts of the world.[53]

At around the same time in early July when Attlee warned Truman about the nature of the Soviet threats, the British government was approaching the Soviet government on its own initiative to secure a settlement in Korea. The British policy-makers felt that if Moscow were willing to co-operate to establish the *status quo ante* in Korea, then the West should be more flexible on Taiwan and the question of Chinese rep-resentation in the UN. On 8 July, Bevin, who was still in hospital, probed Acheson's opinion on this by sending him a message which asked whether Washington would reconsider its policy towards Taiwan if Moscow agreed to exert their influence in finding a solution to the Korean conflict.[54]

The Americans were not prepared to make concessions to the Soviet Union. Recalling this episode in his memoirs, Acheson wrote: 'One can easily imagine that this message did not please either the President or me'.[55] Acheson gave Bevin a firm 'no', telling him that any retreat 'would have disastrous consequences that might easily place in jeopardy the entire venture of resistance to aggression'. On the question of China, he bluntly said: 'In all frankness, I do not see any likelihood of harmonizing our policies in the basic attitudes on which US policy is founded'. When Ambassador Lewis Douglas relayed Acheson's reply personally to Bevin, who was still in hospital, he also questioned the wisdom of admitting the Beijing government to the Security Council. Douglas told Bevin that Acheson felt that the implications of Bevin's message and its possible consequences on Anglo-American relations might become very serious.[56] The American response was far stronger than Bevin had expected; the British Foreign Secretary was, in Douglas' words, 'somewhat surprised' and 'a little taken aback' by the vigour of Acheson's reply.[57]

The future of Anglo-American relations was not something the British government could take lightly. Younger and other senior officials responsible for Far Eastern affairs expressed their concern over the US response during a lunch meeting with Douglas a few days afterwards. They insisted, however, that a clash between the People's Republic and the US over Taiwan would have 'disagreeable consequences' for the position of the West. They also emphasized the importance of the support given to the US resolution in the UN by India and other Asian countries and the difficulties created for these countries by Washington's stance. Douglas retorted that the US and UK governments should reach a common view on Taiwan and should concert their efforts to influence the other governments in favour of their view.[58]

In his reply to Acheson, Bevin dropped earlier hints that some concessions might be needed to get Soviet cooperation over a peaceful settlement of the Korean War. He agreed that the question of Chinese representation should not be connected to the Korean problem. This reply also reassured Acheson of Britain's intention by saying that North Korean troops must be pushed back to the 38th parallel and that it was not going to submit to 'Russian blackmail'. Yet it also reiterated the British government's view that Beijing should be seated in the Security Council, and that the West should not 'add China to our enemies by our actions or attitudes of ours'.[59]

Anglo-American relations and co-operation were not seriously affected, partly because of Bevin's conciliatory reply, and partly because the Soviet Union did not respond positively to Britain's approach and a parallel Indian initiative. Towards the end of July, the British government decided to commit ground forces to the fighting against the North Koreans.[60] By now the prospect of a peaceful solution to restore the *status quo* in Korea had vanished.

Anglo-Chinese Relations after the Outbreak of the Korean War

London's diplomatic initiatives to establish proper diplomatic relations with Beijing came to a halt when the Korean War broke out. In early July the British government imposed controls over the export of strategic goods to China.[61] British policy-makers, however, did not see why a confrontation with the People's Republic should necessarily follow the Korean War.

In mid-August 1950, the Foreign Office conducted a comprehensive study of possible Chinese 'overt aggression' in Korea or in Southeast Asia, where considerable British interests were at stake. The study maintained that the Beijing government, while it generally had supported Moscow on many international issues, had not compromised China's independence. The assessment was: 'China would not commit an act of overt aggression against any state or territory at the dictation of Moscow, and unless she conceived such an act of being in her own interest'. The study also said that the Chinese revolution was still in its infancy and the Beijing government had to concentrate on internal consolidation. It concluded that apart from Taiwan there was no evidence that Mao would wish to launch military adventures outside of China.[62]

The Beijing government also seemed to have responded to the Korean conflict in a cautious manner. Britain's support for American policy and later its direct military action in Korea were, interestingly enough, not made use of by the Chinese propaganda machinery to step up their criticism of British policies in Hong Kong and Malaya. This prompted Hutchison to conclude on 25 July that, 'the Chinese may be almost as much in the dark as regards the future of Sino-British relations, and consequently be unwilling to do anything at this juncture which might disturb the tenuous and delicate relations which at present exist, and which it seems to me they obviously regarded as at least potentially valuable, since they have abstained from terminating our negotiations'. During this time, junior Chinese Foreign Ministry officials in fact continued to be courteous in their dealings with British diplomats. Senior members of the Ministry also continued to accept official British communications which were not related to the Anglo-Chinese negotiations on diplomatic relations.[63]

Back in London, Hutchison's colleagues, however, remained frustrated with the lack of progress in Anglo-Chinese talks. Colin Crowe bluntly pointed out that, 'few entry permits have been received, while acceptance of official communication does not take one far if there are no replies'. Yet the restraint shown by the Chinese did not pass entirely unappreciated. An official who had returned to London from Guangzhou argued that, 'I do not think there is any doubt that the Chinese Communists wish to maintain a British connection if only as a counterweight to Russian influence in China, which is not too popular among the mass of the population'.[64]

Senior Foreign Office officials who had argued for voting in favour of the Chinese government in the UN maintained that the question of Chinese representation should be separated from the Korean War.[65] Accordingly the British government on 19 September voted in favour of an Indian resolution in the General Assembly which called for the admission of the Beijing government to represent China in the UN. However, Britain's abstention when a Soviet resolution calling for the expulsion of the Kuomintang representative was put before the Assembly, fell short of what the Chinese wanted.[66]

Nevertheless, the Chinese government refrained from further straining Anglo-Chinese relations. On 30 September 1950, the eve of the national day, when Zhou Enlai delivered his political report to the Chinese National People's Conference, he made special reference to Sino-British relations, reporting that nothing had come out of the 'long-drawn-out negotiations' with Britain. Zhou stressed that Britain's attitude towards Chinese representation in the UN 'makes it difficult to commence formal diplomatic relations between China and Britain'. He then went on to say that the British government's 'unjustifiable' and 'unfriendly' attitude towards Chinese residents in Hong Kong and other places had attracted the 'serious attention' of the Chinese government.[67]

By suggesting that 'normal diplomatic relations' had not come out of the negotiations between Britain and China, Zhou seemed to have acknowledged the existence of some kind of Sino-British diplomatic relations. Hutchison was quick to point this out to the Foreign Office and he felt that the statement was 'moderately worded and certainly does not shut the door'. The fact that no reference was made to the CNAC and CATC affair, and that Britain's attitude towards Chinese residents in Hong Kong was not specifically mentioned as an obstacle to normal relations was, to Hutchison, a sign for optimism. He still believed that as long as Britain could consistently support Beijing's claim at the UN and vote for the expulsion of the KMT representatives, then establishment of diplomatic relations would follow without further difficultly.[68] Making use of the opportunity on this first anniversary of the People's Republic, Hutchison sent a simple message of congratulation to the Vice-Foreign Minister. The NCNA's report on Hutchison and his Dutch counterpart's messages of congratulation described both of them as 'Charge d'Affaires ad interim'.[69]

In mid-October, British commercial officials in Shanghai were also able to speak of 'considerable improvements' regarding British enterprise. In a memorandum to the Board of Trade, they reported that there was a reduction of various taxes, and a revival of trade. They also found Chinese officials had become more accessible and easier to approach, and as a result many difficulties were resolved.[70]

The fact that the Chinese continued to allow the presence of British diplomatic representatives in various parts of China and provided them with basic diplomatic facilities after the onset of the war was a clear indication that Beijing did not want the British to withdraw completely. The British played their part. They did not pull out; nor did they act in ways that the Chinese would find unacceptable. The outbreak of the Korean War had certainly hardened the views of those Foreign Office officials who had doubted the Chinese government's sincerity in wishing to establish diplomatic relations and were concerned that Anglo-American solidarity would be affected by their differences over China.[71] Senior officials responsible for Far Eastern affairs no doubt also shared this concern. Nonetheless, they still saw Washington's China Policy as unwise and continued to explore options which might improve Anglo-Chinese relations and, perhaps, bring revolutionary China into closer contacts with the West.

The Korean conflict brought Cold War confrontation to the battlefield. Britain and China took antagonistic sides in the war, and the Anglo-Chinese talks were discontinued. Yet Britain's relations with China were not broken off; unofficial diplomatic relations between them were maintained. In October 1950, a 'friendship delegation' from the People's Republic led by Liu Ningyi visited Britain. Their visit was not a success, and even the left-wing Labour magazine, *Tribune*, described them as 'the worst mannered delegation ever to visit this country'. Nevertheless, the group was able to meet several Cabinet members at a lunch party with the Labour Party Executive.[72] At around the same time the British government were actually preparing to make another attempt to break the deadlock in Anglo-Chinese relations.

ESLER DENING'S SECRET CHINA MISSION

In October 1950, one of the key architects of the policy of 'keeping a foot in the door', Esler Dening, was assigned to a secret mission to visit Beijing for talks with Chinese leaders. As the decision to send him to China was secret, his trip to Beijing was made part of a Far Eastern tour. It was such a well-guarded plan that Michael Wilford, Bevin's junior private secretary, and Dening's own private secretary, Michael Paton, who accompanied him on his tour, were not aware of it. Paton thought that Dening was being sent to the Far East because he had been appointed Ambassador to China but was not able to take up his post. He later said, 'I didn't at any point, gather that there was any likelihood that we should get to Peking and that Dening would meet senior Chinese leaders'.[73]

In early October the Foreign Office announced that Dening, who had just been knighted, had been given the rank of an Ambassador on a Far Eastern tour. In a press release the Foreign Office said it was a familiarization tour similar to the one William Strang had undertaken when he assumed his post as Permanent Under-Secretary of the Foreign Office in 1949. The press release also said Dening was going to visit Hong Kong, Japan, Korea, India, Australia and various South-east Asian countries, omitting any reference to China. Dening's secret itinerary provided for him to go to Hong Kong first and then from there to China before other places. A few days later on 11 October, reports speculating that Dening might visit Beijing appeared in several newspapers but these reports did not draw much public attention.[74]

The British government not only kept the purpose of Dening's trip a secret, but there was also no prior Anglo-American consultation on it. The British Embassy in Washington was instructed to inform the Americans of Dening's secret mission after it had been finalized. Later in Bangkok when Dening had given up all the hopes of getting to China, he told the US Ambassador about the mission. The Americans themselves, however, were also trying to develop a direct link with the Chinese government on their own in early October. Loy Henderson, the American Ambassador to India had approached the Indian government to act as the intermediary to arrange a meeting between him and the Chinese Ambassador in India. This approach was flatly turned down by the Chinese.[75]

The idea of sending a special envoy to Beijing had been in Bevin's mind before the outbreak of the Korean War. The business lobby had repeatedly pressed the Foreign Office to send a senior representative to China. The Foreign Secretary brought up this idea in mid-June with Younger after he had approved the recommendation to vote in favour of Beijing in specialized UN agencies. Bevin suggested sending a senior official to Beijing to talk to the Chinese leaders directly because 'Britain needed a man of more weight and experience than Hutchison so as to make a stronger impression'. Foreign Office officials, however, advised against it, arguing that it would not be meaningful.[76] This idea was revived when Dening, the Ambassador-designate to China had to make way for others and leave his job as Superintending Assistant Under-Secretary for the Far Eastern department.

On 6 October, the Foreign Office instructed Hutchison to apply for Dening's entry permit. Although the Foreign Office felt that the Chinese government might reject this request, but even if that happened no great harm would have been done. The instruction to Hutchison stated that the object of sending Dening to Beijing was 'to make informal contact and to exchange views pending the establishment of formal diplomatic relations'.[77]

A few days before Dening left for his trip, he discussed his strategy for Beijing with William Strang. He told Strang, 'I think I should encourage the Chinese to vent their grievances, whether real or imaginary, and try to convince them that their suspicions are unfounded and that a measure of good will on their part is likely to find a response in the rest of the non-communist world'.[78] Dening might have had a carefully thought out strategy to approach the Chinese when he got there. The problem was that by the time he left London on 25 October, the Chinese government had not yet issued his entry permit.

The mission was aimed at improving Anglo-Chinese relations and it represented an effort to prevent the further widening of the gap between China and the West, but it had come too late to save the situation. Developments in Korea had reached a critical stage with UN forces advancing beyond the 38th parallel to threaten China's border. In early October the Chinese leaders had already taken the decision of intervening directly in Korea.[79] They were also planning to gain control of Tibet. By the time Dening arrived in Hong Kong on 29 October, the People's Liberation Army had already entered Tibet.

When Dening learnt of the development in Tibet, he suggested that the situation there may 'widen the gap between China and the Western Powers'. Such a development might have given him an additional incentive in seeking to visit Beijing. Reporting to London, he proposed to force the Chinese to make clear their position by telling the press that he had requested a visa to visit China, but the Chinese government had not replied. This proposal was overtaken by reports of direct Chinese military intervention in Korea. By early November, Dening had realized that he was probably not going to make it to China. In a personal letter to Hutchison he said, 'I am very sorry to have got so far and to have failed to get to Peking'. He admitted that in view of events in Korea it was not a propitious moment to go and he was not surprised that the Chinese had not responded to his visa application. He noted that the Chinese government's unwillingness to reply had added 'another touch of black paint to a darkening picture'. The fact that he was known as the Ambassador-designate to China perhaps made the Chinese even more cautious in issuing him a visa. He wrote: 'I have tried to kill that story with the press here, but the Chinese government may conceivably think that I intend to be the cuckoo, so to speak, in my own nest'.[80]

Without an entry permit to visit China, Dening left Hong Kong for Japan. While in Tokyo he asked the Foreign Office whether he should still visit Beijing if the Chinese government should grant him permission in view of the situation in Korea. Rob Scott, the new Assistant Under-Secretary in charge of Far Eastern affairs, told him not to exclude going to Beijing. Scott felt that the visit should take priority over other arrangements in Dening's Far Eastern visit. He also added that the final decision rested on Bevin who would take into account the behaviour of the Chinese delegates who were on their way to New York to speak on the Taiwan question in the UN. In reply, Dening, who apparently had not given up all hopes, agreed with Scott and wrote that the most important objective for his trip was still Beijing.[81]

By the end of November, the Chinese government had still not made any reply. Meanwhile the military situation in Korea was entering a critical stage. Joining the North Korean troops, the Chinese launched a massive counter-offensive. By then the political climate and military situation in Korea could hardly provide a more inauspicious moment for Dening's mission to China, and he gave up all hopes of reaching there.[82]

There was an indication that the Chinese leaders did not totally ignore the British government's approach to send Dening to Beijing. In mid-November, Hutchison reported to the Foreign Office that during a meeting with a foreign visitor, Zhou Enlai had mentioned that, 'an important British official would soon be visiting Peking'. This prompted Hutchison to say that 'I can only assume he meant Sir Esler Dening'.[83]

Even if the entry permit for Dening's visit had been granted the realization of its objective would have been forestalled after the Chinese troops had crossed the Yalu River in 14 October. In the event, with a British military presence in Korea, China's massive military intervention had made the two countries direct adversaries. It was most unlikely that a meeting at this juncture between Dening and Zhou Enlai would have changed the positions of the two governments.

Dening's secret mission was the Labour Government's last direct diplomatic initiative in implementing its policy of 'keeping a foot in the door' in China. The departure of Dening from the Far Eastern Department also symbolized the end of a period in Anglo-Chinese relations during which the British Government's objective had been to secure full diplomatic relations with the People's Republic. From the end of November onwards, British policy-makers were to realize that there was no hope for an early settlement on formal Anglo-Chinese diplomatic relations.

CONCLUSIONS

The British policy-makers' commitment to an Anglo-American alliance was a crucial factor contributed to the failure of the Anglo-Chinese talks. The British government had not been able to implement the policy of 'keeping a foot in the door' consistently after their recognition of the Beijing government. The balancing act between pursuing a close relationship with Washington while establishing a workings relationship with Beijing was clearly no easy task.

After several months of fruitless negotiations with the Chinese in the first half of 1950, British policy-makers came to the realization that the continuation of the unsatisfactory state of Anglo-Chinese relations was not serving British interests. Their decision to recognise Communist China had annoyed their American ally, and had failed to bring any improvement to Britain's position in China. Meanwhile, frustrated by the lack of proper official channels to air their problem with the Chinese authorities, the business lobby were pressing the government to establish official relations with Beijing as quickly as possible. At the same time the Parliamentary Opposition was able to attack the policy of recognition as a failure. Thus, in early June British policy-makers came to the conclusion that they had to take the initiative in breaking the deadlock in the Anglo-Chinese negotiations.

At the initial stage, Chinese representation in the UN was the most important obstacle in the negotiations. The Chinese side was not entirely without justification for their response. As a newly established state, they were naturally anxious to be recognized by the UN. British announcements that recognition was not necessarily an act of approval were clearly also not well received in Beijing. Moreover, as mentioned in Chapter 1, the Communist leadership had already decided in early 1949 that they did not want to be hurried into diplomatic relations with the 'imperial powers', even though they were quite ready to establish relations with non-socialist and other Western countries. India, Burma, and those Scandinavian countries which were willing to support Beijing's claim in the UN had no problem in establishing official diplomatic relations with the People's Republic.

Just before the outbreak of the Korean War in June 1950 both Beijing and London seemed to have prepared for an improvement in Anglo-Chinese relations. The Korean conflict was thus a crucial turning point; any hope that Britain and the revolutionary China might have had for establishing diplomatic relations in 1950 was shattered when North Korean troops crossed the 38th parallel. At the end of September and early October, Chinese policy-makers were engaged in an internal debate over direct military intervention in Korea. It was thus hardly surprising that Britain's affirmative vote in the UN General Assembly in support of Beijing's claim for the China seat, and Dening's attempt to get to China, did not evoke a favourable response.

By this time the establishment of diplomatic relations with Britain was clearly not a priority in Chinese foreign policy-thinking, even though the fact that British diplomatic presence in China was still tolerated showed that the Chinese had not closed the door completely. At the end of 1950, following China's military intervention in Korea, British policy makers concluded that a reappraisal of their China policy was inevitable.

4 From Confrontation to the Establishment of Diplomatic Relations

Revolutionary China became engaged in a direct military conflict with the West over events in Korea at the end of October in 1950. Soon after crossing the 38th parallel in June North Korean troops had driven the South Koreans towards the southern tip of the peninsula. The North Korean victory did not last long. The military situation was changed dramatically when American forces under the command of General MacArthur landed at Inchon on 15 September; very quickly the tide of military fortunes turned against the North Koreans. By the end of the month UN forces which were primarily comprised of American troops had pushed them back to the 38th parallel. The UN objective of restoring the *status quo* in Korea had been achieved. The question then was whether or not its forces should push on to eliminate the North Korean regime and establish a unified Korea friendly to the West. The US decision to advance northwards beyond their initial objective prompted China's military involvement in Korea.[1]

British policy-makers were anxious to find a political solution to the Korean problem. The escalation of the Korean conflict into a military confrontation with China created a dilemma for policy-makers in London. They could not afford to risk a split in Anglo-American relations over the Far East, yet to fight a war against China would divide the Commonwealth and divert Western resources. Anglo-Chinese relations also entered a most strained phase at the end of 1950. The environment in which British policy-makers had formulated their China policy in 1948 had changed drastically by 1951. China's military involvement in Korea hardened the confrontation between the East and the West. Equally significant was the fact that Britain's political leaders who had presided over the formulation of the policy of 'keeping a foot in the door' in China had been replaced by a Conservative government which came to office in November 1951. The two countries only managed to establish formal diplomatic relations in 1954 after the international atmosphere had become more relaxed.

In attempting to implement their China policy of 'keeping a foot in the door' between late 1950 and 1954, British policy-makers had found it

necessary to adjust their positions and revise their policies continuously
in response to the changes in the international environment and domestic
climate. This chapter looks at how Britain's and the revolutionary China's
policies towards one another were revised as a result of the outbreak of
the Korean War, and how under different circumstances the two sides
eventually established official diplomatic relations in 1954 after the Geneva
Conference.

CHINA'S INTERVENTION IN KOREA

Initial British Attitude

British military planners had warned that a military venture crossing the
38th parallel in Korea would involve grave risk, arguing that the ultimate
military commitment for the West would outweigh the political advantages.
Chief of the Air Staff, Air Marshall Sir John Slessor, proposed that since
the *status quo ante* had been restored, the Korean conflict should be settled
by a political solution through the UN.[2] But the temptation for establishing
a unified Korea friendly to the West ended the search for peace in 1950.
Beijing's warnings from late August and a categoric message that it
intended to intervene militarily in Korea during a dramatic mid-night
meeting between Zhou Enlai and the Indian ambassador K. M. Pannikar
on 2 October were largely ignored. Both British and American political
leaders regarded the warnings as pure bluff. The British government was
at that time trying to push through a resolution in the UN to bring about
a permanent political settlement in Korea which carried the implication
that UN forces should cross the 38th parallel if necessary. In a personal
message to a much alarmed Indian Prime Minister, Bevin suggested that
the Chinese warning might have been, 'deliberately directed towards
weakening the front which is opposed to North Korean aggression'. As late
as mid-October, a US Central Intelligence Agency report concluded that
barring a Soviet decision for global war; a massive Chinese intervention
in Korea would probably be confined to continued assistance to the North
Koreans.[3]

   The Chinese leadership did not make a final decision to send troops to
Korea until early October. Military planning for the intervention had begun
in early August, but some members of the leadership were apprehensive
about such a venture. The Acting Chief of Staff at that time, Nie Rongzhen,
later wrote that the newly established People's Republic needed, 'a period
of prolonged peace' for economic reconstruction. However, the advance of

UN forces towards the Yalu River was seen as a serious threat to national security. This sentiment was expressed strongly by Marshall Peng Dehuai, later Commander of the Chinese 'volunteers' in Korea, during a meeting of the Party Central Committee on 5 October 1950. Speaking in favour of intervention, Peng said, 'the US will find a pretext to launch a war [against China] at any time if its troops are poised along Yalu River and in Taiwan.' To the revolutionary leaders in Beijing, the survival of the new government was at stake and the People's Republic had to demonstrate its ability to safeguard its national interests.[4]

By early November when it had become clear that Chinese troops had entered Korea, the British government still thought that a massive intervention would not occur and that UN forces should continue their military operation as long as their intention was made clear to Beijing. As late as mid-November Bevin was still anxious to develop direct communication with the Chinese government. He proposed making contacts with the Chinese delegates who were on their way to New York to speak on Taiwan in the UN as well as approaching the Chinese government directly in Beijing on the possibility of establishing a de-militarized zone in North Korea.[5] The Foreign Secretary's efforts were to prove futile; he had underestimated the strength of Chinese reaction to developments in Korea. At this stage both the Chinese and the US governments had committed themselves to a military solution. The momentum of military operations in Korea had become too advanced to be stopped.

Washington strongly opposed to the idea of establishing a de-militarised zone, arguing that 'it would be harmful' to put forward the proposal when General MacArthur's troops were preparing an offensive. Acheson told the British Ambassador in Washington, Sir Oliver Franks, that the proposal would be regarded 'as a starting point for bargaining for something more' by the Chinese. More importantly, Washington was still thinking that the Korean War would be ended quickly through a decisive military victory. Acheson asked Franks to urge Bevin 'not to proceed with this proposal pending further US-UK consultation'.[6]

Hutchison delivered Bevin's message to Zhang Hanfu in Beijing on 22 November. The message explained that the objective of the UN forces was 'to restore peace and order in Korea' and that 'the fulfilment of this objective was no threat to the security of China nor would it endanger Chinese interest in the area'. Zhang expressed some interest in the idea of a de-militarised zone which was brought up by Hutchison 'in a personal capacity', but the Chinese did not make any response afterwards.[7] Given the military situation at that time, it was not surprising that Beijing did not respond to these 'personal remarks' by Hutchison which were made unofficially and not very concrete. General MacArthur was soon to launch an offensive with the aim of ending the war and 'bringing the boys home for Christmas'; the Chinese were also busy preparing for their first major battle since their troops had already crossed the Yalu River.

The Chinese counter-offensive of 26 to 28 November ended all hopes for an eleventh hour peace proposal. On 29 November, Acheson delivered a public speech in Cleveland describing the Chinese intervention as a 'premeditated act of brazen aggression'. The Truman administration were convinced that it was a communist challenge to the West linked with developments in Tibet and Indo-China. He later wrote, 'we were seeing a pattern in Indo-China and Tibet timed to coincide with the attack by the Communists aimed at intensifying the smouldering anti-foreign feeling among most Asian peoples'.[8] The next day Franks reported from Washington that Acheson had ruled out any possibility of a diplomatic solution to the Korean problem for the time being. Acheson thought that there would be 'no opportunity for negotiations or diplomacy' while the military situation was 'fluid and in favour of the Chinese', adding that only when the Chinese attacks had been blunted and the new situation stabilized would there be 'a real opportunity for the exercise of the political act'.[9]

Events in Korea now seemed likely to lead to a war between China and the US. Such a prospect greatly alarmed British officials in charge of Far Eastern affairs. Describing the British dilemma in the event of a Sino-American military clash, Rob Scott said, 'apart from the immediate effects on our interests in the Far East, we should be faced with the choice between a serious split in Anglo-American relations, or joining reluctantly in a war which would divided the Commonwealth, dissipated Western resources, and weaken our defences without any corresponding strategic gains'. To Scott, a political solution was still the preferable alternative.[10]

The Attlee-Truman Talks

On 30 November, during a House of Commons debate about Korea, MPs learnt that President Truman had suggested the possible use of the atomic bomb against China. The President's remark had been made in response to a question at a press conference. The White House later clarified that it did not represent a change in US policy, but the remark greatly alarmed both sides of the House. Roy Jenkins recalled that the mood in the House was 'near panic' with MPs 'crowding and clucking around the main tape machine like animals around a meal'. At the end of the debate Attlee announced that he had proposed visiting the US to meet President Truman.[11]

Attlee in fact had wanted to visit Washington to meet Truman as early as mid-August, but the plan was dropped when the Americans did not respond in a positive manner. Truman's remark offered the Prime Minister an opportunity to visit Washington. Urged on by Hugh Dalton and other MPs during the Commons debate, Attlee called a Cabinet meeting to discuss the suggestion on the same day. The Cabinet agreed that the Prime Minister should go to see Truman; he was not only to discuss the use of atomic weapons, but also the supreme command in Europe and international arrangements for raw materials.[12]

Attlee had talks with Truman from 4 to 8 December. He returned to report US assurances that there was no intention to use atomic bombs, calming the apprehensive mood at home. His diplomacy was hailed in the press and in Parliament. Kenneth Younger who was present on the second day of the talks noted in his diary that Attlee's visit had been a success. Later in an interview he further suggested that Truman and the UN land Commander in Korea General Omar Bradley might have extended the war had it not been for Attlee's intervention.[13]

Anglo-American relations, as Acheson suggested, became 'substantially closer than would have appeared' after Attlee's Washington visit. Their differences over China, however, were not resolved during the meeting. The two sides continued to disagree on Chinese representation at the UN, China's relations with the Soviet Union, and on Taiwan's status. As far as their policies towards China were concerned, the Attlee-Truman talks, Acheson later wrote, 'ended without any meeting of minds'.[14]

The British Dilemma

To Attlee it was of prime importance to avoid a major war with China. He was anxious to find a political solution to the Korean problem. Reporting to the Cabinet after he returned from Washington in December he stated that, 'the broad choice was between a settlement of the Korean problem or a general drift to world war'. It turned out that the choice was not as clear as Attlee maintained.[15]

Britain was perhaps better placed than other major western countries to seek a political solution with China to the Korean problem. Despite Beijing's intervention in Korea, the Chinese government had not abruptly changed its attitude towards British diplomats stationed in China. Although British officials in Beijing did not enjoy formal diplomatic status, they continued to enjoy basic diplomatic privileges. They were able to bring their government's views to the attention of the Chinese authorities and explain these views. Since from the Chinese point of view they were British representatives officially and technically only in China for the negotiations on the establishment of diplomatic relations, the Foreign Ministry seldom gave them written replies on other matters. Nonetheless, quite often, the British diplomats were able to 'learn from other sources that the Ministry have done what we have asked'.[16] It was clear that the Chinese government was not in a hurry to develop full diplomatic relations with Britain, but no attempt was made to force British diplomatic representatives out of China. Chinese military operations in Korea did not seem to have an immediate adverse effect on the British diplomatic mission in Beijing. At this point it seemed that the possibility of bridging the gap between Britain and China still existed.

Britain's objective of reaching a negotiated settlement with China over Korea was in jeopardy when Washington wanted to introduce a resolution in the UN branding China as an 'aggressor'. London had misgivings about castigating Beijing, but American pressure was too hard to resist. When the Cabinet discussed the dilemma in late November the general agreement was: any major divergence of British and American policies over the Far East would prejudice American support for Britain in Europe, a risk Britain could not afford to bear.[17]

BRANDING CHINA AS AN AGGRESSOR

Efforts for a Negotiated Peace in Korea

In mid-December 1950 thirteen Asian and Arab states proposed a cease-fire resolution in the UN and a three-nation Cease-Fire Committee headed by the Iranian President of the UN General Assembly was set up. After consultations with the Americans and the Commonwealth Prime Ministers, the committee produced a statement of principles for the settlement of the Korean conflict in early January 1951. These included the withdrawal of all foreign troops from Korea by stages and an invitation to the Chinese government to take part in discussions on problems such as the future of Taiwan and Chinese representation in the UN. The Cease-Fire Committee secured US approval to put forward these principles as the basis for a peaceful settlement of the Korean problem. The proposal also maintained that a cease-fire must come into effect prior to any negotiations. These principles were accepted by the UN Political Committee and sent to Beijing on 13 January 1951.[18]

The Chinese government did not recognize the Cease-Fire Committee, for it was set up without their participation. Nevertheless, Zhou Enlai issued an official reply which insisted that there could not be a truce without prior political negotiations. It rejected the idea of an immediate cease-fire, saying that it was an attempt to give the Americans time to breathe. The Chinese government stated that, 'as a basis for negotiating a peaceful settlement of the Korean problem, all foreign troops must be withdrawn from Korea'. The reply linked Korea with US military presence on Taiwan, and the China seat question in UN. The Chinese government called for a seven-nation conference to be held in China, which should recognize Beijing's claim in the UN, for the negotiation of these problems.[19]

The reply thus rejected an immediate cease-fire, but did not close the door of negotiations entirely. By putting forward a counter-proposal, it created a division among UN members. The US government quickly denounced it as an outright rejection of the UN proposal. Bevin also felt that the Chinese had rejected the UN proposal by demanding conditions which could not be accepted. On the other hand, the Indian Prime Minister saw it quite differently. In a personal letter to Attlee he wrote, 'I do not consider the reply to be outright rejection. It is partly accepted, partly request for elucidation, partly counter proposal, and leaves room for future negotiation'. Nehru cautioned that, 'all of us must have time to consider them before determining further line of action'.[20]

Attlee felt that Nehru's view on the Chinese reply was a 'very charitable interpretation', but he also wanted to explore any room for negotiations. He agreed that the Chinese reply was 'not entirely clear' and further elucidation from Beijing was necessary. Attlee believed that if the Chinese wanted a peace settlement they should demonstrate and show their sincerity. Canada's External Affairs Secretary, Lester Pearson, who was also a member of the Cease-Fire Committee, felt that 'the Chinese response was sufficiently ambiguous to warrant further investigation'.[21]

Immediately after the Chinese government had announced its reaction to the UN peace proposal, the US government tabled a resolution condemning China as an aggressor. Washington pressed hard for British and Canadian support for their resolution which was scheduled to be put to a vote on 22 January. The US motion to castigate Beijing put British policy-makers in a very difficult position. It was a critical moment, for if the resolution was adopted it would destroy the chance for a diplomatic solution to the Korean problem. The British government did not want to make a final decision to close the door on negotiations before China had elucidated its position regarding the UN proposal.[22] In early January, Younger noted in his diary that although the whole Cabinet supported the policy of trying to prevent the 'Americans from pursuing a limited war against China', there was 'great reluctance to be tough with the Americans'. He felt that, 'we have in effect brought no pressure on the Americans at all'. Eventually the British government informed Washington that British support for condemning China as an aggressor in the UN and calling for consequent sanction measures could not be assumed.[23]

Britain, together with India who also acted on behalf of Canada, made a last attempt seek clarification from Beijing. The British and Indian governments approached the Chinese authorities separately in late January. The three issues they sought to clarify were: whether China's call for the withdrawal of all foreign troops included the withdrawal of Chinese 'volunteers'; whether Chinese insistence on negotiations meant negotiations for a cease-fire or on political issues; and whether the Chinese regarded recognition of their legal status in the UN as a precondition for negotiations.[24]

On 21 January Hutchison called on the Foreign Ministry in Beijing and requested for an urgent reply. It appeared that the Chinese had indeed sensed the urgency of the situation as they worked out their reply on the same day. Less than three hours after reporting the meeting with Zhang, London received the Chinese reply. Hutchison sent his report of the meeting at 4:20 pm, 22 January, Beijing time (London: 8:20 am, 22 January). At 6:47 pm (London: 10:47 am) the same day he sent China's reply to the joint Indian and Canadian approach to London. Just more than two and a half hours later Hutchison was able to send off a similar-worded but separate Chinese reply to the British government at 9:14 pm (London: 1.14 pm). On this occasion the Chinese government responded with extraordinary speed and seemed to have clearly taken into consideration the time differences between Beijing, London and New York.[25]

The Chinese government's clarification confirmed that the withdrawal of all foreign troops in Korea would include Chinese troops. It proposed that a peaceful settlement of the Korean problem could proceed in two steps: a cease-fire for a limited period, and seven-nation conference negotiations for a settlement of the Korean problem and other political issues in East Asia. The questions for negotiations, the Chinese suggested, should include: the withdrawal of all foreign troops in Korea, internal settlement of the Korean problem, and the withdrawal of US forces from Taiwan. The Chinese government also added that their legal status in the UN had to be ensured.[26]

By late January, the military situation in Korea had become more difficult for China after its initial success on the battlefield. It appeared that at this stage the Chinese leaders had not ruled out a negotiated peace and were seriously considering an alternative to a military solution. Neither the British nor the joint Indian Canadian approaches were rebuffed. In fact the speed of the Chinese response was rather uncharacteristic of their past dealings with western countries. Beijing no longer insisted that negotiations had to take place in China and agreed to work out a cease-fire immediately. All these factors seemed to suggest that the People's Republic was prepared to consider entering into negotiations with the West over the Korean problem.

Peace Initiative Aborted

The British press saw hopes for a peaceful settlement on learning of the latest Chinese proposal. The UN correspondent of *The Times* reported on 23 January that at first sight China had moved closer to the position adopted by most UN members that a truce should precede a negotiated settlement in the Far East. On the next day the newspaper's editorial found that, 'careful examination of the new proposal shows that at many points they do come nearer to the offer made by the Political Committee'.[27]

The Canadian and Indian governments also saw China's response as a promising sign. Canada's Lester Pearson felt that the Chinese government had 'come a long way in the right direction'. He believed that they might well be induced to respond in this way by 'the fairly tough line taken up by the Americans and others as a result of their previous intransigent communication'. Pearson was optimistic that 'a new situation has been created, on which negotiations leading to a peaceful solution were on the horizon'. This view was shared by the British UN representative, Gladwyn Jebb.[28] On 22 January, India's UN representative B. N. Rau announced the latest Chinese reply at the UN and proposed a forty-eight hour adjournment before the US resolution condemning China as an aggressor was put to a vote. The US representative Warren Austin objected to this request saying that the Beijing's clarification was not an official communication directly addressed to the UN. The Assembly, however, accepted the adjournment with twenty-seven for and twenty-three against.

The British Cabinet were divided on how to react to this latest Chinese reply. In a Cabinet meeting on 23 January, two different opinions emerged. There was suspicion that Beijing was trying to 'bring about a division within the UN between Asiatic powers and Western powers' and its stance towards UN representation and Taiwan was still uncompromising. But others felt that the reply was at least an offer of a time-table for negotiations on a cease-fire, and argued that in the long term the question of Taiwan and Chinese representation had to be settled. Summing up the discussions, the Prime Minister put his foot down firmly, saying that the reply 'suggested the door to negotiations had not been finally closed; and we must do our utmost to keep it open'. Attlee said that Britain could not support the US resolution because it contained a paragraph saying that the Chinese government had rejected the UN proposal. He was emphatic that the government should not support sanctions against China, but conceded that, 'we should be prepared to support some condemnation of Chinese actions in Korea'. Jebb was instructed 'to avoid committing himself' to any formula which would formally censure China in the UN.[29]

The difficulty for British policy-makers was again that they wanted to keep the door of negotiations with China open, yet they were not prepared to risk Britain's relationship with the US. On 25 January, the Cabinet held two meetings on the same day to discuss whether or not to support the US resolution in the UN. The Cabinet concluded that 'the possibilities of arranging for a conference should be fully explored before a vote was taken on the US resolution'. In the second meeting, the policy-makers agreed that, 'the resolution as a whole represented a mistaken approach to the problem of Chinese intervention in Korea' and decided to vote against the US resolution in its 'present form'.[30]

However, the tough stance adopted against supporting the castigation of China in the UN was not supported unanimously by all Cabinet members, and the government's determination to explore the possibilities for a negotiated settlement in Korea was not to be sustained for long. After the meeting, the Chancellor, Hugh Gaitskell, who was prepared to threaten to resign over this, tried to convince several colleagues that the government should support the Americans. When an Israeli compromise resolution was put forward in the UN, the Cabinet met again the next day and decided to support it. The Israeli resolution would still condemn the China as an aggressor, but included the provision that sanctions against China would only be considered after all attempts to open further negotiations had failed. After the Israeli compromise had been rejected by the US, the British government finally decided to support a marginally revised US resolution. Instead of stating that the Chinese government had rejected all UN proposals, the resolution now said it had not accepted all of them. The US government also gave an assurance that it would genuinely try to reach a peaceful settlement.[31]

From the outset, however, Washington was not enthusiastic about the initiative of the Cease-Fire Committee. Acheson recalled in his memoirs that the American government supported the initiative 'in the fervent hope and belief that the Chinese would reject it' and that 'our allies would return' to 'comparative sanity and follow us in censuring the Chinese as aggressors'. The US government thus quickly tried to push through the resolution putting all the blame squarely on the Chinese.[32]

Washington was in no mood to find a common basis for a negotiated settlement of the Far Eastern problems with Beijing. During a meeting with the Canadian Ambassador Hume Wrong, the US Assistant Secretary for Far Eastern Affairs, Dean Rusk, spelt out the US anti-Beijing position. At this stage, the Americans were convinced that the Beijing regime was under a pro-Moscow leadership hostile to the West. The US considered the existence of the Beijing regime as 'disadvantageous to the Western world' and it would not be 'wooed away from Moscow' by making concessions over Taiwan and Chinese representation in the UN. Although the US government did not intend to undertake any overt commitment to bring down the Beijing regime, Rusk suggested, it 'could do something to confuse and impede its activities'.[33]

The Attlee government's decision to vote against the US resolution on 25 January was the last serious attempt by British policy-makers to find an alternative solution to the US approach to settle the Korean problem. When it became clear that the US government had opted for confrontation with China, the British government backed down. London's policy objective was still to limit the conflict in Korea, but by joining the US to condemn Beijing, Britain had become a party to a 'limited war' against China. In a way the decision to support the US resolution condemning China marked the end of Britain's attempt to ride two horses at the same time. The priority of Britain's foreign policy was clear: the choice was between closing ranks with its American ally or exploring the possibility of further compromise with the Chinese, thus straining Anglo-American relations to the limit.

After the castigation of China as an aggressor in the UN, *The Times* lamented that, 'at the moment the way forward seemed blocked'. Echoing this the *Manchester Guardian* also viewed that the UN resolution would have a negative effect on Chinese attitudes. The future of peace looked doomed. As *The Times* put it, 'without a truce Peking cannot hope to secure either a seat on the UN or a settlement for Formosa and Western troops cannot be withdrawn from Korea for urgent defence duties elsewhere'. The resolution had darkened the prospect for finding a negotiated settlement in Korea. It had also cast a long shadow on Anglo-Chinese relations.[34]

A New Phase in Anglo-Chinese Relations

Anglo-Chinese relations entered a new phase in early 1951. Beijing's changing attitude towards Britain first became apparent in December 1950, when the Ministry of Foreign Affairs issued its first official statement on the repatriation and treatment of overseas Chinese in Malaya. The statement accused the British authorities in Malaya of carrying out 'a frenzied persecution' of Chinese nationals there. It further said that the Chinese government held the British government responsible for the 'persecution'. The statement did not represent a change in China's attitude on this question, for the government controlled media had spelt it out repeatedly in the past. Its significance was that for the first time an official statement had been made by the Foreign Ministry on this question, reflecting a change in the Chinese government's policy towards Britain.[35]

In January 1951, two British diplomats in China were expelled by the Chinese authorities on charges of espionage. The expulsions were, perhaps, not too surprising since the two men were residing in sensitive areas, one in Urumuqi in Xinjiang, close to the main road from the Soviet Union to China, and the other, in Shenyang, North-Eastern China, close to Korea. Indeed the British admitted that the expulsions of their consul in Shenyang was essentially a security measure. A telegram from Beijing to the Foreign Office suggested that the British government, 'wished to leave him in Mukden [Shenyang] not so much to protect British interests . . . as to act as a listening post . . . We had therefore no good ostensible grounds for keeping him there'.[36] While agreeing that the Chinese government had the legal right to expel British officials from China, the Foreign Office was nonetheless upset that the expulsions had been undertaken in a 'high-handed fashion' and saw them as 'clearly unfriendly' and 'unjustified'. Hutchison was subsequently instructed to make a formal protest.[37]

The downturn in Anglo-Chinese relations, however, came about only when the dialogue between China and the West broke down at the end of January. The Foreign Office learnt later that Zhang Hanfu was so certain that he was going to London as ambassador that his wife had been buying clothes in Shanghai for it. Whether or not Zhang had been Ambassador-designate was probably not the most crucial question; it was very clear that the Chinese attitude towards British diplomatic staff in China worsened markedly after the UN resolution condemning China had been passed.[38]

The departure of Hutchison in February symbolized the state of deterioration in Anglo-Chinese relations. When he went to bid goodbye to Zhang and other Foreign Ministry officials, he was received 'with strictly formal courtesy', 'a studious lack of any appearance of cordiality' and 'a deliberate abstention from any manifestation of friendliness'. His attempt to test Chinese attitudes about the possibility of reopening the Anglo-Chinese talks did not receive any response. Hutchison thus concluded that, 'it augurs ill for any early rapprochement between ourselves and the Chinese in the present international circumstances'.[39] It was by no means surprising that

Hutchison was not greeted warmly in his farewell meeting with Chinese officials. Indeed it was perhaps somewhat surprising that he did not have a rougher time considering that his government had just joined the US government in condemning China in the UN. The Foreign Ministry officials' formal and unfriendly manners were clearly a calculated response. Walter Graham, who had attended some of the previous interviews between Zhang and Hutchison in Beijing, observed that the Chinese attitude towards Britain had 'undergone an important change for the worse'.[40]

A change in attitude was equally noticeable in London by early 1951 as well. British policy-makers were no longer keen to establish full diplomatic relations with Beijing, even though they were still reluctant to break off all diplomatic links with it. Summarizing the government's position in February, Robert Scott stated that Britain's China policy still aimed at 'exercising a moderating influence on Peking and showing that we for our part are sincere in our wish to see more normal relations established in the Far East'. He maintained that, 'Our foothold, political, commercial and cultural in China is tenuous, but we are reluctant to see these links completely severed since once we abandon this foothold all western influences in China will disappear'.[41] But this policy of 'keeping a foot in the door' and of seeking the establishment of normal diplomatic relations with China was becoming more and more difficult to implement. The Chinese intervention in Korea and subsequently the passage of the UN resolution branding China as an aggressor not only changed the international situation; it also changed the perceptions of policy-makers both in London and in Beijing.

Although Leo Lamb, Britain's newly appointed charge d'affaires to China, was instructed to bring up the establishment of official diplomatic relations, he was told not to 'make too much' of it. The Foreign Office now had mixed feelings on the question of establishing diplomatic relations with China. It felt that a favourable response from the Chinese government would put the British government in 'an awkward position' given the animosity between China and the US at that time.[42]

Additional Measures Against China

At the beginning of 1951 the British policy-makers were still resisting US pressure for further economic and political sanctions against China. London's position was that the UN should still try to secure a negotiated settlement with China before considering punitive measures.[43] After studying the possible effects of political, economic and strategic sanctions against China, British officials concluded in mid-February that sanctions were not likely to have any significant effect other than 'playing Russia's game' by driving 'China more and more into the hands of Russia and her satellites for economic and trading purposes'. During a Cabinet meeting on 5 April, the new Foreign Secretary, Herbert Morrison, presented the case against imposing political sanctions and maintained that the government should not support any economic sanctions other than a selective embargo on strategic materials.[44]

Like the British position towards the branding of China as an aggressor in the UN, British opposition to the imposition of sanction measures soon gave way under American pressure. When the UN Good Offices Committee had failed to make any progress towards a negotiated settlement in Korea, American pressure to sanction China intensified. Throughout March and April, the US delegate to the UN pressed for a full meeting of the Additional Measures Committee to take actions against China. The Labour government was also under considerable pressure from the Opposition in Parliament to adopt a tougher stance towards China in April and May.[45]

The British preference for a united effort to achieve a negotiated settlement in Korea collapsed in early May when the US government introduced a resolution in the UN calling for a selective embargo against China. By that stage Britain's withholding of the imposition of a further embargo against Beijing would not have made any difference; China was essentially fighting a limited war with the West and the stigmatization by the UN had already closed the door for negotiations for the time being. The resolution on a strategic embargo, supported by Britain, was adopted by the UN General Assembly on 18 May. One month later, on 19 June, the President of the Board of Trade announced in the House of Commons that the government had decided to impose license controls on all exports to China and Hong Kong, where China could easily obtain Western goods.[46]

The Chinese Foreign Ministry called the UN embargo resolution 'a malevolent attempt to extend aggressive war' and 'a violation of the Charter of the UN'. The British government was told that 'in agreeing to the embargo, it had closed the door for possible negotiations and had revealed its determination to be the enemy of China'. Apart from the US, Britain was the only other country singled out for criticism in this official statement. Two days later in a most uncompromising tone and one of the most severe attacks on the British government, the *People's Daily* declared that the Labour government was 'the most submissive slave of the United States and her most shameful accomplice'.[47]

The changes in British attitude to China was further displayed when

Morrison agreed to a moratorium arrangement with the US postponing any discussion on Chinese representation in the UN in May.[48] The fighting in Korea would have made any attempt to seat Beijing in the UN impossible, but Britain's acceptance of the US proposal had significant implications; Chinese representation in the UN had been a crucial issue in the Anglo-Chinese talks on their bilateral relations. By agreeing to the moratorium, British policy-makers had virtually abandoned their policy of seeking to establish full diplomatic relations with China for the time being.

In late April, Lamb painted a rather gloomy picture of the prospect for an improvement in Anglo-Chinese relations. He wrote, 'I fail to see what factor exists or is likely to materialize which may induce the Chinese Government to regularize the present anomalous status of our diplomatic relationship'.[49] Beijing's tougher policy towards Britain was reflected in its treatment of British diplomats. The Chinese authorities in Nanjing not only refused to recognize the diplomatic status of the British Consul there, but also accused him of interfering with China's internal affairs when he attempted to intervene over the arrest of a Catholic nun in March. Other disturbing incidents in Shanghai, Kunming, Xiamen and in Chongqing were also reported.[50] Most of these incidents were troubles with local authorities which did not involve the central government in Beijing, yet they revealed growing anti-British feelings and a lack of constraint on the local authorities.

The Beijing government had not made any attempt to drive British diplomatic presence out of China. British officials noted that the Chinese government had continued accepting official communications, representations and protests from the British charge d'affaires on subjects not connected with the establishment of diplomatic relations. Even though the Chinese usually did not reply to these official communications, a British policy brief maintained that there was reason 'to think that our representations are not entirely without effect' and that, in practice the British diplomatic mission in Beijing enjoyed diplomatic status. Nonetheless a changing Chinese attitude was also observed, and the message was clear. From January 1951 Chinese authorities had stopped issuing entry permits for either diplomatic or clerical staff for the British diplomatic mission in Beijing with the sole exception of Leo Lamb.[51]

In 1951, the British business community had come to a bleak conclusion about the prospects for doing business in China. The British Chamber of Commerce in Shanghai conceded in May that even though different views had been expressed about the status of foreign enterprises in China, it had become obvious that foreign businessmen in China could not 'look forward with any degree of confidence to remaining in China as free agents, enjoying such rights as are normally granted by most countries to foreign nationals admitted to trade in those countries'.[52]

Meanwhile the tide of military fortune had changed again in Korea. UN troops had forced the Chinese and North Korean troops to retreat, and a stalemate was established along roughly the 38th parallel by June 1951. Both the Chinese and the Americans had been intransigent during the course of the war; neither side had been prepared to enter negotiations when the military situation was favourable to them. With the stalemate, time had come for a negotiated settlement of the Korean problem. On 23 June 1951 the Soviet UN delegate Jacob Malik sent up a trial balloon for a negotiated settlement in a radio address in which a proposal for cease-fire talks between the belligerents in Korea was put forward. Subsequently talks were held in Kaesong; and later in Panmunjom. Military confrontation continued, but apart from a brief period in 1953, shortly before the Korean armistice was signed in June, the battleground had shifted to the diplomatic arena.

Despite the armistice talks, no immediate improvement occurred in Anglo-Chinese relations. While British diplomatic presence in China continued, no attempt was made by either side to re-open talks on the two countries' diplomatic relations. For the British government the policy of 'keeping a foot in the door' was maintained in a way, but it had shifted from a positive approach seeking to establish a closer and working relationship with China to that of damage limitation to avoid the complete alienation of China from the West. It was during this period of uncertainty that a Conservative government came to power in Britain.

THE KOREAN ARMISTICE

The Conservative Government's China Policy

The return of Winston Churchill as Prime Minister in October 1951 did not mark a radical change in Britain's China policy. As the new Foreign Secretary Anthony Eden later wrote, he shared the foreign policy objectives of his predecessor and was in agreement with most that Bevin had done.[53] The Conservative government continued to perceive the Soviet Union as the greatest threat to the security of Britain, and to regard the US as their most important ally. Churchill's private secretary recalled that one reason why the ageing Churchill decided to remain as Prime Minister was 'to have time to re-establish the intimate relationship with the United States, which had been a keynote of his policy in the war'. The maintenance of a close Anglo-American alliance continued to be new Conservative leadership's foreign policy priority.[54]

No attempts were made to reverse the Labour government's policy of maintaining Britain's diplomatic presence in China. This was not without controversy since some members of the Conservative party had openly opposed the policy of recognizing the People's Republic. Lord Salisbury remained opposed to recognition even after he had become Minister of State at the Foreign Office.[55] Churchill himself who had earlier supported the recognition had also become more sympathetic to the Kuomintang regime in Taiwan. In a letter to Gladwyn Jebb he expressed support for the US effort to preserve Taiwan as 'a refuge for those with whom the US and ourselves were allies in the war'.[56]

One of the first decisions that the new Foreign Secretary, Anthony Eden, had to make was about China. Expecting that Chinese representation would be raised in a forthcoming UN General Assembly meeting to be held in Paris in November 1951 which Eden was to attend, the Foreign Office recommended continuing the existing Anglo-American moratorium arrangement to postpone the discussion of the question. Approving the recommendation, Eden remarked that it was 'a carefully balanced compromise' between Britain's recognition of the Beijing government and its common front with the US.[57] These remarks were to set the tone for Britain's China policy under his Foreign Secretaryship. He did not want to undo the former government's efforts to establish a working relationship with Beijing, but the new Conservative government attached an even greater importance to Anglo-American co-operation and were most anxious to avoid risking Britain's friendship with the US because of China. This position corresponded closely with the views of the Foreign Office officials who were beginning to favour a tougher China policy.

The change in attitude among British officials responsible for Far Eastern affairs was not merely a result of the Korean conflict, but also a result of their frustration over the fruitless Anglo-Chinese talks as well as the personnel changes in both London and the Beijing 'embassy'. By the end of 1951 not only was the Labour leadership replaced, many of the officials who had been directly involved in formulating the policy of 'keeping a foot in the door' in China and implementing the policy of recognition had also left the Far Eastern department. A new team under Leo Lamb also took over in Beijing. Most of the original staff who moved on to Beijing from Nanjing with Hutchison had been replaced. The team led by Lamb with Michael Gillett as Consul General, Joe Ford as Chinese Secretary, and Colin Crowe as Head of Chancery were in Crowe's own words, 'pretty hard nosed, and were to experience the less agreeable aspect of the Communist regime'.[58]

Britain's China Policy Revised

During a visit to the US soon after returning to office, Churchill made a speech to the US Congress on 17 January 1952. Referring to what the British government would do if the Chinese crossed the Yalu again, Churchill declared that 'our reply will be prompt, resolute, and effective'. This created an uproar back in Britain when opposition MPs criticized the remarks as representing a new commitment to play a more active role against China. The Chinese reacted strongly to Churchill's speech. A *People's Daily* editorial – headlined 'British Imperialists warned against trying any trick' – bluntly said Churchill had made 'a declaration of support for US war policy'.[59]

Behind the rhetoric, however, the situation in Korea had become more stable after the armistice talks had started. At the end of 1952 the Foreign Office began a reassessment of Britain's China policy. Responding to questions from the Foreign Office, Lamb suggested that the Chinese leaders had been taken aback by Britain's recognition and were embarrassed. The various explanatory statements made by the Chinese government at different times were only, Lamb believed, 'opportune pretexts'. Thus he did not have much hope that China would offer to discuss seriously an exchange of ambassadors.[60]

In London different views about Lamb's hypothesis were being discussed in the Foreign Office. One was that Beijing had expected British recognition because London's intention had been made very clear over a period of time before January 1950. Another was that even though the Chinese might have been aware of the intention of the British government, they found recognition by a country in the Western camp embarrassing. Some officials believed that an armistice in Korea might provide an opportunity to re-open Anglo-Chinese talks on diplomatic relations, but others felt that the existing informal relations with China were serving British interests well. The general consensus appeared to be that as long as the fighting in Korea continued, establishing full diplomatic relations with Beijing would be embarrassing for the British government.[61]

Reviewing Britain's policy of recognizing Beijing, Robert Scott felt one major problem had been the way in which the policy was implemented. He believed that, 'whilst our policy was right our tactics were hasty and legalistic'. If the government had allowed an interval to elapse before committing itself publicly to establishing diplomatic relations, Scott suggested, it could have been 'free to withdraw without a public reversal of policy.' As far as the negotiations were concerned, Scott observed, the lesson was: the Chinese government did not play the game by established European rules and customs, and therefore Britain should not necessarily have to abide by these conventions in dealing with China. Thus he proposed: "If the Chinese prevent British press agencies from functioning in China, let us do the same to them. Similarly over visas, restrictions on British banks and traders, and so on'.[62]

There was no doubt that British policy-makers did not want a complete break with China; Beijing had not adopted an entirely uncompromisingly hostile attitude towards Britain. The Foreign Office still considered that 'the maintenance of tenuous official and commercial contacts with China is of importance to the West generally'. Yet British attitude towards China had undergone significant changes by 1952. When the US suggested that all UN members should sever diplomat relations with Beijing and impose a total embargo in mid-1952, Churchill rejected the American proposal only after much persuasion by Eden.[63]

After the Korean Truce

The Korean truce in 1953 led to a more relaxed international climate; the possibility of an escalation of the Korean conflict into a general war was greatly reduced. The war, however, had lasting effects on international politics and on Anglo-Chinese relations which could not be undone over night. China's intervention had failed to expel UN forces from the Korean peninsula, but it had thwarted the advance of UN forces beyond the 38th parallel. This boosted the Chinese revolutionaries' confidence and international prestige. After the war, few would dispute that the People's Republic had become firmly established. Most governments now reasoned that China would play an important role in Asia. Unfortunately, the conflict had further widened the divide between revolutionary China and the West.

The general relaxation in international tensions after the truce did not immediately lead to any dramatic improvement in Anglo-Chinese relations. The more favourable climate was countered by the changing perceptions of British and Chinese policy-makers, who had adopted a much tougher line towards each other. Scepticism created by Beijing's refusal to establish immediate official diplomatic relations was fortified by the fighting in Korea. British support for branding China as an aggressor in the UN had convinced the Chinese leaders that Britain's China policy was guided by the Americans. This view was further reinforced when the British government supported US proposals to impose a shipment embargo against China. Against this background of mistrust the prospect for Anglo-Chinese relations was most uncertain even after the armistice was signed.

In August 1953, Humphrey Trevelyan replaced Leo Lamb as Britain's Charge d'Affaires to China, or as the Chinese called him, 'the British representative for the negotiations on the establishment of diplomatic relations'. Three and a half years had passed since Britain had recognized the People's Republic, and the two sides still had not established proper diplomatic relations. As they had maintained *de facto* diplomatic ties throughout these years, British officials now felt that 'the anomaly over the question of diplomatic relations has corresponded fairly well with our desire to maintain relations of a sort with China despite the circumstances of the Korean war'.[64] British policy-makers were not yet ready to revive the question of official diplomatic relations with China. This question was considered to be extremely sensitive because it 'would be strongly criticized in the United States'. London believed that the Chinese government, in any case, might reject any such approach or demand too high a price as *quid pro quo*. The British thinking, in Lord Reading's words was: 'silence is the best policy'.[65]

Thus, Trevelyan was instructed not to take the initiative to revive the question of diplomatic relations and an exchange of ambassadors, and not to commit himself if the Chinese raised it. The instruction explained: 'the establishment of diplomatic relations . . . belongs to a later stage when the Korean armistice has led to a more general improvement in the situation in the Far East'. Policy-makers in London could not forecast a definite time-table for that general improvement and therefore did not wish to lay down new precise conditions which had to be fulfilled in advance. Their attitude was: 'the Korean armistice has not in itself ushered in the new stage in which mediation of our policies would be appropriate'. The British government were not prepared to change their previous stance. It would continue to support the moratorium to postpone the discussion of Chinese representation in the UN and controls on strategic exports were to be maintained until international developments become more favourable.[66]

The first meeting between Trevelyan and Zhang Hanfu was thus a non-event. Neither side mentioned the question of the establishment of full diplomatic relations. The Chinese side appeared to have become more conciliatory, but nothing concrete was discussed or resolved.[67] In a personal letter to Denis Allen, who had replaced Rob Scott as Assistant Under-Secretary, Trevelyan reported that the Chinese officials had been polite and friendly, and official relations had improved slightly, but he did not expect any change in the Chinese position on exchanging diplomatic representatives unless Britain could modify the embargo and vote for the admission of China in the UN.[68]

As long as the Korean conflict was not resolved, and the estrangement between China and the US continued, the existing unofficial Anglo-Chinese diplomatic relations suited the British government. It served Britain's need for diplomatic representation in China on the one hand, and carried no risk of antagonizing American opinion on the other. The problem was that the situation could not be maintained indefinitely, and would hardly be a basis for a long-term China policy. Foreign Office officials, however, had actually refrained from asking for a decision from ministers on this question. One thing did seem clear: if China revived the question, Britain would be obliged either to respond favourably or to withdraw their mission from Beijing.[69]

GENEVA AND ANGLO-CHINESE RELATIONS

The Policy of 'keeping a toe in the door'

While there were no clear commitments or policy decisions on the question of diplomatic relations with Beijing, Britain's general objective of seeking to establish a working relationship with China was maintained. Towards the end of 1953, a Cabinet paper spelt out the British position on this question. The British approach was: 'based upon acceptance of the facts of the situation, the avoidance of provocation, gradual progress towards more normal trading and diplomatic relations, and the need to keep a toe in the door in case divergences between China and Russia develop and can be exploited'.[70] While this approach seemed similar to earlier versions of Britain's policy papers on China in late 1949 and early 1950, it reflected a change in both the British perception and position. The China policy formulated in late 1949 had been based upon three considerations: legal, economic and political. The legal position, namely that recognizing Beijing constituted a recognition of facts, and not necessarily an act of approval, still stood; but the economic consideration of protecting British commercial interests in China and the political reasoning that recognition would encourage a Sino-Soviet split did not seem valid any more.

The economic argument had been weakened by the virtual collapse of British commercial interests in China. On 19 May 1952, the British government informed the Chinese government that all British firms in China had decided to close their businesses. It was quite clear that the situation for foreign business in China would improve little. There was also no doubt that China needed to trade with the West. Thus, despite the difficult situation for British businessmen, those who wanted to trade with China continued to press for the lifting of government prohibitions on exports to China.[71] The Chinese government, however, were trying to by-pass the established British firms to trade with those who had no previous trading relations with China. This created suspicion in London. In early 1953, the Foreign Office had found it necessary to advise British businessmen not to attend the Beijing economic conference when invitations were issued through the British Council for the Promotion of International Trade, an organization considered by the government as a communist front body. In early 1954, the Foreign Office also advised against inviting Chinese representatives to attend the 1954 British Industrial Fair even though the Board of Trade were in favour of it. Arguing against the invitation, Denis Allen mentioned the possible adverse effects from US reaction and the fact that the business prospect remained uncertain.[72]

Of the three considerations which had led to Britain's recognition of the People's Republic, the change in the political argument was most notable. The main reason was that British perception of the Sino-Soviet relationship had undergone a fundamental change since the outbreak of the Korean War. As far as the Foreign Office was concerned, the detachment of China from the Soviet Union had become unlikely.[73] In late 1949, the British government had been anxious that China should not be driven into the arms of the Soviet Union. By early 1954 the Chinese were considered to be already in Soviet arms. British policy-makers thus concluded that they could only seek to exploit any possible divergences between China and the Soviet Union that might develop.

In the process of attempting to 'keep a foot in the door' in China, the British policy-makers had shifted their position to merely 'keep a toe in the door'. They had by now adopted a more cautious approach. Despite the Korean armistice, neither the British nor the Chinese governments took any initiative to revive the question of official diplomatic relations. The armistice, at least, provided the international climate for the two governments once again to test each other's intentions and policies. The breakthrough eventually came in 1954 at Geneva.

The Geneva Conference 1954

The Geneva Conference in 1954 was the first major international meeting that representatives from the People's Republic attended. It was convened to discuss the problems of Korea and Indo-China. International efforts at Geneva failed to find a solution for Korea, and despite an agreement on a cease-fire and a regroupment of opposing forces, peace was not established in Indo-China. The conference, however, provided the opportunity for ministerial meetings between Britain and China which ultimately led to a formal exchange of Charges d'Affaires.

British officials were not to foresee that one outcome of the Conference would be the establishment of official diplomatic relations with China. At the beginning of 1954, Denis Allen defined the twin objectives of Britain's China policy as 'containment' and 'seeking a *modus vivendi*'. Elaborating on these two objectives, Denis Allen wrote: 'On the one hand, we seek to prevent the spread of Communism outside its present confines', but on the other hand, 'we strive, so far as circumstances permit, to establish something more like normal relations between China and ourselves and between China and her neighbours in Southeast Asia and the Pacific'. These two objectives, however, were to be implemented subject to the overriding consideration of Anglo-American solidarity.[74]

British officials believed that any improvement in Britain relations with China had to wait until a general improvement in the Far Eastern situation. The Geneva meeting was not seen as an opportunity to explore the question of Anglo-Chinese relations, but as a testing ground to see whether a more favourable international climate was to come about. Any change in British policies would depend on the outcome of the Geneva talks since Britain did not intend to alter its policies towards either Chinese representation in the UN or the shipment embargo against China, if the Chinese stepped up their support for the Vietminh. Thus only if the situation in Indo-China stabilized then the British government would have to think hard about their China policy.[75]

The policy brief for the British delegation to Geneva actually made it clear that the government were not prepared to discuss bilateral relations with the Chinese. Full diplomatic relations should be 'the symptom of a real improvement in the relations between China and the United Kingdom' which belonged to 'the hypothetical future stage when there has been a general improvement in the situation'. London's position was that :'The Korean armistice though an important step forward, was not in itself sufficient to usher in this new stage'. British officials even suggested that an offer by the Chinese to exchange ambassadors might prove 'extremely embarrassing given the situation in Indo-China.[76]

The Chinese, however, were prepared to take a step forward to improve Anglo-Chinese relations. Earlier in March for the first time the Vice Foreign Minister and other senior Foreign Ministry officials accepted Trevelyan's invitation to a buffet party after which they were shown a film about the Coronation. A week later Zhang invited the Trevelyans and three other senior British officials in Beijing to a dinner in the Foreign Ministry, a function normally only given for the heads of recognized missions.[77] British officials in London were not too impressed. Colin Crowe, now head of the China and Korea department, maintained that the gestures were 'deliberate acts of policy, probably in preparation for Geneva'. But the change in Chinese attitudes was noted. As another official, Joe Ford, pointed out, 'the Chinese have shown a desire to cultivate better relations with the UK'.[78]

British officials, however, remained cautious about the prospects for an improvement in Anglo-Chinese relations. The willingness of the Chinese authorities to settle the outstanding problems of the British community in China did not have a significant impact on the Foreign Office's attitude. Crowe insisted that 'the fundamental position remains unchanged and the Chinese have only been putting right a few of the wrongs they have done to British subjects'. The Foreign Office's recommendation was: no commitment on Anglo-Chinese relations should be made in Geneva.[79]

The change of Chinese attitudes was even more noticeable in Geneva. Accompanying Eden to the conference, Trevelyan was for the first time able to hold meetings regularly with the Chinese Foreign Ministry's Director of Western European Department, Huan Xiang, and the Vice-Minister of Trade, Lei Renmin. During these meetings many outstanding problems concerning the British community in China were resolved – exit permits were granted, and negotiations for the closure of British firms were made easier.[80]

The Establishment of Official Diplomatic Relations

It was at the ministerial level that the deadlock in Anglo-Chinese diplomatic relations was eventually broken. The Geneva Conference provided an opportunity for the foreign ministers of the two countries to develop personal contacts and to discuss bilateral relations. Anthony Eden and Zhou Enlai appeared to have impressed one another. In their first meeting, Zhou indicated that China was prepared to work with Britain when Eden asked him whether Chinese officials would be willing to talk to Trevelyan who had accompanied him to Geneva. Eden's objective in Geneva was not to seek the establishment of official diplomatic relations, but he believed that any improvement in China's relations with the West would help to lessen international tensions. During a private dinner meeting with Zhou later, Eden found that he could not avoid mentioning the question of diplomatic representation. In his memoirs Eden recalled that the meeting had been most agreeable, and when he 'twitted' Zhou with not having a representative in London, the Chinese Foreign Minister said the Chinese government was willing to send one.[81]

Geneva was the first occasion on which the Chinese Communist leaders emerged onto the international scene. There was an air of uncertainty about the possible outcome of the meeting. Denis Allen recalled that as the Conference went on the Chinese delegation became gradually more open and forthcoming. He felt that the agreement to appoint a Chinese representative to London was developed out of a growth of confidence and understanding between Eden and Zhou during the conference, but not as a direct consequence of the dinner. He later wrote: 'One thing I am certain of: the decision to exchange diplomatic representatives was not taken during or in direct consequence of the dinner'. Denis Allen was emphatic that the meeting 'was simply a convivial affair, useful in helping the leaders to get to know one another in an informal atmosphere but of no more significance than that'. Another member of the British delegation, Joe Ford, also could not recall any agreement on the formal exchange of charge d'affaires.[82] There was no doubt that a formal agreement had not been reached during the dinner meeting, but equally true was the fact that when Eden first mentioned the question of diplomatic representation Zhou responded positively.

The British delegation in Geneva did not inform their American colleagues about the informal exchanges between Eden and Zhou during the dinner party. The next day Denis Allen told the Americans that, 'nothing of particular significance resulted from the meeting'. More specifically, Allen said, 'there was no discussion of diplomatic relations or exchange of Ambassadors or of UN representation for Chinese Communists'. Although Zhou's offer to send a Chinese representative to London did not represent a formal discussion of Anglo-Chinese diplomatic relations or the exchange of ambassadors, it seemed that the Americans might have been misled. Later Allen maintained that the dinner meeting was a social event and as such not an occasion 'for broaching of serious business'.[83] Perhaps British officials did not regard the remarks made during the dinner as of any significance, but the Chinese certainly did, for they immediately followed them up and took the initiative to bring up the matter officially.

A few days afterwards Huan Xiang told Trevelyan that a Chinese official should be sent to London with the same status as Trevelyan in Beijing, and proposed to announce this arrangement. Huan also said that the Chinese government had agreed to Trevelyan's earlier proposal that an extra officer be added to his staff in Beijing who could be sent to head the 'British Government Office' in Shanghai with diplomatic status. The arrangement proposed by the Chinese was most peculiar, since the two countries would have a diplomatic mission in each other's capital, headed by a charge d'affaires, while not formally admitting it. Trevelyan felt that this was illogical, but he supported it, saying that the arrangement appeared to be beneficial for Britain.[84]

Back in London the Cabinet discussed the Chinese offer on 5 June. It was a sensitive issue since an improvement in Anglo-Chinese relations, as Eden put it, 'might give rise to misunderstanding in the United States, where our recognition of the Central People's government was still the subject of unfavourable comment'. Given US sentiments about China, it was not an opportune moment for the British government to receive a Chinese representative in London. But Eden argued that, 'it would be both discourteous and illogical to reject this offer entirely'. Therefore he proposed that the Chinese representative could be accepted on the basis that he would be described, as was the British representative in Beijing, 'as responsible for discussing the practical arrangement for establishing diplomatic relations between the United Kingdom and Communist China'. The Cabinet, however, were reluctant to accept an official Chinese diplomatic representative immediately and decided that the appointment should be deferred until after the Geneva conference.[85]

Following the Cabinet decision, the British delegation in Geneva told the Chinese that the question was being examined in London because the proposal was without precedent and there were certain legal questions involved. The reply was thus delayed, but it could not be delayed for long. On further reflection after returning to Geneva for the conference, Eden told London that the Chinese offer should be accepted quickly because 'hesitation will only raise suspicions with the Chinese'. If their offer was rejected, Eden argued, the Chinese government might react by denying the British charge d'affaires a useful role in China, and making it impossible for the British government to maintain their diplomatic presence in China. If that was to happen then the only option left would be to withdraw the British mission in Beijing. Eden considered that to be 'a counsel of despair' and 'a most serious business for British nationals in China and the abandonment of our policy of trying to get on with the Chinese'. The Foreign Secretary therefore recommended accepting the offer and proposed making a joint announcement with the Chinese while they were still in Geneva.[86]

A few days later Eden told the American deputy Secretary of State General Bedell-Smith that the Chinese government had offered to send a Charge d'Affaires to London. Bedell-Smith agreed that there was no other course that the British government could follow but to accept the offer. He also brushed off Eden's suggestion that it might upset American opinion by saying that there were some who did not want the Americans to have any relations with the USSR. Eden was reassured by Bedell-Smith's attitude and felt strongly that now London should go ahead and accept the Chinese offer.[87]

Reporting Eden's views to the Cabinet on 15 June, the Minister of State, Selwyn Lloyd, pointed out that as the Chinese offer had been disclosed in a newspaper report, it was necessary to make an official announcement without delay. Some members of the Cabinet, however, still had reservations and suggested that the Chinese representative should not be described as charge d'affaires. When Lloyd telephoned Eden then in Geneva to ask his opinion, the Foreign Secretary insisted that the Chinese representative should be called charge d'affaires because this was how the British described their representative in China. He proposed that the position could be made clear by announcing that the Chinese representative would have the same position as the British charge d'affaires. In the end Eden's insistence carried the day. The Cabinet accepted the Chinese offer with the condition that the public announcement of this arrangement should also make clear that the establishment of formal diplomatic relations would remain a matter for negotiations between the two governments.[88]

The technicalities of the positions of the two charge d'affaires were swiftly arranged. Trevelyan's name was added to the list of recognized embassies and legations and the British diplomatic mission in Beijing was described as 'the Office of the British Charge d'Affaires'. The British government also decided that the Chinese representative in London would be treated in 'precisely the same way as any other acting Head of a Diplomatic Mission'. In September Huan Xiang was appointed the People's Republic of China's first Charge d'Affaires to London.[89]

Thus ended a strange chapter in Anglo-Chinese relations. Four and a half years after Britain had recognized the People's Republic of China, the two governments finally established official diplomatic relations of a kind. It was a landmark in the development of Anglo-Chinese relations. The irony was that in early 1954 the British government had been neither expecting nor preparing for this development.

After Geneva, policy-makers in both Beijing and London continued to view the international situation from different perspectives. Reporting to the first session of the First National People's Congress in September 1954, Zhou Enlai cited Britain's support of the formation of a Southeast Asian collective security pact as a problem in Anglo-Chinese relationships.[90] Yet Britain's relations with China greatly improved after the Geneva Conference. When Clement Attlee, now Leader of the Opposition, led a labour delegation to China in August 1954, he was received by Mao; for the first time Zhou also visited the British diplomatic mission in Beijing. Other visits from British business representatives soon followed, and trade between Britain and China reached a new peak in 1955.[91]

The exchange of charge d'affaires, however, was not a dramatic breakthrough. It was, in a sense, a move to regularize the diplomatic relations between the two states which already existed. Bilateral relations between the two countries were to remain at this level for eighteen more years. The second phase of a more favourable international development which would allow Britain to establish full diplomatic relations with China did not arrive until 1971. The two countries upgraded their bilateral relations to ambassadorial level in 1972.

CONCLUSIONS

Britain's China policy was revised from 'keeping a foot' to 'keeping a toe' in the door during the course of the Korean conflict. The Conservative government which came to office in early 1952 basically shared their predecessors' view on China. The revision in Britain's China policy during this period was largely caused by changes in the international environment created by China's military intervention in Korea. The intensification of the East-West conflict, and of Sino-American antipathy, had made it impossible for British policy-makers to pursue their objective of establishing diplomatic relations with revolutionary China. When a more favourable international atmosphere emerged after the Korean truce, the British government had deferred the question of diplomatic relations indefinitely. In the end the Chinese leaders took the initiative when Eden offered them the opportunity in 1954.

For revolutionary China, 1954 marked its entry into international society when it took part in its first major international conference. The new government had firmly established itself and was launching an ambitious five year economic programme. The Chinese revolutionaries were beginning to turn to a new style of diplomacy to cultivate friendship among their neighbours in Asia. After Geneva, with British mediation and assistance, the first series of informal meetings between the US and China began in Warsaw. Zhou's diplomacy of peaceful co-existence after 1954 was to characterize China's foreign policy until revolutionary fervour swept the country again in the 1960s during the Cultural Revolution.

The response of revolutionary China to Britain's recognition and efforts to establish diplomatic relations were in many ways a reflection of how a new revolutionary state reacted to the existing international order. From the early years of uncertainty and suspicion, the People's Republic gradually found itself better established in international society. It was not achieved without bloodshed and bitterness; the Korean War proved to be extremely costly for both the West and China. Once the war was over the Chinese revolutionaries turned their efforts once again to domestic economic and social reform programmes. After establishing China's role as a regional power, Beijing also found it necessary to be accepted as a responsible member of international society and tried to develop a better relationship with the West. Revolutionary China's full participation in global affairs, however, was still blocked by its exclusion from the United Nations.

Part III
Policy Issues

6 Chinese Representation in the United Nations

5 Chinese Representation in the United Nations

On 4 January 1950, two days before Britain formally accorded *de jure* recognition to the People's Republic, the head of the British permanent delegation at the UN, Sir Alexander Cadogan, wrote in his diary, 'I saw a repetition of a telegram to Delhi, from which it appeared we recognised Communist China on the 6th. I think the FO might have given me this information direct'. Not only was Cadogan not directly informed of the date of the recognition, two days after it had happened, he noted, 'A bag after lunch, but nothing of great interest and particularly no guidance about China'.[1]

British policy-makers had not anticipated that the question of Chinese representation in the UN would hamper the establishment of Anglo-Chinese diplomatic relations. As discussed in Chapter 3, in response to Britain's recognition, Beijing insisted that diplomatic relations could only be established after negotiations because Britain had not severed relations with the Kuomintang, citing as evidence the British UN delegate's absten-tion from voting when the Soviet Union raised the question of China's representation at the UN on 13 January 1951.[2]

For Beijing, at issue was its legitimacy and right to represent China abroad, and also its future role in international affairs. Its response to Britain's voting policy in the UN revealed much about the new leadership of China: their attitudes towards international relations and perceptions of the West. For London, two issues were at stake: first, the effective role of the UN as an international organization; second, Britain's long-term relationship with the newly established People's Republic which seemed there to stay. Added to these was a third element in British considerations: its relationship with the US – China's declared enemy number one, which in turn had made public its detestation of the Beijing regime. British policy-makers therefore faced a very difficult situation: on the one hand, Britain had recognized the Beijing government, on the other hand, the US attitude towards the new Chinese government made it extremely difficult for them to support Beijing in the UN. The considerations behind Britain's voting policy on the China seat revealed vividly the predicament its policy-makers had to face. Between January 1950 and

June 1951, the British government revised their voting policy four times and twice withheld implementing their decisions.

Following the scene set in Part II, this chapter analyses the problems British policy-makers faced over Beijing's claim in the UN, a major obstacle which blocked the establishment of formal Anglo-Chinese diplomatic relations. It traces the changes in Britain's attitude towards the question of Chinese representation at the UN, and discusses how these changes affected Anglo-Chinese relations between 1950 and 1954 in general, and the implementation of Britain's China policy in particular. Revolutionary China's response to Britain's policy, and its views on the role of the UN as an international organization, will also be explored in this chapter.

BRITAIN AND CHINESE REPRESENTATION IN THE UN

Initial British Attitudes

The Foreign Office had not entirely ignored the question of Chinese representation in the UN when the decision to recognize the Communist government was taken in December 1949. But British officials did not regard this issue as urgent; they had not anticipated that it would have a serious effect on Britain's relationship with revolutionary China.

As early as November 1949 the British delegation to the UN had suggested that Britain should discuss the question of Chinese representation in the UN with other friendly delegations and with the Secretariat. The delegation told London that, 'we feel that it would be unwise to delay these consultations longer than is absolutely necessary'. The Foreign Office did not share the delegation's sense of urgency; instead of replying immediately by telegram as requested, it responded one month later by letter, and only after receiving a second request from the delegation. The question was discussed in some length in this reply, but it dealt mainly with the procedural problems at the UN and possible American reactions. It was also rather inconclusive, with the Foreign Office admitting that, 'The question is an extremely complicated one and on almost every point it seems possible to argue in either direction, more especially since no precedent of any kind exists and appeal to the Charter is largely fruitless'.[3]

The importance that the new Chinese government would attach to the issue was not fully appreciated by British officials at this stage, and the difficulties that would be posed to the establishment of Anglo-Chinese diplomatic relations were not foreseen. Policy-makers in London soon found that in dealing with Beijing's claim at the UN they were caught between the

Cold War on the one hand, and their policy of 'keeping a foot in the door' in China on the other. Their successive changes of policy towards Chinese representation in the UN between 1950 and 1951 demonstrated clearly the difficulty they faced. Within eighteen months British policy went through three phases: abstention from voting; voting in favour of Beijing; and a moratorium arrangement to postpone the question.

Phase I – Abstention

The British government abstained when the question of who should represent China in the UN was first put to a vote on 13 January 1950. Anticipating that the newly recognized Beijing government would not be too happy about this, the Foreign Office cautioned Hutchison that the Chinese government would probably reproach Britain for not supporting Beijing at the UN, before he left for Beijing in February to begin negotiations with the Chinese. Since the British government intended to abstain again if a motion approving the credentials of a representative from Beijing was put forward in the Security Council, Hutchison was instructed to explain to the Chinese that, 'the problem of Chinese representation in the United Nations cannot be solved unilaterally by individual states' because 'a collective decision of some sort must be taken'. The Foreign Office also suggested that if the atmosphere were favourable, Hutchison might venture to suggest that the Soviet attempt to take positive action on behalf of the Chinese government had bogged down the whole question which might take a long time to solve.[4] It is obvious that at this stage the Foreign Office did not expect that Chinese representation in the UN would become a central issue in Anglo-Chinese relations.

As pointed out in Chapter 3, Beijing had already expressed dissatisfaction through NCNA regarding the manner in which British recognition was accorded, because the announcement of recognition was followed by suggestions that it was not an act of approval.[5] The first indication that the new government attached great importance to the question of Chinese representation at the UN came when they requested the Norwegian government to explain its position over the China seat question at the end of January 1950. Like the British, the Norwegian government had also abstained from voting in support of Beijing in the Security Council on 14 January.[6] When Hutchison arrived in Beijing in February, the Chinese government had still not responded to Britain's abstention from voting in support of Beijing in the UN. The first official confirmation that the new Chinese government had decided to make it an important issue in the Anglo-Chinese talks on diplomatic relations came only in March.

The British explained to the Chinese that it would be useless for Britain to vote for Beijing alone, if the majority of Security Council members would not agree to accept its representative. Nevertheless, after Britain's recognition of the new Chinese government, Cadogan suggested from New York that if the question came up in the form of a resolution accepting the credentials of the People's Republic, and not expelling the Kuomintang representative, he would have to vote in favour of it.[7] Back in London, Hector McNeil, Minister of State at the Foreign Office, unhappy over the fact that the People's Republic had not yet 'recognized British recognition', proposed a policy of 'sitting on the fence' and continued abstention. Cadogan was told that since the Chinese Government were 'in no hurry to establish satisfactory diplomatic relations with us' voting in favour of them in the UN 'might create an impression of over-eagerness on our side'.[8]

Other Foreign Office officials in charge of UN affairs, however, had reservations about this advice. One observation was that the British government's vote and its influence on others might became instrumental in having the Beijing government's credentials rejected in the Council. In Beijing, Hutchison, apprehensive of possible negative effects on his negotiations with the Chinese, advised against the policy of abstention. He feared that such a policy would be very strongly resented by the Chinese Government and might even greatly delay the establishment of diplomatic relations. He went on to say, 'I do not consider they would regard our vote in favour as an indicator of over-eagerness on our side. They would certainly regard our abstention as unjustifiable and as deliberately unfriendly'.[9] After assessing the problem in the light of Hutchison's comments British officials concluded 'there is a case for reversing the decision communicated to Sir A Cadogan'.[10]

A few days later the British Embassy in Washington reported that the US Assistant Secretary in charge of UN affairs John Hickerson had indicated that Washington would not be seriously disturbed if the British were to vote in favour of the credentials of the People's Republic. On the basis of this report, senior British officials responsible for UN, US, and Far Eastern affairs agreed that Cadogan could go ahead and cast his vote in favour of accepting the credentials of the Beijing government.[11] Following his officials' advice, the Foreign Secretary accepted that Britain should vote for accepting the credentials of Beijing's representatives if two more votes in the Security Council were secured.[12]

In March 1950, the British government began an initiative to secure a majority in the Security Council in support of the new Chinese government. British policy-makers had decided to vote in favour of a change-over of representation in any principal organ of the UN and its specialized agencies as soon as a majority in that body were in favour of doing so. Britain began the initiative in the Security Council because 'in a question of this sort the Security Council ought in principle to give a lead and that if it does not do so soon the danger exists of a decision on the question being taken first in some totally inappropriate organ of the UN.'[13] At this stage Beijing had a good chance of replacing the Kuomintang in the Security Council. Representation in the council at that time was, in Evan Luard's words. 'unusually favourable' to the People's Republic.[14] Of the thirteen members in the council, five – the USSR, Britain, India, Yugoslavia and Norway – had recognized the People's Republic. Two more votes for the new Chinese government would mean a majority.

On 7 March, Bevin agreed to approach three other Council members, namely, Egypt, Ecuador and Cuba in order to secure the necessary majority for China in the Security Council. Instructing the ambassador in Egypt the Foreign Secretary said he had made up his mind 'to make a serious effort to resolve the deadlock in the Security Council on the subject of Chinese representation'.[15] Meanwhile, the French and the US governments were consulted on Britain's new initiative. Responses to the British approach, however, were, if not entirely unsympathetic, negative. Other Council members states did not wish their actions to become decisive factors in a matter of considerable international importance, especially since the US and France would still not vote for the new Chinese government.[16] Thus the solution now lay in American and French attitudes. The only certain way to solve the deadlock on Chinese representation in the UN would be for the US or France to recognize Beijing because only then countries like Egypt might be persuaded either to follow suit or at least to vote for the People's Republic's delegate in the Security Council.[17]

In the end the US and France refused to change their stance and the deadlock was not resolved. Indeed, even the British government could not adhere to their decision to vote for the credentials of Beijing's representatives in other UN bodies. Following instructions agreed by the Foreign Secretary, the UK delegations to the UN would abstain from voting to expel the Kuomintang representative, but should vote in favour of the Beijing credentials. In early March, London had agreed that the UK delegation to the UN International Children Emergency Fund (UNICEF) should abstain in both cases.[18] Then in May, the British government manoeuvred to keep the Chinese representation question out of the full meeting of the Economic commission for Asia and the Far East (ECAFE) in Bangkok because of apprehension that it might have 'a disquieting effect in South East Asia', particularly in Indochina.[19]

If British policy-makers could not do anything to influence other members in the UN, could they resolve deadlock in Anglo-Chinese relations by supporting Beijing's claim regardless of the opinion of their allies?

Phase II – Voting in Favour of the Chinese

Britain's manoeuvering to resolve the Chinese representation question in the Security Council had in fact ended in pleasing nobody; it had upset its American ally and failed to satisfy the Chinese. The British government thus had two choices: either to retreat and abandon its policy of trying to get the China into the UN by securing majority support for it or to go further and vote in favour of the new Chinese government irrespective of the policies of other members. Voting for the People's Republic might also bring back the Soviet delegation which walked out of the UN after their motion to expel the Kuomintang representative had been defeated in January.

The need to revise Britain's voting policy had become evident for British policy-makers by May. At this time Ernest Bevin was ill and Minister of State at the Foreign Office Kenneth Younger was, in his own words, 'nominally in charge of the office'.[20] Younger argued that given the Chinese and American positions, 'there is a danger that . . . we will get the worst of both worlds'. He proposed that, 'we should do everything that is practicable to improve our relations'. What Younger had in mind was to support the Chinese at the UN for he believed that Britain would not gain anything by refusing to vote for the Chinese government and he saw the policy of abstention as 'little more than an attempt to ride two horses at once'.[21]

Meanwhile, Hutchison, who was having a hard time negotiating with the Chinese, sent a telegram to the Foreign Office, suggesting that the government should take positive steps in the matter of the UN. The Chinese government had just issued a public statement on the state of Anglo-Chinese negotiations on 22 May, putting the blame squarely on the British side. This, Hutchison felt, called for an official reply. He believed that the UN was the one problem area in Anglo-Chinese relations over which something could be done and recommended that the government should 'vote for the admission of the China Government and for the expulsion of the Kuomintang delegate whenever these questions are brought up' in UN agencies.[22] Two weeks later in another telegram to the Foreign Office he again argued that for the Chinese a necessary consequence of recognition would be an acknowledgement of their representative as 'solely competent to speak for China in international bodies', and they expected the

British government to vote for their representative whenever and wherever the question came up.[23]

In fact, senior British officials in charge of UN and Far Eastern affairs had come to similar conclusions, if for different reasons. Esler Dening of the Far Eastern department argued that, 'there can be no doubt that our attitude in the UN has been one of the main reasons for our failure in establishing relations'. To him the policy of abstention had brought no benefit to Britain for the policy had ended in pleasing nobody at all. He said, 'we are attacked in this country for appeasing China, and attacked by China for doing her less than justice'. William Strang went even further and admitted that in a way British policy towards China had been 'double-faced', noting that 'we do not seem to have gained anything by our subsequent attempt to ride two horses (this is what the Peking press calls our "double-faced" policy)'.[24]

During this time in May and June 1950, the Soviet Union also approached the British government and brought up the question of Chinese representation in the UN. Senior Foreign Office officials concluded that the best solution was to tell Moscow that the British government were prepared to vote affirmatively for Beijing, but the Soviet Union should also urge the Chinese government to establish proper relations with Britain.[25]

British officials were thus prepared to end the unsatisfactory state of affairs in Anglo-Chinese relations, and to enable the Soviet Union to return to the UN. On 26 May, Bevin endorsed the policy to vote for the admission of the People's Republic to other UN bodies. What the Foreign Office had in mind at this time was the meeting of the UN Economic and Social Council (ECOSOC) on 3 July. Later, when British officials found out that the UNICEF meeting would take place before the ECOSOC meeting on 19 June, Bevin agreed that Britain should cast its first affirmative vote on that occasion. In a submission to the Prime Minister in June, Kenneth Younger summed up the rationale behind Britain's new voting policy towards Chinese representation in the UN: if Britain continued to abstain from voting in favour of Beijing in the UN until a majority were secured, the United Kingdom 'should not only please no one but also give the People's Government an additional ground for delaying the establishment of diplomatic relations'. On a more practical note, Younger explained, 'as more member states recognised the People's Government or decide to abstain it becomes increasingly difficult for us to decide in advance which way the vote is likely to go and therefore whether to vote in favour or to abstain'. This new voting policy was officially approved by the Prime Minister on 15 June 1950.[26]

Britain's affirmative vote for the Beijing government in UNICEF, however, did not materialize. Instructions to the British delegation to the UN to support Beijing were rescinded almost immediately after they were sent. Three days after Attlee's approval of the new voting policy, the British government succumbed to American opposition which was far stronger than expected. After Attlee's approval the Foreign Office immediately notified both France and the US of the British government's intention to support the People's Republic in UNICEF. Although French officials found the British modification entirely logical and actually corresponded to their views, the French government declared themselves unable to recognize or vote for the Beijing government because of the situation in Indo-China.[27] The reaction in Washington was stronger than the French; the Americans, perhaps not too surprisingly, were enraged by the British decision.

On 17 June US Assistant Under-Secretary for Far Eastern Affairs, Dean Rusk, summoned the British Minister in Washington to urge the British not to implement the new voting policy. The American position was that during a tripartite talks which took place earlier in London in May, Britain, France and the US had agreed that none of them would take any major initiative in the matter of Chinese representation in the UN. As Truman was attempting to secure a bipartisan approach to China in Congress he feared that a British vote for Beijing would nullify the administration's effort to placate the Republican Senators. The administration was hoping that a bipartisan understanding at home would provide a basis for the administration to approach the UK and France to work out 'some common policy towards the Far East, China and in particular Chinese representation on the UN'. The US government therefore urged Britain not to vote for Beijing at the UNICEF meeting on 19 June.[28]

After some hasty discussions the Foreign Office reversed the decision to vote for the new Chinese government in UNICEF. Bevin conceded that he had given Acheson 'too short notice' of the change in British voting policy, and agreed to withhold voting for Beijing on 19 June. The British Embassy in Washington was, however, instructed to 'make it plain to Mr Acheson that the line of the policy about our affirmative vote in the Economic and Social Council . . . still stands'. On 24 June the Embassy reported from Washington that it was unlikely that the State Department would put pressure on the British again in the forthcoming ECOSOC meeting in July.[29]

The British government almost immediately found it necessary again to withhold voting for the People's Republic following North Korea's invasion of the South on 26 June. As a result of the developments in Korea the State Department bluntly made it clear that they 'do not think any useful purpose would be served by further discussion of voting arrangements at the ECOSOC meeting'.[30] T. Shone of the British UN delegation offered his advice on the situation: 'I cannot but feel that if we were now to vote for seating the Chinese Communist representative in the ECOSOC, and still more if we lobbied to this end, we should run into the risk of riling American opinion considerably'. Bevin had no other choice but to postpone voting in favour of Beijing once again.[31]

Confronted by the new international situation the Foreign Office had to retreat on the question of Chinese representation at the UN. Senior officials, who had proposed voting in favour of the Beijing government, argued that the issue of the Korean War should be separated from that of Chinese representation. Esler Dening believed that the American attitude was 'both dangerous and wrong'. This premonition was based on the assessment that if Beijing were excluded from the Security Council, the Soviet Union could demonstrate to the Chinese that they had nothing to hope for from the West and that would mean that China could be driven further into the arms of Moscow. By abstaining from voting, British relations with India would also be affected, as the Indian government held strong views on Chinese representation. Gladwyn Jebb, head of the British delegation to the UN, summed up the British belief of the importance in having the new Chinese government in the Security Council, by saying that, 'The only real question is one of timing'. It was, however, necessary to explain the British position to Washington and make it clear that sooner or later Britain would have to vote for Beijing. Sir Oliver Franks conveyed the message to Dean Acheson on 11 August.[32]

Dean Acheson found that the positions of Britain and the US were so different that he had already concluded in July that, 'the correspondence clearly had no future, so we dropped it'.[33] The US objection was based on three factors: first, the Beijing government had singled out the US as the major 'imperialist' enemy in spite of past American feeling for China; second, the new government was not in firm control of the whole of China and; third, Congressional and public opinion was strongly against it especially after the outbreak of the Korean war. British officials dismissed the American objections as 'emotional or inadequate' and regarded the American belief that the new communist regime did not have a firm control over the whole of China as based on wishful thinking.[34] By September the British Cabinet had again approved the Foreign Offices recommendation to vote affirmatively for the People's Republic in the UN.

The Indian government, which had always been in favour of voting for Beijing, came in with a timely proposal in September. Prime Minister Nehru had earlier expressed great disappointment when Britain reversed its decision to vote for the new Chinese government. Nehru wanted to see a resolution introduced into the General Assembly proposing the admission of the People's Republic whatever its chances of success. He believed strongly that India could establish a special relationship with the Beijing government and by doing so bring about a more favourable international atmosphere throughout Asia.[35] For the British government, the Indian resolution had its advantages: it would save Britain the embarrassment of having to vote in favour of a resolution put forward by the Soviet Union and attract wider support among other UN members. During the September tripartite talks in New York, Bevin succeeded in securing US and French agreement that each country should feel free to vote independently when the question of Chinese representation arose in the General Assembly.[36]

On 19 September, the United Kingdom voted for the admission of the People's Republic as proposed by India at the opening of the fifth session of the General Assembly. The British delegation, however, abstained on the Soviet resolution to expel the Kuomintang representative and to invite the People's Republic to take part in the General Assembly and other UN organs. Both resolutions were defeated. Canada then proposed that a special committee of seven members nominated by the President and confirmed by the Assembly should be set up to consider the question of Chinese representation; meanwhile the Kuomintang representative should remain in the UN. Britain voted for the first part of the Canadian resolution, abstained on the second part and then voted for the resolution as a whole. The Canadian resolution was finally approved by the Assembly.

Beijing was not admitted, but at least the British had cast their first affirmative vote for it, nine months after Britain's recognition of the new Chinese government. After failing to gather a majority for Beijing in the Security Council, Britain had been on the brink of voting for the new Chinese government twice within a month, but had to call if off at the last minute. What is more significant was that the affirmative vote had been cast while the war in Korea was still in progress. British policy-makers soon found however that they would be obliged to change yet again their support for the Beijing government within a few months. In the event Britain entered into an agreement with the US to postpone any vote in the UN on the question of Chinese representation by way of a moratorium.

Phase III – The Moratorium

Britain's affirmative vote in support of Beijing in the UN failed to impress the Chinese leadership. Two days after the vote in September the Indian Ambassador in Beijing, Pannikar, went to see the Chinese Foreign minister Zhou Enlai. Bitter about the exclusion of the People's Republic from the

UN, Zhou said that Chinese leaders had been waiting patiently for a year and this patience was running out. The Chinese were not favourably impressed by Britain's affirmative vote for them and regarded Britain's abstention over the Soviet motion to unseat the Kuomintang representative as further proof of British duplicity.[37]

On 25 September, the Chinese Foreign Ministry issued a statement expressing great dissatisfaction that the Beijing government had not been recognized by the UN as representing China. The statement blamed the US for obstructing Beijing's admission into the UN, saying that, 'it was a result of the deliberate obstruction, and manipulation of the American government which had decided to be the enemy of the four hundred and seventy-five million Chinese people'. Then, without naming Britain, the statement said: 'Certain countries having declared their willingness to establish diplomatic relations with China, although supporting India's resolution to invite a Chinese representative to participate in the General Assembly refused to support the Soviet resolution to expel the illegal representative in the UN of the Kuomintang reactionary remnant clique, thus facilitating the realization of the American plot'. This was obviously a reference to Britain. The Chinese government made it clear that they were not prepared to improve its relations with Britain as a result of the British government's recent vote in support of the Chinese People's Government at the UN. The statement went on to say: 'The Chinese people are continuing to observe closely the attitude in the UN of these self-contradictory countries'.[38]

British officials were not pleased with the Chinese reaction which indicated clearly that the affirmative vote still did not meet Beijing's expectation.[39] Accordingly, the British government proceeded with a new voting policy and supported a Soviet resolution at the October meeting of the ECOSOC which called for the expulsion of the Kuomintang representative and inviting Communist Chinese representation. This policy was to continue until 1951, even after China had been branded an 'aggressor' by a US resolution in the UN, following its military intervention in Korea.

When the Chinese army crossed the Yalu river in October 1950 to take part in the Korean War, Britain and China became enemies. British officials anticipated that Britain's voting policy on Chinese representation would have to change again in view of Chinese action in Korea. Yet even by early November, after China's direct military intervention had been reported, Under-secretary Dening's successor in the Foreign Office, Robert Scott, still maintained that developments in Korea did not call for a reconsideration of the voting policy.[40] Britain had in fact just begun to take new initiatives to improve Anglo-Chinese relations. As mentioned in

Chapter 3, Esler Dening was trying to visit Beijing to hold talks directly with senior Chinese officials. His mission departed London in late October under the guise of a general trip to the Far East and Southeast Asia. In the end Dening was not able to visit China; he was denied a visa probably because of the new developments in Korea.

Meanwhile the British government continued to vote for Beijing in other UN bodies. In fact, the British delegation to the Food and Agricultural Organization (FAO), a UN body, put out a statement in the general committee making clear their government's views on the Chinese representation question even though the report of the conference credentials committee had not referred to the question. When the Soviet Union presented a resolution on the Chinese question in the Trusteeship Council on 22 November, all other members of the Council, except Britain, voted against the resolution. On 27 November UNICEF's executive board only rejected a motion to seat Beijing's representative after two tied votes with twelve in favour and twelve against, with Britain voting in favour. Events in Korea, however, made it very difficult for Britain to sustain this voting policy. By early February 1951, although the British delegation to the UN was instructed to continue to vote for the Chinese until further notice, London told them that because of the military situation in Korea it was not easy to predict what British voting policy would be in a month's time.[41]

After the British government had supported a resolution in the UN which had castigated China as an aggressor in Korea in January, their argument for recognizing the Chinese Communist's claim in the UN had been greatly weakened. The US quickly tried to establish the principle that the Assembly's condemnation of 'China's aggression' should end all attempts to revise Chinese representation in the UN. Acheson sent a personal message to Bevin, asking him to reconsider Britain's position at the seventh session of the ECAFE due to convene on 20 February. Younger lamented: 'I am sure that no one contemplated when we voted for the US resolution, that we would thereby be obliged to alter our policy about Chinese representation'. The British government, moreover, had always maintained that the question of Chinese representation should be decided on recognition of fact, not on moral judgement. Younger admitted that 'The situation is awkward, but we must, I am sure, stick to our guns'.[42]

The British indeed stuck to their guns, and when the question of Chinese representation was ruled in order by the Chairman at ECAFE's opening session in Lahore, Britain supported the ruling. Yet, Foreign Office officials privately expressed a sign of relief after the ruling was successfully challenged by Thailand and Britain's vote was not decisive. As P. C. Holmer of the United Nations department noted, 'I was glad to see that our vote was not crucial. We were also in quite good Asiatic company in voting as we did'.[43] New thinking about British voting policy on Chinese representation was about to take shape.

Across the Atlantic in New York, Britain's representative to the UN, Gladwyn Jebb, was having a rough time defending his government's position. Urging London to revise its support for Beijing in the UN, Jebb pointed out that it was very hard for him to justify voting to admit a representative of a government responsible for shooting at British troops, which had also been condemned as an aggressor by the highest international tribunal. When Jebb encountered such an argument he always had to ride it off by saying that whatever views the British government might hold on the Chinese representation question, so long as Chinese action in Korea continued the Chinese Communist government would not find a majority voting for it. In any case, as Jebb argued, as long as Britain remained a party to conflict in Korea fighting against China, gestures like voting for the Beijing government would not be very useful in improving Anglo-Chinese relations. On the other hand, such a gesture did serve to exacerbate Anglo-American relations. But Younger insisted that Britain should not reverse its policy. While accepting London's instruction Jebb again pointed out that, 'it is difficult to persuade the Americans that we only preserve our present policy as regards Chinese representation because we know it cannot result in success'. For the time being, the policy of voting for the People's Republic in the UN was upheld. Nevertheless, Jebb's letters sparked off a debate within the Foreign Office; even Robert Scott began to question whether or not the voting policy was logical given the state of Anglo-Chinese diplomatic relations and the situation in Korea.[44]

By the end of May, British officials had already come to the conclusion that the policy of voting for the Beijing government was not leading anywhere. The continuing conflict in Korea and China's failure to respond positively to peace mediation by the UN Good Offices Committee further strengthened this view. As far as Anglo-Chinese relations were concerned, whether Britain's stance towards Chinese representation in the UN would make any difference was highly questionable. The Foreign Office's major concern had become, in P. C. Holmer's words, 'to find a way to revert to our former policy of abstention'. Although Younger still did not want any such move to be seen as a 'capitulation to the American view point', he had accepted his officials' view; what he wanted now was that the change had to be carefully prepared.[45]

The Truman administration, apprehensive of possible trouble over the question of Chinese representation when the Soviet representative took the chair in the Security Council in June, approached the British government at the end of May to discuss the problem. Britain was asked not to vote in favour of the Chinese government as long as the Chinese Communists continued their involvement in Korea. State Department officials suggested that this would save Dean Acheson a lot of trouble when he faced the Congressional hearings which would be held at the same time.[46] Subsequently the US proposed a moratorium arrangement which would postpone any discussion on the Chinese representation in the UN. This proposal also suited Britain's purpose; it avoided the embarrassment for the British government of having to retreat to its former policy of abstention. Senior Foreign Office officials welcomed the proposal. The new Foreign Secretary, Herbert Morrison, who had succeeded Bevin in March, was also delighted at this opportunity to do Acheson a favour in return for American help in the Middle East.[47]

The British policy-makers were still anxious to avoid giving the impression that they had changed their view that Beijing ought to be recognized as the legal Chinese government. But they approved the moratorium arrangement, which took the form of a procedural motion, postponing discussion of the question of Chinese representation in the UN for the time being.[48] After obtaining support from Italy and Denmark, the ground was prepared for Britain's new voting policy. On 5 June the British delegate voted for a US motion to defer discussion on Chinese representation during a UN Trusteeship Council meeting and made a statement explaining that the British government was in favour of a postponement while Chinese forces were fighting UN troops.[49]

This new voting policy did not attract much public attention until about two weeks later when the question of Chinese representation was brought up in UNESCO. Voting was deferred on a US resolution, which apart from calling for a postponement, also urged that Kuomintang representation be sustained. Accordingly the British government's support for the US resolution was seen as support for the Kuomintang. The *Manchester Guardian* reported Britain's vote in UNESCO and called it: 'vote to retain Nationalist', while *The Times* said it was: a 'vote given to the Nationalist'.[50]

As discussed in Chapter 4, the Conservative government which came to power after the general election in October 1951 continued the Anglo-American moratorium arrangements on Chinese representation in the UN. The Foreign Secretary, Anthony Eden, supported the continuation of the 'moratorium' procedure because he found that the rationale for the moratorium arrangement remained valid. Eden's stance was: 'we have now got an established drill for putting this procedure into operation' and 'the procedure was originally evolved as a carefully balanced compromise between the fact of our recognition of the Chinese People's Government and our desire to keep a common front with the US'.[51] The British government's vote to postpone voting on Chinese representation in the Trusteeship Council marked the beginning of a series of Anglo-American moratorium arrangements in the UN which lasted for ten years until 1961.

A full circle had been completed. It took Britain nine months after recognizing the People's Republic before it voted for the new Chinese government in the UN; nine months later, the British government abandoned that policy.

REVOLUTIONARY CHINA'S ATTITUDE TOWARDS THE UN

British voting in the UN did not, in the event, resolve the deadlock in Anglo-Chinese relations. In 1954, when Eden met Zhou for the first time in Geneva, the issue was raised again informally. Referring to Zhou's remark in a speech the day before which maintained that Britain was a colonial power, Eden said: 'Look what we did for India, Burma. We recognized you, I sometimes wonder if you recognized us'. To this, Zhou retorted: 'You don't recognize us in the UN'.[52] It seemed that Chinese leaders did not appreciate Britain's short-lived support for Beijing in the UN from September 1950 to mid-1951. The eventual British decision to postpone discussion about Chinese representation in the UN was adopted partly because of the changing international conditions, and partly because of China's uncompromising attitude. Was the new Chinese government really not interested in entering the UN, as some British officials suspected? If not, why did the Chinese take such an adamant position even after Britain had cast an affirmative vote for them?

During the 1960s, revolutionary China had attacked the UN as an adjunct of the US State Department, and a channel for US economic and cultural penetration into Asia, African and Latin American countries.[53] In his book *China, the United Nations and World Order*, Samuel Kim argues that Mao employed a radical-populist model of world order. Thus, Kim suggested, 'Mao found it difficult to render support to the structures, values and rules of the post-war international system in which China had been prevented from playing her legitimate role'.[54] Kim's reference to China being prevented from playing a role in the postwar international system probably identified a crucial factor behind Beijing's polemical attack against the UN in the 1960s. During the formative years of the People's Republic, its views about the UN had been very different.

Compared to their attitude towards the League of Nations, the Chinese

Communists had a much higher regard for the UN. The CCP had appointed
its own representative to China's delegation to the San Francisco Conference. Under American pressure, the Kuomintang government appointed
the CCP's Dong Biwu to the Chinese team on 23 March 1945. Thus
the Chinese Communists were directly involved at a preparatory stage
in the founding of the UN. Accompanied by his private secretaries Chen
Jiakang and Zhang Hanfu, Dong attended the Conference and a committee
on the organization and procedures of the new international organization.
He represented the Chinese delegation at a press conference on the UN
security system. At the end of the Conference Dong signed the UN Charter
as a member of the Chinese delegation.[55]

Mao Zedong himself had openly made it clear that the CCP appreciated the need for an international organization. Commenting on the San
Francisco Conference on 24 April 1945, when it was in progress, Mao
said, 'The Chinese Communist Party fully agrees with the proposal of the
Dumbarton Oaks conference and the decision of the Crimea Conference on
the establishment of an organization to safeguard international peace and
security after the war. It welcomes the United Nations Conference on International Organization in San Francisco'.[56] Assessing the significance of
the CCP's participation in the San Francisco Conference, Zhou Gengseng,
the Foreign Ministry's legal adviser wrote, 'it represented the Chinese
people's unanimous support for the establishment of the United Nations
Organization'. He said: 'It was a concrete act by the CCP, representing
the Chinese people, to strive for lasting world peace'.[57]

Even though revolutionary China was excluded from the UN, Beijing
continued its support for the organization during the formative years of
the People's Republic. Dong Biwu reaffirmed theofficial position in an
article commemorating the tenth anniversary of the UN. 'Our support
for the purposes and principles of the Charter of the United Nations
is consistent', Dong declared: 'the United Nations should become an
effective international organization and play its proper part in maintaining
international peace and security'.[58]

The new Chinese government had in fact sent a message to the UN
at the earliest opportunity in November 1949 claiming that the Beijing
government was the only legal government representing China. A similar
message claiming that the Kuomintang had no right to represent China was
sent in January, and in the same month, Beijing also informed the UN
Secretariat of the appointment of its delegation to the UN. Subsequently,
the new Chinese government appointed representatives to all important
bodies of the UN. In the three months preceding 27 November 1950,
the first time a representative from the People's Republic had spoken

in the UN, Beijing lodged seventeen complaints through the UN about American 'aggression' carried onto Chinese territory from Korea and over Taiwan.[59]

A detailed look at China's bilateral treaties with other countries during the 1950s also reveals that the principles of the Charter were cited even though the Chinese government was then excluded from the UN. These references to the UN Charter and principles were included in China's bilateral treaties with Socialist countries, such as the Sino-Soviet Treaty of Friendship, Alliance and Mutual Assistance signed on 14 February 1950, and other friendship treaties: with East Germany in 1955, Czechoslovakia in 1957, and Hungary in 1959. Other treaties with non-socialist countries, such as the Sino-Afghan Treaty of Friendship and Non-Aggression contained similar references.[60]

The People's Republic's first representative to the UN, Wu Xiuquan, who was invited to speak before the UN on China's accusation of US aggression in Taiwan, has recalled how he felt on that occasion in his memoirs. Wu was appointed by the Communist Party together with Dong Biwu to join the Chinese delegation to San Francisco in 1945. The Kuomintang government refused to let him join on the ground that he had trachoma, claiming that it was international practice that people with trachoma were not allowed to travel overseas. Recalling that episode, Wu remarked, 'That time I was not able to go; I did not anticipate that in five years' time, I would have become the Central Government of the new China's special representative on a mission to attend the UN General Assembly. My "trachoma" was no longer a problem. Meanwhile, the Kuomintang "central government" which had tried to be difficult with me, now had to stay in that tiny corner in Taiwan, I could not but feel the enormous changes that had taken place, heaven had turned upside down'. There is little doubt that Wu attached significance to attending a UN occasion; he did not disguise his personal joy at being appointed to represent China in an important international body. Wu's first appearance in the UN attracted wide media attention, and Wu had this to say: 'I thought Dulles and the Chiang Kai-shek clique had always portrayed Chinese Communists as a group of horrifying "bandits", now we can let the people of the world have a look themselves, to see what kind of people we are'.[61]

For revolutionary China, the UN had thus provided an opportunity to present its account of controversial issues as well as for some public relations. If British information is accurate, the Chinese had even set up a permanent delegation to the UN in mid-1950, only to disband it in early 1951.[62]

Beijing's communications to the UN and the inclusion of the UN Charter in its bilateral treaties with other governments clearly suggest that the People's government attached considerable importance to the UN as an instrument of diplomacy. China's strong reaction to Britain's abstention from voting over Chinese representation in the UN also suggested that the new Chinese government attached importance to UN membership as a symbol of the new government's right to represent China in the world. Other Western countries which had not voted for the Beijing government at UN meetings received a similar rebuff during their talks on diplomatic relations with the Beijing government.[63] In a study of Beijing's UN policy from 1949 to 1971, Byron Weng suggested that, 'any nation would have behaved as did the PRC under similar conditions'. He therefore concluded that revolutionary China's UN policy was 'normal and not deviant', a conclusion well supported by the Beijing government's insistence for wholehearted British support for their right to represent China at the UN in 1950.[64]

The British government were to support the American moratorium arrangements for ten more years until 1961. After that they continued to maintain for another ten years that Chinese representation was an important issue requiring the approval of a two-thirds majority in the UN. The deadlock in Anglo-Chinese relations was resolved in 1954 when the two countries exchanged charge d'affaires, but the question of Chinese representation was not resolved for many years to come. In 1971 when Anglo-Chinese talks on the normalization of diplomatic relations began, the British government found no difficulty in lending full support to Beijing's claim in the UN, but Chinese representation in the UN remained an important issue in the two countries' relationship up to 1972.

CONCLUSIONS

In implementing their policy towards Chinese representation in the UN, British policy-makers discovered that they had to revise the policy continuously because of Beijing's response, their American friends' objections, and the changing international circumstances. British thinking and manoeuvering in the eighteen months between January 1950 to June 1951 revealed clearly Britain's dilemma of how to reconcile its China policy with its US policy; Britain could not ride two horses at the same time. An independent British policy in the Far East had to be sacrificed for British interests in other parts of the world which were inexplicably tied to

Britain's special relationship with the US. The new Chinese government's attitudes towards the West and treatment of British commercial interests in China certainly did not help overcome Britain's dilemma in China's favour. The whole issue was further complicated by the Korean War which was neither of China's nor Britain's making. But once war had broken out, and given the revolutionary China's perception of the West at the time and Britain's need for American friendship, a train of events got underway which could not be arrested.

Revolutionary China's position towards Britain's voting policy at the UN has to be seen also in the context of the domestic problems that the new Chinese leadership was facing. They faced the daunting prospect of rebuilding the war-torn country, not yet entirely recovered from the Second World War, let alone the civil war. The communist leadership had also to face a hostile international climate amidst the Cold War. For the newly established People's Government to be recognized as the sole legal representative of China in the UN was of paramount importance. The Chinese revolutionaries who came to power in 1949 had clearly wanted to participate in the UN, and hoped to play a role in an international organization to which they had given support when it was founded. Hence their insistence that the British government should recognize the Beijing government's claim in the UN.

6 British Commercial Interests in China

Commercial interests were a major consideration leading to Britain's recognition of the People's Republic. As pointed out in Chapter 2, the business lobby, particularly the China Association, was an influential pressure group which had played an important part in influencing the making of Britain's China policy in 1949. The business lobby had hoped that after diplomatic relations between Britain and the People's Republic had been established, British enterprises in China would have an official channel available through which to draw the attention of the new Chinese government to their difficulties. To their disappointment, recognition led to neither the establishment of diplomatic relations nor an improvement in business conditions in China.

As shown in Part II, the conditions for British business in China deteriorated steadily further during 1950. Economic relations between the two countries worsened even more when the British government supported a UN embargo on the shipment of goods of strategic value to China in 1951. The following year London notified Beijing that British firms had decided to withdraw their operations from China, thus officially winding up the 'great British economic empire in China'.

Despite the liquidation of British business in China, the Korean War, and with China and Britain in opposing camps within a bipolar international system, trade relations continued because of mutual economic needs. This chapter examines the changing nature of Anglo-Chinese economic relations. In assessing the changes of British priorities between 1950 and 1954, this chapter also looks at the role of the British business lobby as a pressure group in influencing Britain's trade policy with China, and the Chinese revolutionaries' attitude towards developing economic relations with the West.

THE CONDITIONS OF BRITISH BUSINESS IN CHINA

Recognition and its Aftermath

In early February 1950, representatives from the China Association went to the Foreign Office to discuss business conditions in China. Their disappointment that recognition had failed to bring the expected improvement for British business was summed up vividly by the Association's Chairman, W. J. Keswick. He told Foreign Office officials: 'although the situation had been very bad for several months, most firms had held on in the hope that there would be a distinct improvement after the British Government recognized the new regime, but unhappily that had proved to be a false hope'. To British businessmen the situation was desperate; they wanted government assistance so that they could continue their business in China. Keswick warned: 'once the British commercial position was broken, it would probably never be re-established'.[1]

In March, when it had become apparent that the Chinese were not prepared to come readily to terms with Britain, Ernest Bevin could hardly conceal his disappointment during a meeting with Keswick and other China Association representatives.[2] At this time a feeling of hopelessness had come to prevail among business firms in Shanghai after months of frustration and inactivity with a constant drain on their resources. The most immediate problem was the Kuomintang blockade of Shanghai, but the changes in the Chinese economy introduced by the Communist leadership, such as new tax regulations and labour laws, were creating difficulties for the foreign business community in China. The Shanghai Chamber of Commerce reported that the blockade had 'reduced Shanghai to a shadow of its former self' and trading was 'almost at a standstill'. Unless the situation improved materially in the very near future,the chamber predicted: 'a great number of British firms, large and small, will have no option but to close their business and quit'. Businessmen in Shanghai were fearful that even if the firms would like to abandon their assets, the Chinese authorities would not allow them to leave before they had settled their taxes and wages. In such cases, they suggested that intervention by the British government might become necessary to assist those business firms which wished to leave China.[3]

At this stage the British government's position was that British firms should not abandon their assets in China. In an inter-departmental discussion between the Foreign Office, the Treasury, and the Board of Trade, officials agreed that it would be a bad bargain for the British firms if they abandoned their assets in China simply to ensure that their employees be allowed to leave the country safely. They were not only concerned about the loss of invisible income from China, but were also worried that, 'any sign of weakness in China would prejudice the position of British concerns all over the world'.[4]

The British government was reluctant to make representations on behalf of British firms through diplomatic channels, for it feared that if the scope of discussions being held between Hutchison and the Chinese government in Beijing were widened, the establishment of diplomatic relations might be further delayed. The Foreign Office believed that the new Chinese government had not applied sudden pressure on the British firms; there was no evidence that foreign firms were being discriminated against specifically by Chinese authorities. The firms' difficulties were due to outstanding problems such as high taxation, forced purchase of victory bonds, and the stringent labour laws covering wages and terms of employment.[5] However, it was clear that foreign business in China could not continue in any viable sense under such tough conditions. British officials accepted that if the British government did not respond to the situation, the Chinese authorities might feel that they need not do anything about it. Nonetheless the Foreign Office still believed that, 'the chances of success of an approach through diplomatic channels would clearly be greater if it were made when diplomatic relations had been established'. It therefore recommended that, 'firms which asked for advice should be induced to hold on for a little longer'. Throughout late March and early April 1950, the British government was thus reluctant to press the Chinese authorities for an official clarification of its policy towards foreign business.[6]

British businessmen became increasingly impatient as their situation deteriorated further in April and May. In early April the China Association received a telegram from Shanghai which stated bluntly that many British firms had come to the conclusion that 'their ability to continue in business is at an end'. These firms believed that even if they were able to make profits in China, they would not be allowed to remit them abroad. Therefore, they felt that if they continued to remain in China, they would eventually become a liability to their parent companies in varying degrees. Their earlier optimism that the new Communist government would allow foreign business to continue their operations in China had vanished. They had now come to the conclusion that the new Chinese leaders intended to govern the country both economically and politically along orthodox communist lines. Thus they have to cut their losses rather than attempt to overcome a hopeless situation.[7]

These firms urged their government to come to their rescue because they were not just unable to continue business, but also unable to 'extricate themselves from their difficulties by their own effort'. They requested that the government should despatch an ambassador to discuss the future of British business in China with top level Chinese officials.[8] The problem was that without official diplomatic relations, the Foreign Office could not send an ambassador to China. In April, London was hoping for a breakthrough in the Anglo-Chinese talks, for India and several Scandinavian countries had just established diplomatic relations with China. These hopes for talks were shattered, however, when the Chinese Foreign Ministry demanded further clarification over Britain's attitude towards Chinese representation in the UN, and by the CNAC/CATC affair in early May.[9]

On 24 May Hutchison, Britain's representative in Beijing, conveyed a note on conditions for foreign business in China to the Vice Foreign Minister. The Chinese government made no reply; when further enquiry was made, they maintained that the question was complicated and that it was being studied. But Hutchison was able to report in mid-June that: 'my impression is that there has been a general all around lessening of difficulties from which British firms out here have been suffering'.[10] While business in Shanghai remained stagnant and an increasing number of business firms, foreign as well as Chinese, were closing down, the picture was not completely bleak. The China Association's monthly bulletin in May reported that there had been 'some slight lessening of the pressure on industrialists for taxes and enforced subscriptions to loans' and because a very large part of China trade was passing through Tianjin, business conditions there were 'difficult but not entirely unsatisfactory'.[11]

There was no doubt that the Chinese revolutionaries were dedicated to applying a socialist ideology in their economic management. In 1950, they still recognized the importance of the private sector for the well-being of the economy. In May the readjustment of China's industrial and commercial structures had begun. Its aim was to enhance the relative power of the public sector against the private sector. Nonetheless, the economic planners were anxious not to let the private sector collapse. The municipal government in Tianjin, for example, had assisted some private firms which were important for the national economy by persuading workers to cooperate with the management. After the Tianjin authorities had established a Public-Private Relations Mediation Committee in early May, the amount of business they conducted with the private sector greatly increased; private firms were given numerous contracts for processing goods and supplying public enterprises with materials.[12]

In June British businessmen noticed official indications that the Chinese authorities might be prepared to adopt a more favourable policy towards foreign business. A government-sponsored national economic conference in Beijing issued a statement which recommended that private enterprise and state trading be better coordinated. Reports to the conference suggested that 'harsh taxation and levies', 'the rapid development of state trading' and 'severe deflation' had led to 'paralysis of all private industry'. This, the reports suggested, had caused an acute problem for China's industry and commerce. It appeared that Chinese planners had come to accept the importance of private enterprises for the country's economic well-being. The statement issued by the Conference said, 'it was unanimously felt . . . . that an adjustment of balance between public and private economy has become the most important issue of the day'. It further stated that, 'public and private enterprise will hereafter be developed under a co-ordinated system which will take into account the interests of both sides'. Observing the conference, some British merchants believed that the Chinese authorities had realized that harsh taxation and strict regulations on business activities had done great damage to China's industry. The China Association quickly issued a press statement welcoming the report and offered to send a small delegation representing British commercial interests to Beijing.[13]

Then the news came that North Korean troops had crossed the 38th parallel. As discussed in Part II, the Korean conflict had a far-reaching impact on China's relations with Britain and the West. It had direct consequences for British commercial interests in China also.

The Korean War and British Business in China

At the time of the outbreak of the Korean War the primary concern of the business lobby was the recall of the British Consul Sir Robert Urquhart from Shanghai. The maintenance of the post of Consul-General in Shanghai was seen as an indication of the government's commitment in China. The Foreign Office explained Sir Robert's recall as 'relief for domestic and other reasons'. Anxious that the government should maintain a strong presence in China, British businessmen were upset that an old China hand was leaving Shanghai. For them the most important implication of the Korean War seemed to be the possible broadening of the conflict into a more general confrontation between China and the West over Taiwan which might cause serious effect on British interests in China.[14]

The Chinese authorities did not tighten the screw on foreign business after the outbreak of the Korean War. A few weeks afterwards businessmen in Shanghai reported that although there had not been any fundamental progress in business condition, they agreed that there had been a lessening of difficulties. The Chinese authorities had also become less troublesome over the closure of foreign firms.[15] Jardine Matheson concluded an agreement with the Chinese authorities to sign a series of barter agreements to a total value of five million US dollars when its head of operation in Shanghai, John Keswick, went to Beijing in July. The British Consulate in Shanghai reported that the agreement 'seems to confirm what we have long suspected, namely that the People's Government are not prepared for general discussion but will respond to concrete trade proposals'.[16] The Korean War had naturally caused anxiety amongst the foreign community in China, and foreign companies continued to face great difficulties in the running of their business. Nevertheless, British businessmen were not totally without hope that China might still be prepared to conduct business with the West.[17]

In the first few months after fighting began in Korea, the Foreign Office's attitude remained that, 'it was politically desirable for British interests to maintain a foothold in China if this was possible'.[18] By September, when it became clear that there was no major improvement in commercial conditions in China, British officials had become far more sceptical of the prospects for foreign business there. The Treasury's view was that it would not recommend any official financial support to the British firms in China. Supporting this view, the Board of Trade put it this way: 'firms must make their own judgement whether it is the better course to hang on or to get out'.[19]

During this period, the Chinese government's official position was that formal negotiations and arrangements about commercial relations with Britain had to wait until diplomatic relations between the two countries had been established.[20] China's military intervention in Korea in late October and early November not only practically ended any realistic hopes for a speedy conclusion of the Anglo-Chinese talks on bilateral diplomatic relations but also had far-reaching implications for Anglo-Chinese economic relations. Following Britain's support of the US resolution in the UN in early 1951 condemning China as an aggressor, Anglo-Chinese relations took a marked downturn, and hopes for the establishment of formal Anglo-Chinese diplomatic relations in the near future were totally destroyed. The UN's decision to impose economic sanctions against China in 1951 further restricted Anglo-Chinese trade.[21]

In May 1951, British businessmen in Shanghai believed that they were facing a crisis which could not be surmounted without official intervention. They therefore urged London to join other Western governments in making a concerted protest to the Chinese government over existing business conditions. This appeal for assistance did not have the support of the British diplomatic mission in Beijing. The mission's report to London said, 'it would be unrealistic to expect the Chinese Government in its present temper to respond to any such request for modification of what is clearly its determined policy, one of the principal items of which is evidently the elimination of American and other democratic foreign influence'. British diplomats in Beijing concluded that as long as major issues such as the Korean War and the Japanese Peace Treaty remained unresolved, 'it seems impossible to devise any constructive remedy for the intolerable attitude of the Chinese Government towards foreign interests'. In fact because of the UN embargo the Chinese government were 'more likely to contemplate measures of reprisal rather than of relief'.[22]

After much prompting from the China Association, the Foreign Office agreed to approach western allies on a possible joint representation to the Chinese government. Earlier, the Indian ambassador, K. M. Pannikar, had already approached the Soviet ambassador in the latter's capacity as the doyen of the diplomatic corps in Beijing over the Chinese authorities' treatment of foreigners. The specific questions raised by the Indian Ambassador included: the withholding of exit permits, imprisonment incommunicado, and lack of response from the Ministry of Foreign Affairs to the representations of foreign missions. The Soviet ambassador not only welcomed Pannikar's initiative in presenting these problems to him as doyen, but also volunteered to raise the matter with the Chinese government at a higher level than that of Vice Minister of Foreign Affairs at an early opportunity.[23]

During a dinner meeting in early August, Pannikar had the opportunity to discuss the treatment of foreigners directly with Zhou Enlai. He was told that the new government would not allow foreign Christian missionaries to continue active preaching in China, but it wanted to encourage trade with the West, and 'bona fide foreign businessmen were welcome'. Senior Chinese officials also told the newly-arrived Swedish ambassador that China was willing to trade with the West.[24]

Since not all other governments represented in Beijing were enthusiastic about the idea of a joint demarche, Hutchison advised that joint or identical representations 'were not feasible and were in fact not desirable'. He proposed that as a matter of tactics interested foreign representatives should 'stagger' their approaches so as to give the appearance of independent action while stressing the same principal points. Eventually Britain's representation was made on 1 September; the other governments presented theirs separately.[25]

Not too surprisingly, the Chinese government did not change its policies towards foreign businessmen after receiving the representations. Towards the end of 1951 there was no general improvement in conditions for foreign enterprises. The year 1951 was particularly bad for British businessmen with commercial interests in China. Not only were British enterprises in China squeezed, but the embargo imposed on China by the UN had also made trading with the People's Republic most difficult. But British merchants in Shanghai were still pressing their government to negotiate an accord with the Chinese government, and to make a public statement to improve Anglo-Chinese economic relations.[26]

There was very little the British government could do. The Chinese government had permitted capitalists to continue their business out of necessity; not only foreign but also private Chinese business enterprises were being squeezed. This policy did not necessarily mean that foreign businessmen would be forced out of China immediately, or that Anglo-Chinese trade would not be revived under more favourable circumstances. A study of China's industrialization in the early years of the People's Republic suggested that, the new leaders sought to 'reorganize a system of state ownership, central planning, and capable and responsible factory leadership'. Another study observed that the CCP's policy towards taking over industrial units in this period may be characterized 'as a continuous move from radicalism to a moderate policy with rank and file cadres tending to be more radical than the centre.'[27] As the British diplomatic mission in Beijing observed in December 1951: '"the British stake" in China will be under constant pressure. The aim of the Chinese . . . will be to try and trade through a few government organizations and thereby eliminate the British middle man in China'.[28]

Politically, the business lobby's request for their government's intervention could not have been more ill-timed. Anglo-Chinese talks over their bilateral relations had been virtually suspended since the outbreak of the Korean War. Britain's support for the American resolution in the UN censuring China as an aggressor and the UN embargo had further strained relations between the two countries. The hardening US attitude towards the Beijing regime as a result of the Korean conflict had also made it almost impossible for London to adopt a more flexible trade policy with China.

Even on purely economic grounds, British trade officials were not particularly keen to develop trade with China at that time. As there was a world-wide demand for machinery and metal goods, trade officials felt that it was in Britain's interest to export to markets offering greater profits. The Board of Trade concluded at the beginning of 1952 that, 'on supply grounds alone, we could not justify the export of scarce goods to China as long as we could sell them in more desirable markets'. By this time the gap between China and the West had so widened that the continuation of normal Sino-British trade had become impossible. Trade officials in London more or less ruled out the possibility of better trade relations with China for some time to come. They pointed out that any public statement on trading with China would be more stringent and restrictive than an earlier one made in June which announced licensing control of exports to China as a result of the UN embargo on shipment of goods of military value.[29]

The End of the British Commercial Empire in China

In early 1952 British firms in China experienced further difficulties and many were forced to withdraw. Yee Tsong Tobacco, the China arm of the giant British American Tobacco Company, had to offer all its assets free to the Chinese. Apart from the worsening Anglo-Chinese relations, the 'three antis campaign' (anti-corruption, anti-waste, and anti-bureaucracy) also made life difficult for many British firms. Many well-known British companies thus made plans to pull out.[30]

In March the China Association again pressed the government to talk to Chinese authorities about the problems British firms were facing in China. But this time their concern had changed. Since many firms had decided to close their businesses in there, their major concern had become how to withdraw from China. Many British firms had decided that there was no hope of carrying on and there was no point in staying if conditions did not improve, but they were concerned that Chinese authorities might hold local managers responsible for the actions and policies of their firms. They requested the government to present a note to the Chinese government on these problems.[31]

After discussing this request, the Cabinet approved the sending of a note to the Chinese government with a list of problems which unless resolved would make a continuation of British business in China almost impossible. These included: (i) the making of each individual manager personally responsible for the policy and acts of his company; (ii) the increasing restrictions on the entry and exit of foreign staff; (iii) the cancellation by the Chinese Government's trading organization of former contracts, even though raw materials have been paid for and processed; (iv) uncertainty caused to British subjects by the fear of arrest and detention incommunicado and without charges being proffered; (v) pressure by the labour unions and reluctance by the local authorities to give any protection to firms who were accused by the unions of malpractice.[32]

This note was delivered by the British Charge d'Affaires Leo Lamb in Beijing on 12 April. The Chinese government was told that if the situation for foreign business continued 'it can only result, sooner or later, in the elimination of British business interests in China to the detriment of friendly relations between China and the UK'. When there was no reply after more than one month, Lamb informed the Chinese government that most British firms with commercial interests in China had decided to leave and requested assistance for their withdrawal.[33]

On 24 May 1952, the British government announced in Parliament the withdrawal of British firms in China. The news was greeted with lamentation by the press on the collapse the great economic empire which Britain once controlled in China. But there was a consensus that the end of trade 'in' China did not necessarily mean end of trade 'with' China.[34] Apparently British business interests had not given up hope entirely. On behalf of the firms, the British government also proposed the setting out of a 'new form of organization' for Sino-British trade. This new organization, the British government suggested, would be an 'association of representatives of manufacturers and overseas buyers, which would maintain direct contact with the appropriate Chinese authorities' and act as a permanent trade mission. In the event, not all the companies withdrew; some decided to carry on in spite of the difficulties they faced.[35]

Nevertheless, it became clear that the once dominant British economic presence in China was in ruins. Beijing did not change its policy towards foreign business. A good indication of the state of British business in China was the fortunes of the British Chamber of Commerce in Shanghai. In 1948 the Chamber comprised one hundred and sixty member firms. Four years later at the beginning of 1952 there were only sixty-eight member firms, by October twenty-four of them had closed down or applied for the liquidation of their interests. Of the remaining forty-four firms, about ten or more would ask to pay a reduced fee or to resign. Therefore towards the end of 1952, its executive committee 'had no option but to take a decisive step to wind up the Chamber'.[36] A small number of British firms might still be able to continue business, but the majority of them had felt obliged to leave. The British commercial empire in China had indeed fallen.

SINO-BRITISH TRADE

The end of the British commercial empire in China did not mean an end to Sino-British trade. British traders had made a distinction between trade in China and trade with China. Well before British firms had decided to pull out from China, they had been pessimistic about the prospect of continuing trade in revolutionary China, but hopeful about trade with it. When John Keswick of Jardine Matheson was interviewed in May 1952, he maintained that, 'the natural evolution of the firm's business showed that the emphasis had changed from "trading in China" to trading with China'. He referred to the decision by British firms to get out of China as 'desirable adjustments in a realistic manner', and maintained that the company was not making any sudden reversal in policy'.[37]

Chinese political leaders had in fact stated unequivocally that they wanted to continue China's trade relations with other countries. The Common Programme adopted by the People's Political Consultative Conference which outlined the new government's major policies stated that it 'may restore and develop commercial relations with foreign governments and peoples on a basis of equality and mutual benefit'. But the Programme also made it clear that foreign trade would be promoted under the direct control of the state through a protective trade policy.[38]

The new Chinese government's stated objective in continuing trade relations with other countries was straightforward: to serve the development of China's industry, in particular heavy industry. It was important, according to China's economic planners, to export in order to import necessary materials and equipment to carry out the government's industrialization programme. In the words of Foreign Trade Minister Ye Jichuang, 'Export is for the sake of import, which in turn, is for the socialist industrialization of our country'.[39] Nevertheless, trading with the West, in particular with Britain, was a more complicated question. As the predominant Western imperial power in China, Britain's victory over China in the Opium War was regarded by the Chinese as the beginning of their country's humiliation at the hands of Western powers. This view was clearly shared by the Chinese Communists, whose revolutionary aspirations included the elimination of western economic influences in China.

An article in *Xin Jianshe* [*New Construction*] in January 1950 provided an indication of the Chinese economic planners' views about Sino-British trade. The article outlined several features of Sino-British trade in the past. First, China had allowed Britain to acquire a privileged position. Second, Britain had been an exporter of manufactured goods to China, while China had been an exporter of raw materials. Third, Britain had controlled China's exports through its predominance in finance and shipping. Fourth, direct Sino-British trade had been in decline before 1949. Finally, because of the predominance of Britain's position in China's external trade, the needs of Britain's traders had dictated the nature of China's economy with negative consequences. The article suggested that all these factors had to be changed under the People's Republic, stressing that the new government was to play a direct role in controlling and co-ordinating China's foreign trade. By emphasizing that the new government wanted to conduct trade with Britain on a different basis, the article at least indicated that the Chinese government did want to continue trade with Britain.[40]

The 1952 Moscow Economic Conference

Foreign trade played an important part in China's economic rehabilitation between 1950 to 1952. During these two years, the annual value of China's foreign trade surpassed the level before the Sino-Japanese War, but a major shift in China's trade direction had occurred. The Soviet Union had replaced the US and Britain as China's major trading partner (see Appendix 2). When the People's Republic completed its basic rehabilitation, Chinese economic planners moved on to the next stage in their strategy: industrialization. In order to obtain the machinery, equipment, and materials for its new economic programme, revolutionary China not only needed to trade with the Soviet bloc, but also to trade with the West.[41]

Beijing's initiative to develop trade with the West began in 1952 when it took part in an international economic conference in Moscow, an event staged by the Soviet bloc. The Chinese government made use of the opportunity to stress that the UN embargo against China was damaging the West's economic interests, and expressed its willingness to trade with the West. An editorial in the magazine *Shijie Zhishi* [World Knowledge] pronounced: 'the conference is in line with the principle of peaceful co-existence among countries with different systems'. The need to improve normal trade relations between capitalist countries and the people's democracies was highlighted. The magazine suggested that China had successfully lifted itself from past reliance on capitalist countries and was ready to trade with the West on a basis of equality and mutual benefit. Another article in the same issue of the magazine further suggested that China's new foreign trade policy of trading with the West was an important tool in its attempt to accelerate the country's industrial development.[42]

Indeed Chinese trade officials went to Moscow with concrete plans to establish trade relations with the West. Despite the gloomy business situation in China which eventually led to the withdrawal of British firms in China in May, many British businessmen succeeded in negotiating trade deals with Chinese trade officials in Moscow. As a result of these negotiations, trade deals to a total value of ten million pounds on each side were concluded. The goods which the Chinese were interested in included textiles, chemicals, and metals. In return the Chinese were willing to supply the British side with goods like frozen eggs, egg products, bristles, and hog castings.[43]

On 7 April Lord Boyd-Orr, head of the British delegation to the Moscow Economic Conference, cabled the President of the Board of Trade informing him of the Chinese side's interest in British textile products and urged responsible representatives to be sent immediately with samples. The

Board replied the next day stressing that the UK would be willing to trade with China, and British traders in Hong Kong and Shanghai had been seeking business for some time and were experts in arranging trade transactions. The reply also stated that if the Chinese government were unwilling to trade through these well-established channels, the British government would be glad to make other arrangements through their representatives in Beijing.[44] The British government preferred to see Sino-British trade conducted through existing channels. The fact that traders negotiating with the Chinese in Moscow were businessmen without connection with British firms with interests in China was alarming to Britain's established China traders. The China Association cabled Lord Boyd-Orr on 9 April, asking him to draw the attention of the Chinese delegation to the ability of British firms in China and Hong Kong to handle such business.[45]

On 8 April, John Keswick of Jardine Matheson wrote to his brother Tony on the trade discussions between Chinese trade officials and those British businessmen without previous experience in China trade. He obviously resented the fact that these newcomers were stepping into the China market while established British firms had to operate in very difficult conditions. 'It is irksome', he told Tony Keswick, 'that these ridiculously uninformed businessmen should go hobnobbing with the Chinese at a time when we are being squeezed to death by them.' With resignation he remarked: 'I suppose that is the way the world goes round'. He thought that the Chinese were putting out an 'attractive bait'. 'Most of us who have really been taken for a ride', he wrote, 'will not relax our efforts to endeavour to extricate ourselves.'[46]

Chinese trade officials in Moscow however, went further than putting out an 'attractive bait'. After the conference, the Chinese government set up a branch of the China National Import and Export Corporation (CNIEC) in Berlin to deal with contacts with Western countries which had been developed as a result of the Conference. It was clear that CNIEC was established to put foreign trade firmly under the direct control of the state and indicated that Beijing wanted to establish new channels and new contracts in trading with Britain. The establishment of CNIEC was a concrete step towards developing trade with the West.

Responding to Chinese trade officials' suggestion that China wanted to improve trade relations with Britain, Lamb approached the Chinese for a clarification of their statements made in Moscow on 18 April. British officials felt that, 'we cannot afford to ignore or appear to ignore the possibilities that the Chinese genuinely wish to expand trade, although UK exports of strategic value must be of course ruled out'. Lamb was instructed to ask the Beijing government for 'an early intimation of the nature of its proposals and of the channels through which it intends to pursue the suggestions outline in Moscow'. The British government maintained that many established British firms in Shanghai and Hong Kong were 'well qualified' to negotiate trade arrangements with the Chinese government.[47]

On 5 July, the Chinese Foreign Ministry issued a statement in response to the announcement that British firms had decided to pull out from China. The Chinese government said that it had repeatedly declared that China was willing to restore trade relations with other countries on a basis of equality and mutual benefit, and all law-abiding foreign residents and firms would be protected by the government. The Chinese government referred to the agreement with British representatives in Moscow for a trade exchange as an example of China's willingness to trade with Britain. It blamed Britain's policy of supporting the UN embargo against China, plus bad management, as the causes of hardship for British firms in China. Firms that wished to wind up their businesses were advised to apply to local authorities which would examine their cases according to their own merits and regulations. The Chinese government also maintained that state and private trade organizations were willing to conduct trade with British firms and organizations representing their interests.[48] The Chinese government obviously had no intention of changing its policy towards foreign business in China, but trade with the West was a separate issue that they wished to develop.[49] As *The Times* commented, 'The Chinese answer, though argumentative in form, is conciliatory in content'.

In August, the London Export Corporation, an approved agent of the CNIEC, approached the Board of Trade over the possibility of allowing the CNIEC to open a branch in London. The Board was in favour of the proposal because it would help the extension of Sino-British trade by saving British businessmen the trouble of conducting business discussions through East Berlin, and facilitate direct contact between the two governments on trade matters. Moreover accepting the proposal would also be consistent with Britain's declared policy of promoting all legitimate trade with China.[50] Foreign Office officials also saw political advantages in allowing China to set up a trade office in London because by establishing a link with the Chinese government, the British government would have a means of exerting pressure on them. There was the feeling that the British government had been regarded 'as a negligible quantity', by the Chinese. In the words of the China and Korea department's head, Charles Johnson, 'the more links we have, the more pressure we can exert through them'.[51]

Two problems stood in the way of a permanent official Chinese trade mission in London: first, a presidential election campaign was being held in the US at that time; second, the China trade question might be brought up in a forthcoming UN General Assembly meeting. Announcing a decision to accept a permanent trade mission from China would be sensitive and highly unpopular in the US. The Foreign Secretary agreed that while the proposal should be accepted in principle, the Board of Trade should only give an oral reply because the question of timing had to be carefully thought out and a final decision should wait until after the UN discussion.[52]

Not too surprisingly, the British Embassy in Washington advised against the proposal for a Chinese trade office in London. After the US presidential election was over in November, the embassy urged that nothing should be done about the trade mission before the new US administration had taken over. Accepting an official Chinese government trade agency in London whilst Chinese Communists were still actively intervening in the Korean War would cause serious problems for Anglo-American relations and generate adverse public criticism in the US. The Embassy warned that the risk was hardly worth taking if there was 'little serious hope of achieving more than a more convenient method of conducting our present volume of trade with China'.[53]

In the event the Board of Trade did not even have the opportunity to reply to London Export Corporation's approach because the proposal had not been followed up. Summing up the whole affair in late October, the Foreign Office's Charles Johnston concluded: 'In the present circumstances, the right course seems to be for us to sit tight and see if any more feelers are put out to us on this subject'. British officials seemed to have accepted that the setting up of an official Chinese trade mission in the UK was desirable in principle, but the British government should avoid giving the impression that it was keener than the Chinese on the idea.[54]

Although the establishment of an official China trade agency in London did not materialize in 1952, discussions within the British government were indicative of the official thinking that there was a need for developing further trade links with China. The Moscow Economic Conference had not changed trade relations between Britain and China in any dramatic manner, but it confirmed the desire of the People's Republic to trade with the West and provided an opportunity for it to express its willingness to trade with Britain despite the conflict in Korea and the fact that official diplomatic relations with Britain had not been established yet. The conference thus paved the way for an improvement in Sino-British trade relations.

The Dilemma of Britain's China Trade Policy

At the beginning of 1953, the British government were under increasing pressure from business circles on the one hand to relax export controls to China, and from the American government on the other to tighten those controls. British businessmen argued that Britain's commercial competitors were getting China's orders for goods because the Board of Trade's license controls were too strict. But with the Korean conflict continuing, Washington clearly did not want London to relax its trade controls against Beijing.

In March, a Cabinet paper submitted by the Board of Trade stated that the government had controlled British exports to China more severely than any other country in Western Europe, and had introduced transhipment controls over the most important items to prevent other countries from sending these goods through British ports. The paper also suggested, 'To the extent that other countries in Europe allow their traders to sell these goods to China, the effect of our controls is not to deny the goods to China but to divert the trade from our merchants to merchants on the Continent'. British policy-makers were facing a typical problem in the enforcement of economic sanctions.[55]

The Board therefore recommended that the government should only extend further controls on the export of strategic goods to China if other European countries agreed to do the same. However, trade officials argued that Britain's trade with China was useful and that the exports were not helping China's military operations. More importantly, trade officials worried that a trade embargo against Beijing would weaken Britain's power to resist US pressure for a similar embargo on exports to the Soviet bloc which would have serious consequences for essential supplies that Britain needed from that area. A complete embargo would cripple Hong Kong's economy which in turn would have grave consequences for the colony.[56] Thus, even though the British government were not prepared to break ranks with the US on the export of strategic goods to China, they were reluctant to go further to impose a complete embargo, and were quite willing to trade with China in non-strategic items.

The British government's ambivalence towards trade with China was best illustrated by their response to the Beijing economic conference in 1953. Foreign Office officials reacted very strongly when British business groups who had established new trade contacts with the Chinese government during the Moscow conference issued invitations to other businessmen to attend the Beijing conference. Representatives of these groups such as the London Export Corporation and the British Council for the Promotion of International Trade were regarded by the Foreign Office as 'covert members of the Communist Party'. Within the Foreign office those who were concerned about the Cold War aspect of the conference regarded it as 'a manoeuvre in a political warfare campaign directed against this country and its friends'. Other officials who were not opposed to attending the conference favoured a concerted policy with other NATO countries. The Board of Trade, however, believed that in the interest of British trade, leading British firms should send representatives to the conference. This view was shared by Leo Lamb in Beijing. In a telegram to London he said, 'I can see considerable advantage in the visit by British businessmen of reliable calibre who would take the opportunity of trade talks to press for the removal of disabilities with which established British commercial firms are now overwhelmed'. After much deliberations, the government decided that firms which had decided to send representatives to Beijing should be briefed, but they should not be prevented from going there so.[57]

In mid-1953, the international tensions generated by the Korean conflict were beginning to ease, and it seemed to be a suitable moment for Britain to relax trade restrictions and to improve trade relations with China. British policy-makers had shifted their policy of 'keeping a foot in the door' by then, both because of the difficulties in their dealings with the Chinese, and because of the changing international environment after the outbreak of the Korean War. But the policy had not been completely reversed; the policy-makers still aimed at developing better political and trade relations with China.[58]

But 1953 was also a year when US politics was still dominated by McCarthyism. Britain's trade relations with China had been severely attacked by Senator McCarthy, who alleged that British ships had carried strategic goods to China and British-owned ships had transported communist troops to Chinese ports. The predicament of the British policy-makers was that although they wanted trade with China, the government could not afford to be seen as encouraging such trade. Eventually the Foreign Office issued notices through the Federation of British Industries (FBI) to advise against participation in the Beijing Conference, even though trade deals would not be discouraged.[59]

The Beijing economic conference may have had a Cold War element in it, but there was little doubt that China was interested in increasing trade with Britain. The China Association observed that Chinese news media were emphasizing the benefits of Sino-British trade and recalling its long history and potential. The Association concluded: 'the Chinese authorities were adopting a more friendly approach'. Nineteen British businessmen, who were referred to as communist-sponsored by the Foreign Office, went to Beijing in June to hold trade discussions with Chinese officials and concluded a commercial agreement for trade to a value of 30 million pounds. Well established British firms were not very pleased to see that China was developing more trade links with what they considered to be 'less reputable firms' which were new to the China market. In September the China Association reported unrest among its members because the newcomers might be able to get an 'undue' share of trade with China.[60]

There was no doubt that the British policy-makers also preferred to see the established firms which had regular contacts with the government conducting Sino-British trade. The main problem was not which was the most desirable channel to conduct trade with China, but how far Britain could go to improve trade relations with China in the context of the international situation and Britain's alliance relationship with the US.

The Turning Point in Sino-British Trade Relations

The most delicate problem in developing Anglo-Chinese trade was US estrangement with China. British officials were divided on whether better trade relations with China would affect Britain's close relationship with the US. In early 1954 trade officials suggested that Chinese representatives should be invited to attend the British Industrial Fair, but the Foreign Office was reluctant to endorse the invitation.

The Foreign Office argued that while business prospects with China were still uncertain, the government should not do anything which might provoke ill feelings in the US. Another worry was that the Chinese might only place orders for strategic goods which were on the embargo list. This, in the words of Colin Crowe, head of the Far Eastern department, would embarrass the British government and encourage traders to 'agitate against our controls'. A second concern was that a large proportion of Anglo-Chinese trade was conducted through organizations regarded as communist fronts by the British government. In March 1954, with the government's approval, the Federation of British Industries, the China Association and the London Chamber of Commerce addressed a letter to the Chinese Minister of Foreign Trade proposing that a trade mission should visit Beijing and a joint organization should be set up to assist the development of Anglo-Chinese commercial relations.[61]

The Geneva Conference on Korea and Indo-China which began in April 1954 provided an opportunity for the British government to probe China's stance towards trade with Britain. The British delegates were briefed that if the Chinese expressed a desire to expand Anglo-Chinese trade, the delegates should agree that they shared that goal as a long-term objective, but should refuse to be drawn into any discussion of the UN embargo and also bring up the Chinese treatment of British firms. The government's position was that fair treatment of British firms in China was a prerequisite to an improvement in Anglo-Chinese relations.[62]

In the event, the Geneva Conference provided an opportunity for an improvement not only in Anglo-Chinese diplomatic relations, but also in trade relations. When Humphrey Trevelyan, the British charge d'affaires in China who accompanied Eden to the Conference, met China's Vice-Minister for Foreign Trade, Lei Renmin, on 1 May, they discussed the possibilities for British traders to send a trade mission to China and set up a new business organization to conduct China trade. Lei told Trevelyan that it was acceptable in principle, but he would like a fuller explanation about certain points. The Foreign Office promptly arranged a meeting for Chinese trade officials with representatives from the Federation of British Industries.[63]

The meeting between the Federation's Peter Tenant and Lei took place on 6 May. Lei made it quite clear that the Chinese government wanted to expand China's trade with Britain. He added that British traders who wished to set up an economic organization to further Anglo-Chinese trade need not wait for a reply from Beijing; they could go ahead with their plans. He also expressed the hope that the two sides would have frequent visits to one another's country. The meeting agreed on further talks on technical matters, and that the two sides would meet again to discuss the question. Trevelyan, who was present together with Joe Ford, was still a bit sceptical about the Chinese side's motivation. After the meeting he remarked that the Chinese seemed to be keen on signing an inter-governmental agreement and might try to make political propaganda out of it.[64]

In the second meeting, the two sides agreed to prepare lists of goods available so that they could know in advance the possible scope and volume of Sino-British trade. They also agreed to develop direct contacts between British businessmen and Chinese trade officials, and exchange visits to each other's country. The Chinese side preferred a trade agreement, but by not insisting on it demonstrated that their primary objective was economic rather than political. They then proposed to send a trade delegation to Britain in May or June because China's trade contracts with British commercial representatives concluded in 1953 had expired and they had to plan in advance for their purchases for the rest of the year.[65]

The trade talks impressed Trevelyan as a serious attempt by the Chinese to develop trade with Britain. Although he believed that 'the Chinese will no doubt make incidental political capital where they can', he thought their principal motive was not political. He recommended to the Foreign Office that the trade visits should be arranged before the end of June because the practical results would be better sooner than later, and also because the British side could demonstrate that they were serious about developing trade with China.[66]

The arrangement of trade visits was not without problems. A visit by China's Vice Minister for Foreign Trade would be too politically sensitive. The Chinese were later told that although the British government hoped that Lei would visit Britain, suitable arrangement were not possible in June. The business groups sponsored by the government to enter into trade talks with the Chinese did not want other competitors who had developed trade links earlier with the People's Republic separately to have any part in organizing the trade visits. They had by then formed an organization called the Sino-British Trade Committee, and demanded the Chinese delegation not to meet representatives from the British Council for the Promotion of International Trade. The Chinese accepted that the Council would not take part in organizing the visit, but they did not want to be prevented from seeing other firms in Britain.[67]

The Chinese delegation which went to London at the end of June attracted wide publicity. They stayed on for five more days after the programme arranged for them by the Sino-British Trade Committee was over and met representatives from the so-called 'communist fronts organi- zations' such as the British Council for the Promotion of International Trade and the London Export Corporation during their spare time. But there was little doubt that they went to London primarily for trade purposes. In a press statement, the delegation announced that the object of the visit was 'to ascertain the requirements of both sides and to examine trade possibilities'. They extended an invitation to British businessmen to visit China in autumn. While their visit was exploratory and no trade deals were concluded, it paved the way for concrete deals. Following the visit, official media in China also indicated that the Chinese government were willing to develop further Sino-British trade.[68]

Most British traders who went to Beijing in November reported that they were satisfied with the business concluded or preparation made for future business. The Chinese also adopted a more realistic stance about confining the trade negotiations to items not on the embargo list. The *Financial Times* reported that this Chinese position marked, 'a notable change from the experience of earlier British business visitors to China who came back with masses of conditional contracts which were never fulfilled'.[69]

The total value of Anglo-Chinese trade in 1954 was just under 16 million pounds. This figure was slightly less than the 1953 figure. But as Robert

Boardman observed in a study of Anglo-Chinese relations bewteen 1949 and 1974: 'The 1954 arrangement marked a fresh departure in Sino-British trade'.[70] Further trade visits from both sides to each other's country were arranged. The following year the value of Anglo-Chinese trade reached 20 million pounds, the highest figure since the end of the Second World War (see Appendix 3). One last barrier in Sino-British trade remained: the British government were not yet prepared to relax export controls over strategic goods to China. A decision towards that direction could only be taken after further consultation with the Americans. That decision was eventually taken in 1957 after domestic business and political opinion had asserted greater pressure on the British government.

CONCLUSIONS

Britain's recognition of revolutionary China had not brought any improvement to business conditions for British firms or helped to maintain the British commercial empire in China. The new Chinese government were determined to implement an economic programme which provided very little opportunity for foreign private business enterprise. This was not entirely unexpected by British policy-makers. Any hope that the establishment of diplomatic relations with China would affect Beijing's economic policies was clearly unrealistic since by 1952 Anglo-Chinese relations were still maintained at only an unofficial level. At this time British firms gave up all hopes for continuing their business in China and decided to withdraw. In 1953 Foreign Office officials were talking in terms of 'keeping a toe in the door' instead of 'a foot in the door' when they presented policy papers on China to their ministers. Between 1950 to 1954, the government's position was revised from urging British businessmen not to abandon their assets in China to ensuring that they could get out of China safely. During this period, as far as Britain's commercial position in China was concerned, the government's emphasis, like the merchants', had also shifted to trade with rather than in China.

There was no doubt that the British business lobby formed a pressure group which had a strong influence on their government's policy towards China. Pressure group politics, however, was only one of the many factors which influenced the policy of the British policy-makers' calculations of Britain's interests in China. Even though the business lobby's connections with the government remained close, its influence in Britain's China policy was reduced significantly when it became clear that the prospect for foreign business in China was doomed. Their effectiveness was further weakened as political considerations came to dominate British thinking on the China question as a result of the Korean conflict. Beijing's attitude towards foreign business was also another important factor which forced the British government to shift the emphasis of their policy from protecting existing commercial interests in China to improving trade relations with that country.

Fundamental changes in China's external trade took place after the Chinese Communist Party came to power. The Soviet Union quickly replaced the US and Britain as China's leading trade partner in the early 1950s. Still, the development of Sino-British trade relations from 1949 to 1954 demonstrated that revolutionary China's economic planners were quite willing to trade with Britain despite its role as the imperial power which had dominated China's economy for almost a century, and its alliance with the US in Korea. The most important difference after 1949 was that Britain's relative importance as a trading partner declined. Another novel feature in Anglo-Chinese trade was that the new Chinese government tried to channel trade away from well-established British firms with a long history in China, which were associated with Britain's past domination. Beijing's policy towards foreign business and foreign trade indicated that even though the Chinese revolutionaries were determined to implement a socialist economic policy, they were also prepared to trade with the West when necessary and convenient.

7 British Colonial Interests in Southeast Asia

The presence of a large ethnic Chinese population in British territories in Southeast Asia and the traditional links between overseas Chinese and their country of origin meant that internal developments in China had always affected local politics in places like Malaya and Singapore. Hong Kong, situated on the doorstep of China, was even more vulnerable to political changes on the mainland. This was true when the Kuomintang was in power; the communization of China accentuated the linkage. Precisely because of the different locations of these territories, their distinctive domestic political situations, and degrees of dependence on China, British colonial administrations in Southeast Asia reacted differently to the London's decision to recognize the Beijing government. As demonstrated in Chapter 2, while the Hong Kong government supported the decision, the administrations in Malaya and Singapore accepted it with great reluctance.

After the Second World War British policy planners had concluded that Britain's major interests in the Far East lay south of the Tropic of Cancer in its dependent territories in that area. Political developments in there took an unexpected turn when a communist regime was established in China; the balance of power in Asia was altered in favour of the communist bloc. The prospect of an attendant increase in communist influence in Southeast Asia was most uncomforting for policy-makers in London.[1] But British officials in charge of colonial affairs and Foreign Office officials looked at the problems from very different perspectives. The two Departments' priorities, as reflected in their divergent approaches to the China problem, led to intense bureaucratic in-fighting. The way in which they resolved their discord provides a good example of the influence of bureaucratic politics in foreign policy-making. Also interesting is the attitude of the People's Republic towards British colonial possessions in Southeast Asia for it provides a good indication of the priorities of the newly established revolutionary regime. As revolutionaries adhering to a Marxist ideology, China's political masters should have supported other revolutionary movements in Southeast Asia against colonial rule. Yet, they failed to provide concrete assistance for the insurgent Malayan Communist Party.

By looking at the problems arising from British territories as an issue in Anglo-Chinese relations, this chapter discusses how Britain's colonial problems and conflicting bureaucratic interests within Whitehall affected its China policy, as well as revolutionary China's attitude towards those British territories with a sizable Chinese population.

MALAYA AND BRITAIN'S CHINA POLICY

The Importance of Malaya to Britain

Malaya was one of Britain's 'principal dollar-earning sources' during the post-war years. In April 1949 the Foreign Office's Economic Intelligence Unit reported that Malaya was 'overwhelmingly the greatest dollar earner among the colonies'. The unit estimated that in 1948 Malaya's dollar earnings were about 178 million. Given that the total sterling area dollar deficit in that year was 1,800 million US dollars, the total dollar earnings of Malaya and Singapore, estimated at about 230 million, i.e. 12.8 per cent of the deficit, were very substantial.[2]

Malaya was not just an important dollar-earner for Britain, it was also a principal source of raw materials for the UK and the West. Thus, on economic grounds alone the British government had strong reasons for keeping Malaya out of communist hands. Given China's traditional influence in Malaya, the Foreign Office's policy of 'keeping a foot in the door' in China, was viewed with scepticism by colonial authorities there. The Malayan administration's relationship with China had never been comfortable; Kuomintang activities were banned in Malaya before the Second World War. But by the time the Chinese Communists came to power Chinese Consuls appointed by the Kuomintang government had been accepted by the Malayan authorities.[3]

The different priorities of the colonial administration and the Foreign Office resulted in heated policy debates between the Colonial and Foreign Offices. Three major problems dominated those debates: the acceptance of Chinese Communist consuls in Malaya, the issue of transit visas to Chinese diplomats passing through Singapore en route to destinations elsewhere, and the repatriation of Chinese Communist activists to China. Of these three issues, the question of whether Chinese Communist consuls should be accepted in Malaya was the most controversial. The colonial authorities' apprehension about the appointment of communist consuls was so strong that colonial officials sought in 1950 to reverse the recognition of Beijing, which was a fundamental element of the Foreign Office's China policy.

The Chinese Communist Consul Controversy

The controversy surrounding the question of whether Malaya should accept Chinese consuls appointed by the Beijing government centred on two issues. In the first two months after the British government had accorded recognition to the Beijing government, the Malayan authorities wanted a public declaration of the functions and privileges of Chinese consuls. When the Anglo-Chinese talks on diplomatic relations failed to produce any concrete results after three months, the colonial authorities pressed London to exclude Chinese Communist consuls from Malaya.

British colonial administrators had expressed reservations about London's decision to recognize the People's Republic. They feared that it would jeopardize their effort against the communist insurgency in Malaya and Singapore because the local Chinese community might misinterpret the act of recognition as an act of approval. One of their major worries was that the arrival of diplomatic representatives from China might stimulate anti-British feelings within local Chinese communities. As pointed out in Chapter 2 during the Bukit Serene meeting in November 1949, the decision to recognize Beijing was approved by UK representatives in Southeast Asia, but the decision was only accepted reluctantly by the colonial administrators in Malaya and Singapore who had remained unconvinced by the Foreign Office's argument that the advantages of recognition outweighed the disadvantages.

Almost immediately after accepting that recognition of the People's Republic was inevitable, British officials in Southeast Asia began their effort to delay the appointment of Chinese consuls in Malaya and Singapore. Before the decision of recognition was announced, the High Commissioner in Malaya, Henry Gurney, told the Colonial Office that the expectation of the arrival of Chinese diplomats would have 'an adverse effect on cooperation of the public in anti-bandit and anti-communist measures'. He said that public co-operation had been growing and it would be 'most unfortunate' if the proposed special effort to enlist public co-operation after the Chinese New Year (in mid-February), were to coincide with the arrival of Chinese consuls.[4]

He therefore suggested that as soon as possible after the decision to recognize Beijing had been announced, London should issue a statement making clear that Chinese consuls would have no rights of intervention on behalf of Chinese citizens who were British subjects. They would only be concerned with making sure that their nationals were being dealt with fairly under local law and would not be permitted to operate information or propaganda departments to disseminate communist propaganda. This recommendation was fully supported by Malcolm MacDonald, the UK Commissioner-General for Southeast Asia.[5]

Gurney's suggestion was not received favourably by Foreign Office officials for they were concerned that Beijing might retaliate with some 'unwelcome definition of the function of our consuls in China'. Issuing a statement as suggested by the colonial administrators might also 'afford an excuse for further restrictions on our consuls in Iron curtain countries'. For the Foreign Office, attempts to define the functions and privileges of consuls was likely to lead to trouble. Supporting this view in Beijing, John Hutchison urged against a unilateral declaration to limit the functions of Chinese consuls as it would be inconsistent with the British government's offer to establish diplomatic relations on the basis of equality.[6]

After consultations with the Foreign Office, the Colonial Office advised the Malayan authorities to use other ways to reassure the public. But Gurney insisted that an official statement was necessary to encourage the Chinese in Malaya to join in the 'anti-bandit month'. The Foreign Office, however, remained unsympathetic. Rob Scott, Head of the Southeast Asian department at that time, asserted that a statement would not help Gurney in Malaya and would have repercussions on British consuls in China. He maintained that, 'sooner or later we are going to have Chinese consuls in Malaya. Let us keep our powder dry till then, and meanwhile say nothing that may be brought up and used in evidence against us'. If a statement was necessary, the Foreign Office suggested that it could say that Chinese Communist consuls would be 'given exactly the same treatment as other Chinese consuls in Malaya'.[7]

The Malayan authorities, for their part, wanted more than just a declaration that Chinese Communist consuls would not be treated any differently from their Kuomintang predecessors. They decided to make their views known in the form of a reply to a formal letter by an anonymous Malayan Chinese asking some questions about the government's policy towards the activities of communist agents. This however did not attract as much publicity as the Malayan government had hoped for; it also did not provoke any reaction from the Chinese government or the official Chinese press.[8]

The stalemate over the negotiations for the establishment of Anglo-Chinese diplomatic relations in early 1950 gave colonial administrators another opportunity to revive their argument against the acceptance of Chinese consuls. In March, Gurney wrote to the Colonial Office saying that he had changed his mind over accepting Chinese Communist consuls in Malaya, which he had agreed to earlier only reluctantly anyway.

Reporting to London, the High Commissioner warned that the appointment of Chinese consuls to the Malayan Federation would 'amount to a major setback in the anti-communist campaign'. The Chinese Advisory Committee, which was composed of leaders of the Chinese community in Malaya, had discussed the issue in February and came to the conclusion that 'pressure would be brought to bear on the Chinese in Malaya by Consuls through threats of reprisals on their property or relatives in China'. Chinese Advisory Boards in several states had also passed resolutions urging the government not to accept Chinese consuls. Gurney said their appointments would inevitably affect the Chinese community's confidence in Britain's determination to fight the Malayan Communists and would be interpreted as an act of weakness. This, Gurney warned, would amount to 'suicidal folly' and 'the Chinese might decide that the time had come to make their peace with the other side'.[9]

For the Colonial administrators the exclusion of Chinese Communist consuls from Malaya was essential, at least for the duration of the Emergency, even if it were to affect the Anglo-Chinese talks on diplomatic relations in Beijing. The authorities in Malaya feared that the presence of these consuls were bound to have a grave effect on their anti-communist campaign. The High Commissioner's view was: 'we should be risking the loss of support of law-abiding Chinese and without that there can be no prospect of an end to the present state of affairs within any reasonable space of time, however many more troops may be forthcoming'.[10]

The proposal to defer the acceptance of Chinese Communist Consuls to Malaya had the full support of other senior British officials in Southeast Asia. Gurney's telegram to the Colonial Office was immediately followed by telegrams, with similar arguments, from the Commissioner-General for Southeast Asia Malcolm MacDonald, and the Governor of Singapore, Frank Gimson. MacDonald went as far as to say that Britain's recognition of Beijing had contributed to the deterioration of the situation in Malaya *vis-à-vis* the communists. This view was supported by the Commander-in-Chief, Far East Land Forces, John Harding, who had earlier suggested that London's recognition of the Beijing government amounted to 'substantial reinforcement for the enemies', and was apprehensive that Chinese Communist consuls might assist in organizing and directing 'bandit activities'. In MacDonald's recommendation, he went one step further than Gurney by proposing the exclusion of Chinese Communist consuls from all British protected territories in Southeast Asia.[11]

The colonial administrators' efforts to block the appointment of Chinese consuls to British territories in Southeast Asia was viewed by Hutchison with dismay. He told the Foreign Office that it was extremely improbable that the Chinese government would be willing to accept it once diplomatic relations were established. Given the large number of Chinese nationals in Malaya the Chinese government had a legitimate concern there. There was no chance, Hutchison suggested, that the British government could exclude Chinese consuls from Malaya except at the price of sacrificing British Consular posts in China. He warned that it 'might result in the Chinese Government breaking off the present discussions and refusing to agree to the establishment of diplomatic relations'.[12]

Naturally, Foreign Office officials were alarmed at the possible repercussions for Britain's position in China, if Chinese consuls were to be excluded from British territories in Southeast Asia. Esler Dening warned that if such a policy were to be carried out, ministers 'must be prepared and willing to reverse the whole of their policy in regard to China, even to the extent of breaking off such tenuous relations as have been established with the Chinese People's Government'. In that case, Britain would have to regard 'China as closed territory, both from the point of view of trade and of all other contacts, possible for a considerable number of years'. Dismissing the arguments put forward by the colonial administrators as 'lacking reality', Dening maintained: 'there is nothing we can do if in the event the Chinese People's Government should establish normal diplomatic relations and confirm the status of our Consuls in China'. The Foreign Office's position was that only if the Chinese attempted to restrict British consular functions in China, then similar actions could be taken in Malaya based on reciprocity.[13]

In a telegram to MacDonald, the Foreign Office stated that the consequences of carrying out his recommendation might not be confined to the closing down of British consulates in China. If Beijing declined to establish normal diplomatic relations with Britain, then the British government would have to break off all contacts with China and to write off its trading interests there, and the Chinese Communist leaders would no longer have any reason to restrain themselves over Hong Kong and Southeast Asia. The Foreign Office argued: 'There might well be a stepping up of the terrorist campaign in Malaya and the more open support of Ho Chi Minh in Indo-China, while the position in Hong Kong would probably deteriorate and might prove untenable unless we were prepared to devote major resources indefinitely for the maintenance of our position'.[14]

The Foreign Office's response did not soften MacDonald's resolve to block the appointment of Chinese consuls to British territories in Southeast Asia. In a brusque reply, he asked, 'whether His Majesty's Government consider that the maintenance of probably a rather precarious foothold in China outweighs the importance of winning the struggle in Malaya'. He asserted that trade relations with China had become less important, and questioned the argument that China's support for subversion in

Southeast Asia and policy towards Hong Kong would be affected by the establishment of normal Anglo-Chinese relations.[15]

British colonial administrators regarded the issue of Chinese Communist consuls as more than a question of whether on not these consuls might give assistance to local communists. The issue had, in the words of MacDonald, 'became the touchstone of our ability and determination to protect those people here who are willing to cooperate in defeating the terrorist menace'. He warned that acceptance of the consuls would defeat the authorities' efforts to encourage public co-operation and the authorities would then only be able to maintain their position by force indefinitely. Gurney expressed similar sentiments in a separate telegram.[16]

In April 1950 the Foreign and the Colonial Offices spelt out their differences in a joint Cabinet paper, and recommended that a decision on the issue of Chinese consuls in Malaya should be delayed after the Foreign Secretary's forthcoming meeting with the US Secretary of State which was to take place shortly. During the Cabinet meeting at which this paper was discussed, James Griffiths, the new Colonial Secretary who had replaced Arthur Creech-Jones after the general elections in February, not only wanted to exclude Chinese consuls in Malaya, but also to make a public announcement about it during his forthcoming visit to Malaya. The Colonial Office's position received strong support in the Cabinet. Kenneth Younger, who represented Bevin at the meeting, said that the Foreign Office accepted the objection to the appointment of Chinese consuls in Malaya, but the Office was adamant that 'if at a later stage it became clear that refusal of this facility was the only obstacle preventing the establishment of full diplomatic relations with the Chinese People's Government' then it should be granted to the Chinese. It was clear that the Foreign Office was not ready to concede defeat easily. The discussion ended without a meeting of minds and the Cabinet agreed to delay the decision until the Foreign Secretary had the opportunity to discuss the China question with the US Secretary of State.[17]

If Foreign Office officials had been obliged to give in under the combined pressure of almost all senior British officials in Southeast Asia, they found it very hard to swallow a public announcement on the exclusion of Chinese Consuls from Malaya. Foreseeing that such a declaration would cause difficulties in the Anglo-Chinese negotiations, the British charge d'affaires in Beijing, Hutchison, advised strongly against it.[18]

As the Cabinet had failed to make a decision, the Colonial Office intensified their campaign to exclude Chinese consuls from Malaya. In this, they had the support of the Ministry of Defence and senior military staff. As a result of a report by John Harding, the Commander in Chief of Land

Forces in the Far East, the Chief of Staff recommended in late April that the admission of Chinese consuls to Malaya should be delayed indefinitely as it was 'militarily unacceptable in the present circumstances'. Eventually the Minister of Defence, Emmanuel Shinwell, secured the Prime Minister's approval to the Colonial Office's request.[19]

While Foreign Office officials feared that the exclusion of Chinese consuls from Malaya might have a detrimental effect on Britain's relations with China, the colonial authorities actually hoped for a breach in Anglo-Chinese relations. Thus the authorities in Malaya insisted on a public announcement of the decision, arguing that rupture of diplomatic relations with China could have a beneficial effect in strengthening Chinese co-operation in Malaya. Gurney maintained that as far as Malaya was concerned, breaking off relations with the Beijing government 'would remove a lurking suspicion that concessions which are being made to the Chinese both politically and in such matters as land for squatter settlement are to appease Communist China'. Supporting this view, the Governor of Singapore went as far as to suggest that a breach with the Beijing government would raise British prestige in Malaya more than anything else.[20]

These views were strongly contested by the Foreign Office which feared that the contemplated public announcement would have serious repercussions on Anglo-Chinese relations. Inter-departmental consultations eventually broke down: the Colonial Office went ahead to produce a draft Cabinet paper for the Colonial Secretary who was about to visit Malaya, recommending both the exclusion of Chinese consuls from Malaya during the Emergency, and the public announcement of this decision. In a note to his counterpart in the Colonial Office, Dening stated that the Foreign Office could not possibly agree with the second recommendation. He said, 'This puts us to the necessity of drafting for the Foreign Secretary a paper which essentially is in flat contradiction to yours'.[21]

The Foreign Office considered that the effects of admitting Communist Chinese consuls to Malaya had been exaggerated by Gurney and Gimson. Although it now accepted that the consuls had to be excluded, it would not yield on the question of a public announcement. Since the British government had no proof that the Chinese government was actively supporting the terrorist campaign in Malaya, the Foreign Office felt that, 'If we were to make a public announcement, it would be equivalent to saying to the world at large that the Chinese government are appointing officials for subversive purposes'. The Chinese, Dening suggested, would retaliate because such an announcement would not be tolerated by any self-respecting government and the Beijing government would almost certain regard it as an unpardonable affront. The Malayan authorities' suggestion that the Chinese community could be won solidly to their side by excluding Chinese consuls and breaking off diplomatic relations with Beijing was regarded by the Foreign Office as ridiculous.[22]

At this juncture it seemed that the Foreign and Colonial Offices were heading for a showdown. Or, as Dening put it, the Cabinet papers with opposing views would have to be 'thrashed out' in Cabinet if the two Secretaries of State could not find an agreed proposal.[23]

Foreign Office officials were ready for a showdown. They prepared a paper on the political and economic implications of a break in relations with China in early May which, in Dening's words, was drafted on 'the assumption that the Cabinet would decided at its 18 May meeting to exclude Chinese Consuls in Malaya'. This was not only an assessment of the consequences of a breach in Anglo-Chinese relations, but also an attempt to influence the final outcome of the Cabinet decision, if not on the exclusion of Chinese consuls, then on the wisdom of making a public announcement of such a decision. The paper suggested that Beijing might be provoked into demanding the withdrawal of British consular officers from China or even breaking off relations with Britain. The Foreign Office warned: China would be 'irrevocably lost to the Soviet camp' and the Cold War in the Far East and Southeast Asia would be intensified. Foreign Office officials also sought support from other ministries by asking them to provide assessments of implications for Britain's strategic and financial interests as a result of a break with China.[24]

The showdown was averted by the two Secretaries of State themselves. On 15 May, just three days before the question was to be discussed in Cabinet, Bevin talked to Griffiths about the problem. The Foreign Secretary did not want the two Offices to go to the Cabinet with a paper showing a divergence of views. Since China had still not yet established diplomatic relations with Britain, Bevin suggested that the question of the appointment of Chinese consuls to Malaya had not yet arisen. He told Griffiths that when the time came he would have to consider the matter in the light of existing circumstances and possible reactions of Britain's allies. The problem was settled with the understanding that no Chinese consuls would be accepted while the Emergency was in force, but the decision was not to be made public. The public statement eventually merely suggested that when the question of the acceptance of Chinese consuls arose, the British government would take the opinion expressed in Malaya fully into account.[25]

On this occasion, the 'consensual style' of Whitehall officials, which William Wallace has described in his book *The Foreign Policy Process in Britain,* broke down; instead of being 'suppressed as discussion rises', the differences of opinion between the Foreign and Colonial Offices were presented to their respective Ministers. In the end, the consensual style was reasserted by the Ministers themselves.[26] The controversy over the appointment of Chinese Communist consuls did not became an issue in Anglo-Chinese relations; Beijing made no request to send representatives to Malaya. Moreover, negotiations on the establishment of diplomatic relations between Britain and China were interrupted by the outbreak of the Korean War. Nonetheless, this episode demonstrated the role of bureaucratic politics in Britain's China policy.

The Question of Transit Visas for Chinese Diplomats

As soon as the row about Chinese consuls in Malaya had subsided, new problem emerged. In June the Chinese government requested transit visas for their Ambassador to Indonesia, Wang Renshu and his staff, travelling en route through Singapore. Similar requests for access for their diplomatic representatives en route to India and Burma were made in early July. The Singapore authorities were reluctant to grant the transit visas because they believed that the unrestricted presence of Chinese diplomats could be exploited and 'may touch-off the whole question of Chinese representation which is at present dormant and thus shake confidence once more'.[27]

Arguing against this view strongly, Hutchison suggested that Chinese diplomats would not become involved in activities which would embarrass the colonial authorities because 'foreign representation abroad is a new development for the People's Government and they are I think anxious to behave correctly in the eyes of the world'. He was worried that if visas were refused or special restrictions were imposed on them Beijing would regard it as an act of great unfriendliness, and that the establishment of diplomatic relations would be made even more difficult and might result in direct retaliation affecting British diplomats in China. The Foreign Office felt that although there was some justification for Singapore's argument, it was not 'realistic' to refuse to allow Chinese diplomats to pass through Singapore. When Gimson learnt about the Foreign Office's view, he sent another telegram reporting that the Chinese Ambassador to Indonesia who was known as Wong Yan-seok locally was 'well known as a dangerous communist'. Gimson said Wang had previously been resident in Singapore and later in Medan, Sumatra, where he had been deported to China by the Dutch for subversive activities.[28]

It soon became clear that the colonial authorities' opposition to transit visas for Chinese diplomats was not just directed against Wang. When the Chinese Counsellor to India passed through Singapore unexpectedly en route there on board a ship, Gimson suggested that the Beijing government should be asked to give notice of the transit of their representatives through Hong Kong and that Chinese diplomats might not be allowed to land unless prior permission had been obtained. Foreign Office officials were rather disturbed by Gimson's request, pointing out that it would be an unusual diplomatic practice. The Foreign Office's Southeast Asia department decided against Gimson's suggestion; the Colonial Office was told that Singapore was 'making very heavy weather'.[29]

Towards the end of July, the Chinese government requested transit visas through Singapore for their ambassador to Burma, Yao Zhongming and his staff, and other diplomatic representatives. Despite the misgivings of the Singapore authorities, senior Foreign Office officials finally decided that transit visas should be granted to all Chinese diplomats as a matter of ordinary international courtesy. The Foreign Office suggested that if the Singapore authorities were worried, they could make arrangements for police surveillance.[30]

In a letter to the Colonial Office, the Foreign Office said that even though Wang had a long record of communist activity in Malaya and Indonesia, as he was an accredited ambassador proceeding in a normal way to a new post, the British government had no justification for treating him as an exceptional case by refusing transit facilities. The Foreign Office's view was: the 'damage which the Ambassador might do in passing through Singapore should be small', whereas the refusal of a visa would undoubtedly have an undesirable effect on Britain's efforts to establish relations with Beijing as well as on the position of British diplomats in China.[31]

The Colonial Office eventually agreed that transit visas through Singapore should be granted to all three Chinese diplomats limited to a short period. However, British authorities in Southeast Asia still felt so strongly about this problem that MacDonald telegraphed the Foreign Office to put on record his concern at 'the grave risks' involved in the granting of transit visas to the Chinese diplomats. He warned that he would ask the government to review what he referred to as 'this potential dangerous traffic' if necessary. The Foreign Office did not reply to MacDonald and the matter was closed when the Chinese diplomats passed through Singapore uneventfully and peacefully.[32]

Repatriation of Chinese from Malaya

After the authorities in Malaya had declared a state of emergency in June 1948, the Malayan authorities were empowered to expel 'undesirable elements' and their dependants from Malaya. This power, the authorities felt, was an effective weapon in their campaign against the Malayan Communists. Before the inauguration of the People's Republic in Beijing, the Malayan authorities had repatriated a number of Chinese nationals from Malaya to China. After October 1949, repatriation stopped when shipping companies refused to accept Chinese detained in Malaya as passengers to China. In November 1950, one shipping company obtained permission to carry Chinese deportees to Shantou, and between November 1950 and mid-January 1951, almost three thousand people were deported to China from Malaya.[33]

For the Malayan authorities the repatriation of suspected communists detained was of paramount importance: this would 'contribute more than any other single step to ending the Emergency in Malaya'.[34] The problem was that since the arrival in China of these people from Malaya, the Chinese press had begun to make allegations about atrocities committed by the Colonial authorities against overseas Chinese.

Then on 29 December 1950, the Chinese Foreign Ministry issued an official statement accusing the British authorities in Malaya of 'carrying out a frenzied persecution' of Chinese nationals. Referring to the number of Chinese deported, Beijing accused the Malayan authorities of embarking upon a policy of 'expelling overseas Chinese in large number'. The statement enunciated: 'whether from the point of view of brutality or from the magnitude of its scale and the number of persons involved, this persecution surpasses the persecution suffered by Chinese nationals at any time in the past in the countries of Southeast Asia'. The Chinese government declared that the British government would be held responsible for the policy of the Malayan authorities.[35]

While the statement had not gone further than the other allegations already published in China's publicity organs, as Hutchison submitted, it was 'the first time there has been an official statement on the subject'.[36] It was probably not a coincidence that the announcement was made when Anglo-Chinese relations were heading for a downturn as the Korean conflict worsened. The British government were in fact about to support a UN resolution condemning China as an aggressor in Korea.[37] At the end of January, upon instructions from Beijing, the local authorities in Shantou stopped granting permission to admit deportees from Malaya.

Two months later, NCNA announced that an investigative team had been organized by the Red Cross Society of China and the Chinese People's Relief Administration to find out in detail the extent of British persecution in Malaya. Throughout March, April and May the mistreatment of Chinese nationals in Malaya received widespread attention in the Chinese press. In April, the *People's China* described British administration in Malaya as: 'Fascist Police Rule'. At the end of the same month the Foreign Ministry even requested the British government to issue entry visas for Malaya to an investigative group known as 'the Chinese People's Relief Committee for the Overseas Chinese Refugees of Malaya'. Beijing was probably not expecting a positive response to their application but a refusal to provide entry visas would make good publicity material; it insisted on a written reply, but the British government decided not to respond.[38]

The most interesting feature of the repatriation question was perhaps that despite all the public attacks on the 'atrocities' of the colonial administration in Malaya, China's official statement was a mere protest against the treatment of Chinese nationals, rather than a denouncement of British colonial rule in Malaya. This certainly did not constitute official support for the revolutionary cause of Malaya's Communists.

The Chinese Communist and the Malayan Communist Party

The Malayan Communist Party (MCP), formed in 1930 by former members of the South Seas branch of the Chinese Communist Party was predominantly ethnic-Chinese. Given the two parties' historical ties, the ethnic Chinese connection, and Cold War perceptions about communist expansionism, the Malayan authorities were not without justification for their fears that the Beijing government would support the MCP.[39]

Although China's official media had repeatedly attacked the colonial authorities for 'the murder and mass imprisonment' in Malaya, the emphasis was on 'the infringement of the rights of Chinese nationals' in British territories by British authorities, not the revolutionary cause of the Malayan Communists. In fact the Chinese government had not condemned the British authorities in Malaya officially until December 1950 when the Korean conflict entered a critical stage and the British government were about to support a UN resolution condemning China as an aggressor.[40]

Beijing's public support for the MCP was not just unenthusiastic; it had also not provided any substantial material aid to them. The British government were not able to find any solid evidence that the Chinese government were providing any such support to the MCP. In October 1949 Gurney reported to the Colonial Office that as far as the Malayan authorities were aware, the MCP had not received any material support from either Moscow or China. He stated that MCP leaders were 'local fanatics, who live and maintain their gangs on money and supplies extorted by threats and common banditry'. The Foreign Office believed that the MCP's 'campaign of violence' was approved of and encouraged by the Kremlin and the CCP, but it did not receive any material support from either the Soviet Union or China.[41]

The joint effort by the Colonial Office, the Foreign Office, and MI5 to gather information on the CCP's role in the Malayan Communist movement had failed to produce any concrete results. In November 1949, the Joint Intelligence Committee (JIC) responsible for the Far Eastern area suggested that the CCP would naturally encourage the Malayan Communists' campaign against the colonial authorities and would supply the MCP with small quantities of arms via Thailand or by sea. But this conclusion was largely speculative without clear evidence. As far as British officials were concerned Beijing was capable of supplying the MCP with sufficient aid, and they would work out their counter-insurgency campaign on that assumption. As late as March 1950, the JIC were still unable to produce any actual evidence to suggest that Beijing had supplied material aid to the MCP.[42]

Anthony Short, in his study *The Communist Insurrection in Malaya, 1948 to 1960*, has concluded that the lack of support from Beijing was one important reason why the MCP's campaign against the colonial authorities had failed. He wrote: 'China, in the form of the People's Republic provided little more than fitful encouragement for the insurrection'.[43] It seemed that the MCP's struggle against imperialism and colonialism in Malaya was not an important concern for revolutionary China.

Beijing's attitude can be justified by the Maoist dictum that revolutions cannot be exported; Mao had maintained that under the general guidance of Marxism-Leninism the peoples of every country had to find their own path to liberation. Moreover, in the formative years of the People's Republic, the revolutionaries in Beijing had other more urgent problems – such as the consolidation of their rule and the rehabilitation of the country's economy – to attend to. These problems were exacerbated after China had become involved in the Korean conflict. The revolutionary leaders thus could hardly afford to provide substantial aid to the MCP even if they had wanted to.

HONG KONG IN ANGLO-CHINESE RELATIONS

Britain's Position in Hong Kong in 1949

Hong Kong used to be referred to as the Berlin of the East, by British
officials and politicians. The British Foreign Secretary Ernest Bevin had
in fact taken this line in a general discussion about the situation in Southeast
Asia and the Far East during a meeting with Dean Acheson in September
1949.[44] There was no doubt that Hong Kong was an important political
symbol; if the colony had fallen into the hands of a communist regime,
it would have been shattering to the morale of British administrations in
other parts of the Far East. The determination of policy-makers in London
to defend their country's position in Hong Kong was not, however, based
simply on political and strategic reasoning.

As a crown colony right on the doorstep of China, Hong Kong was a
valuable trade centre in the Far East for Britain. For British officials, the
colony had been turned from a barren rock into one of the most important
and thriving ports and markets of the world because of British enterprise.
Post-war Hong Kong's value to Britain, in the eyes of Colonial Office
officials, was more than just a stable trade centre serving British trade
interest at a time of great turmoil in the Far East, it was also an operating
base for British businessmen to prevent Japan from acquiring a dominant
position in the commerce of the Far East in the future. According to the
Colonial Office's estimate in 1949, the total amount of British capital
invested in the colony was about 156 million pounds; British commercial
and shipping interests there were important to Britain's economy. The loss
of all the British capital, and the possibility of trade which would disappear
if Britain lost the colony would, in the Colonial Office's words, be 'a
serious blow to our economy'.[45]

Following the Amethyst incident in April 1949, the British government
decided to reinforce the garrison in Hong Kong.[46] In June the Defence
Minister, A. V. Alexander, paid a four-day personal visit to Hong Kong
to review the position of its defence. To improve military coordination
in the Far East, London also appointed a Commander-in-Chief for the
armed forces of Hong Kong who was responsible to the British Defence
Co-ordination Committee through the Commander-in-Chief in the Far
East.[47]

Nevertheless, British policy-makers were well aware that even if they
were prepared to use force to defend Hong Kong, to maintain the colony
as a trading centre under British rule would be impossible without China's
acquiescence. The aim therefore was 'to find a basis on which a communist

government of China would acquiesce in our remaining in Hong Kong'. British decision-makers felt that if Britain's possession of the colony were to be made as a matter of prestige, then China might find it necessary to force the British government to withdraw. Yet they had to make a stand in Hong Kong for economic, political and strategic reasons which required practical evidence of their determination to defend Hong Kong. A demonstration of Britain's determination to defend the colony was necessary partly because it might deter a direct attack on Hong Kong by communist forces, and partly to rally the local community to the British side. Britain's position in the colony was not the only consideration policy-makers had in mind: the maintenance of Britain's position in the colony would demonstrate its determination against 'communist encroachment' elsewhere in Asia.[48]

Thus, on the eve of the communist victory in China Britain's position *vis-à-vis* Hong Kong was somewhat paradoxical. On the one hand, it sought to remain there to protect British commercial interest and to check communist expansion in the Far East. On the other hand, it could only remain there on the sufferance of the Chinese government. In a Cabinet discussion in August, the British government decided not to 'discuss the future of Hong Kong with a central Chinese government unless that government were friendly, democratic, stable and in control of a unified China'. Later the word 'democratic' was omitted.[49] For the time being, London decided to maintain Britain's position in Hong Kong as far as possible for economic, political and strategic reasons.[50]

The Chinese Communists' Attitude towards Hong Kong

Before the Chinese Communists took power, Hong Kong had been a useful base for them from which to organize their activities in China. As long as they did not interfere with local affairs, they had the protection of the British authorities against Kuomintang repression. From the end of the war to early 1949 communist propaganda against the British authorities in Hong Kong was remarkably restrained. The Chinese Communists' main objective was, as Hong Kong historian Steve Tsang noted, 'the winning of the civil war in China, not the subversion of Hong Kong'.[51] In mid-1949 after the Hong Kong government had raided several leading communist officials' homes and imposed restrictions on communist activities, the communist criticism of the colonial authorities was still 'measured and unprovocative', according to the then Colonial Secretary of Hong Kong. A secret directive dated 21 June 1951, nine months after the communists had seized power in China, urged local communist cadres in charge of trade union affairs to be careful about their activities, and they were instructed to impress on the colonial government that they were not subversive.[52]

In November 1948, a leading communist representative in Hong Kong assured the British government that a future communist regime in China would not cause any trouble in Hong Kong. The *de facto* chief representative of the Chinese Communists, the head of the local branch of the New China News Agency, Qiao Mu (who became better known later as Qiao Guanhua, China's Foreign Minister) approached Reuter's correspondent in Hong Kong, H. C. Bough, to relay this message. Bough was told that the Chinese Communists were willing to have perfectly normal relations with the British government, and they had no intention of taking Hong Kong by force. Qiao suggested that the status of Hong Kong was only a minor diplomatic issue and paid high tribute to Britain's policy of neutrality in the Chinese civil war. He also said that the communists would understand if the Hong Kong government granted refuge to Kuomintang leaders in the colony in future.[53]

Qiao's initiative in reassuring the British authorities on the Chinese Communist Party's policy towards Hong Kong was obviously a considered move. As Peng Zhen, a member of the Politburo of the Party explained in 1951, 'to take Hong Kong now would not only bring unnecessary technical difficulty in the enforcement of our international policy, but also increase our burden'. Allowing Hong Kong to preserve the *status quo* would also be of advantage to China's economic reconstruction programme. Peng therefore maintained that it was 'unwise for us to deal with the problem of Hong Kong rashly and without preparation'.[54]

The treatment of Chinese nationals in British territories, and the British authorities' attitude towards Kuomintang organizations in Hong Kong, were in fact brought up by the Beijing government during the Anglo-Chinese negotiations on the establishment of diplomatic relations.[55] The Chinese government also issued an official protest in May 1950 when the Hong Kong government introduced new immigration legislation to restrict Chinese citizens from entering Hong Kong; the Chinese government announced that it regarded the Hong Kong authorities' new measures as an 'unreasonable and unfriendly act'. After 1951 pro-Beijing groups in Hong Kong increased the tempo of their activities and became more aggressive, but their criticism of the colonial authorities were confined to specific acts of the government rather than general attack on colonial rule. None of these issues created any direct problems in Anglo-Chinese diplomatic relations.[56]

The CNAC and CATC Affair

The most important issue arising out of Hong Kong which became a critical problem in the Anglo-Chinese diplomatic negotiations involved some seventy civil aircraft based in the colony which belonged to two Chinese organizations. These two, the China National Aviation Corporation (CNAC) and the Central Air Transport Corporation (CATC) were former agencies of the Kuomintang government. While CNAC was a company based in Hong Kong incorporated under Chinese law, the Kuomintang government held eighty per cent of its shares, and Pan-American Airways held the remaining twenty per cent. The CATC was an official agency directly under the control of the Kuomintang government.

In 1949 eight civil aircraft that CNAC and CATC had purchased under American lend-lease were based in Hong Kong. In November, just one month after the establishment of the People's Republic, the managing directors of CATC and CNAC flew to Beijing with eleven aircraft. This set off a round of claims and counter claims over the ownership of the remaining seventy aircraft which involved not only the Communist and Kuomintang governments, but also the US government. The whole issue became more complicated after London accorded diplomatic recognition to the communist government in early January 1950: the British government were caught in the middle, facing diplomatic pressure from both sides.[57]

After the defection of their managing directors, four thousand employees of CATC and CNAC promptly claimed that the remaining aircraft were the property of the People's Republic. The government in Beijing immediately announced that these aircraft in Hong Kong were their national property and maintained that the British government were responsible for them. The aircraft were detained in Hong Kong when both the pro-Kuomintang boards of the organization, and the employees obtained injunctions from the courts to prevent the other side from removing them.[58]

On 1 December, the US government approached the British Embassy in Washington to express their concern about the planes and to inquire whether the Hong Kong authorities could prevent them from 'falling into the hands of the communists'. Shortly afterwards, the Kuomintang government sold all the assets of CNAC and CATC to General Claire Chennault, a American war hero associated with the China lobby, and his business partner Whiting Willauer. Chennault and Willauer in turn sold their interests under this contract to an American company called Civil Air Transport (CAT) in which they had a controlling interest.

With the support of the US government, CAT pressed the Hong Kong and British governments to influence court proceedings and to take executive action in its favour. Even though the US government had not formally associated themselves with these demands, during an interview with the Hong Kong Governor on 4 January, in the presence of the US Consul-General, CAT's representative General Donovan threatened that the US would withdraw Marshall Aid if the Hong Kong government refused to take action to hand over the aircraft to the company.[59]

In the event, the Chief Justice of Hong Kong ruled that the planes were property belonging to the Chinese central government, and removed the injunctions on them. Washington, however, did not want to see the aircraft and other assets of CNAC and CATC fall into the hands of the Chinese Communists. The State Department categorically warned the British Ambassador that if the British government failed to keep the aircraft in the colony, the continuation of Marshall Aid and the Military Assistance Programme might be seriously endangered. Reporting to London the British Ambassador added that a decision favourable to the Beijing government would have a serious effect not only on Anglo-American relations, but also on the personal position of the US Secretary because of internal politics in the US.[60]

The dilemma for the British government was that apart from the fact that claims to the ownership of the aircraft had become a question for the courts, a decision in favour of CAT might affect the British position in Hong Kong, and Britain's relations with China. As a joint Cabinet paper of the Foreign and Colonial Offices put it: 'The strength of our position in Hong Kong depends largely on our not becoming involved in Chinese political issues, the maintenance of an impartial administration and on insisting that the rule of law must prevail'. British officials feared that the Chinese government might be provoked 'to organize strikes, disturbance and sabotage' or to impose an economic embargo on the colony. Then there was the question of Anglo-Chinese diplomatic relations to consider. The Chinese government had made the ownership of the aircraft a major issue in the Anglo-Chinese talks on diplomatic relations. The officials therefore warned that any executive action by the British government which could be seen as partial in favour of the US government 'might stultify the whole of our policy towards China'.[61]

On the one hand, British policy-makers did not want to be seen to be interfering with the decisions of the courts, but on the other hand American pressure proved to be too strong for them to resist. Legal officers were asked to examine what statutory power the Hong Kong Governor could use to keep the planes in the colony. When they failed to come up with a satisfactory answer, the Governor of Hong Kong was instructed 'to hold up the aircraft by any means in his power which did not involve the formal use of statutory powers'. The Attorney General, Hartley Shawcross, then proposed that London should obtain an Order-in-Council which 'would not only provide for the detention of the aircraft, pending an adjudication as to the title to them, but would set up machinery for the trial of this issue'. This advice was accepted by the Cabinet on 24 April 1950 and an Order-in-Council to keep the aircraft in the colony was made on 10 May.[62]

The Cabinet's decision to obtain this Order-in-Council was obviously made under political pressure from the US government. To the newly appointed Minister of State, Kenneth Younger the issue was relatively minor, but he noted in his diary that it had raised the question of the British government's capacity to resist undue pressure from the US. He also wrote: 'In addition this particular matter highlights the fact that we and the Americans are running two inconsistent policies towards the Far East'.[63] Again, the British government was not able to resist American pressure over this issue. It is relevant to note that the Governor of Hong Kong Sir Alexander Grantham, was unhappy about London's intervention over the CNAC and CATC affair. In his memoirs he wrote: 'The British have always been realistic, but if they do a thing of which they have reason to be ashamed, they like to wrap it up in a legal covering'.[64]

Following the announcement that an Order-in-Council had been made to detain the aircraft in Hong Kong, the Chinese government issued an official protest. Their statement said that the British government's action was an unfriendly act towards the People's Republic of China. The CNAC and CATC affair probably had a greater impact on Anglo-Chinese diplomatic relations than Younger could have realized. The Order-in-Council was also particularly ill-timed, for on 8 May the Chinese government had just delivered a note asking the British government to further clarify their position over Chinese representation in the UN and the Chinese government's property rights in Hong Kong. This affair was probably not a decisive factor in the Anglo-Chinese diplomatic talks in Beijing, but without doubt it had contributed to creating difficulties for the negotiations.[65]

The British government's action in keeping the aircraft in the colony and later the Privy Council's decision to hand over the planes to the Americans in 1952 were resented by the Chinese. But they did not make any attempt to incite trouble for the Hong Kong authorities over the CNAC and CATC affair. Throughout that affair Beijing's policy largely followed Qiao's promise. It was obvious that revolutionary China's attitude towards Hong Kong in the early 1950s was pragmatic. It observed standard proprieties in its behaviour towards the British colony in the immediate

post-revolutionary period and has done so ever since, with perhaps the
exception of a turbulent period during the Cultural Revolution. With
China's agreement Hong Kong will remain a crown colony until July
1997 when the 1898 Peking Convention, which gave Britain a ninety-nine
year lease on that large part of the colony known as the New Territories,
expires.[66]

CONCLUSIONS

Britain's China policy was severely tested by events in Malaya and Hong
Kong. The controversy surrounding the appointment of Chinese Communist consuls to Malaya demonstrated clearly that bureaucratic politics were
important in the formulation of Britain's China policy. Foreign Office
officials had to accept the exclusion of Chinese consuls in Malaya, even
though the colonial authorities later also complied with their wish to
grant transit facilities to Chinese diplomats pasing through Singapore.
The Colonial Office and Britain's colonial administrators in Southeast
Asia were able to affect the Cabinet's decision in their favour, which in
effect was a denial of Beijing's diplomatic right, partly because they had
powerful allies in Whitehall in the form of the Ministry of Defence and
senior military advisers to the government. But a crucial factor in this case
was the fact that for British political leaders the defence of Malaya was far
more important than an uncertain improvement in Anglo-Chinese relations.
In short, policy-makers accorded priority to an acute immediate problem
in Malaya rather than to a less urgent one concerning the establishment of
diplomatic relations with China.

Malaya and Hong Kong were important issues in Anglo-Chinese relations. The People's Republic's severe criticism of the colonial authorities'
treatment of Chinese nationals and the British government's handling of
the CNAC and CATC affair were certainly not conducive to better
Anglo-Chinese relations. The treatment of Chinese nationals and the
detention of aircraft in Hong Kong were presented by the Chinese as
problems which had to be resolved before diplomatic relations between
Britain and China could be established. In the case of the CNAC and
CATC affair, once again, the role of US in influencing Britain's policies
towards the Beijing government was evident. The decision to deny the
People's Republic the aircraft was clearly a political decision made under
strong American pressure.

By 1954 a more favourable international atmosphere, plus the fact that
revolutionary China had consolidated its political position and needed

Western trade to industrialise, contributed more to the improvement in Anglo-Chinese relations than a settlement of the Malayan and the Hong Kong problems. Malaya and Singapore ceased to be a direct problem in Anglo-Chinese relations when they attained independence. As far as Hong Kong was concerned, when in 1971 China and Britain established ambassadorial diplomatic relations, the questions discussed were the China seat at the UN and Taiwan, rather than the political future of the colony.

Throughout the Emergency in Malaya, the CCP did not give any substantial material support to the MCP. During the early 1950s China's official statements on Malaya were mainly directed at the treatment of Chinese nationals rather than at supporting the revolutionary movement. In Hong Kong, the People's Government also avoided direct involvement in local political activities, allowing the colony's status quo to continue undisturbed. The Beijing government's attitude and conduct towards British colonial territories in Southeast Asia seemed to indicate that in the formative years of the People's Republic, the Chinese political leaders were more pragmatic than revolutionary.

Conclusion

Britain's policy towards the People's Republic of China, and the response of the newly established revolutionary regime to that policy as described and discussed in this book has raised a number of important issues. This study has attempted first, to identify the main features of Britain's China policy between 1949 and 1954; second, to bring out the implications of Britain's China policy for the theoretical study of foreign policy; and third, to examine the attitude of revolutionary China towards the existing society of states.

So far as the first task is concerned this study has not provided a totally new interpretation of the nature of Anglo-Chinese relations. Nonetheless, the way in which the British policy-makers formulated and implemented their China policy has been explained in much greater detail than in any previous studies on this subject, illuminating the degree of indecisiveness exhibited in the process. In addition, the work has also revealed several hidden episodes in Anglo-Chinese relations such as Esler Dening's abortive secret mission to China, and the way in which the appointment of Chinese Communist consuls in Malaya threatened a rupture in Anglo-Chinese relations.[1] At a theoretical level, this study has highlighted the importance of policy implementation in foreign policy decision-making, an area where foreign policy theories have not been developed adequately.

Another interesting issue which has been raised by this book concerns China's role as a revolutionary power. The response of the Beijing government to Britain's act of recognition, and its subsequent attempts to establish diplomatic relations, suggests that although the People's Republic was a revolutionary communist state it was not out to challenge the conventional rules of international relations in any fundamental way. Revolutionary China in its formative years exemplified a state which both sought to revise the basis of established international order and to become a member of the existing international society. Above all, China's conduct was governed by the determination to confirm without any reservations its rightful international status – hardly a revolutionary goal.

Britain's China Policy, 1949–1954

As suggested in Part I, Anglo-Chinese relations were not a priority in post-war British foreign policy. In fact many studies of Britain's immediate

192

post-war foreign policy have largely ignored the China question. Victor Rothwell's recent book, *Britain and the Cold War, 1941–47*, does not devote one single chapter to the Far Eastern problem, let alone to China. This study has revealed that towards the end of 1948 developments in China began to attract the attention of British policy-makers. The setting up of the China and South-East Asia Committee chaired by the Prime Minister himself was a good indication of the importance British policy-makers attached to the China question. Even though China was relatively less important than other foreign policy issues such as the Anglo-American alliance, the security of Western Europe, the Soviet threat, or the unity of the Commonwealth, it was clearly not discarded as insignificant. The reason, as argued in Part I was that the communization of China would not only seriously affect Britain's interests in China and Southeast Asia; it would also have far-reaching implications for British foreign policy in other areas of the world. The formulation of the policy of 'keeping a foot in the door' in China illustrated British policy-makers' concern for their country's direct interests in the Far East, but the lengthy consultation process with their allies over the recognition of the Beijing government indicated their awareness that developments in China were closely interwoven with wider international politics.

In 1949 British policy-makers were convinced that the Chinese Communists were orthodox Marxists, and therefore in the same ideological camp as the Soviet Union. The policy of 'keeping a foot in the door' was based partly on the calculation that by keeping the door of China open to the West, the new government in Beijing would not be driven to the arms of the Soviet Union. In essence, however, Britain's policy derived primarily from pragmatic calculations of direct British interests and from the assumption that China would act on a corresponding basis.

The fact that British policy-makers had expected the People's Republic to observe conventional diplomatic practice and establish diplomatic relations with Britain immediately after it had been recognized suggests that they had not fully appreciated the aspirations of China's new political masters who were not solely Marxist revolutionaries, but ardent nationalists as well. Britain's policy towards Beijing in the early 1950s was a response to a change of government in China, but it neglected the intertwined revolutionary and nationalistic dimension of that change.

On 6 January 1950, when the British government accorded recognition to the new Chinese government, Sir Hersch Lauterpacht wrote to *The Times* summarizing the legal position that since the communists had effective control of China, *de jure* recognition of the new government was justified in international law. Lauterpacht's article was in fact written

Conclusion

at the Foreign Office's request.[2] Despite the fact that Britain was not able to establish official diplomatic relations with the Beijing government, British policy-makers' attitude to the legal aspect of their recognition of the People's Republic remained unchanged. The revision of Britain's China policy in this period was a result of international factors and the new Chinese government's attitude; it was not a repudiation of the legal position.

Another feature of Britain's China policy in the period covered by this book was the extent to which the British government attempted to retain relations with Beijing despite bilateral differences. Between January 1950, after Britain had accorded recognition, and September 1954, when the two governments formally exchanged charge d'affaires, they did not have any official diplomatic relations. Yet, informal relations were maintained. Significantly, this situation continued despite the fact that Anglo-Chinese negotiations over the establishment of formal diplomatic relations had been suspended as early as June 1950, and certainly after the China had become involved militarily in Korea. Paradoxically, Britain and revolutionary China maintained unofficial diplomatic relations, while their armies were fighting on opposing sides in Korea, and even after the British government had joined in the UN's condemnation of the People's Republic as an aggressor and had imposed export sanctions against it.

London's policy towards Beijing has been regarded as a major source of conflict in post-war Anglo-American cooperation. H. G. Nicholas has suggested that Britain and the US had 'two quite different sets of attitudes, interests, and expectations' in Asia which 'surfaced in contradiction of policies'. In a study of Anglo-American defence relations, John Baylis also suggested that the different perspectives of the two countries over recognition of Beijing, Chinese military intervention in Korea, and the Taiwan question, created important difficulties in the Anglo-American alliance.[3]

There was no doubt that British policy-makers had attempted to pursue an independent policy in the Far East; they were prepared to go a long way in pursuit of their policy of 'keeping a foot in the door' in China in spite of American sensitivity. In January 1950, regardless of American misgivings, they recognized the new Chinese government. In March they tried to persuade other members of the UN Security Council to support the Beijing's claim to the China seat. In September, after the outbreak of the Korean War, Britain voted in favour of the Beijing government in the UN General Assembly. In October, without prior consultation with the Americans, the Foreign Office tried to send a special envoy on a secret mission to upgrade Anglo-Chinese talks on diplomatic relations.

In June 1954, the British government accepted China's offer to send a Charge D'Affaires to London even when Washington and Beijing were still deeply hostile to each other.

A closer look at Britain's policy towards revolutionary China, however, also reveals that while Britain's view and policy in the Far East differed from those of the US, they never seriously threatened Anglo-American cooperation before 1954. In late 1949, the US government objected to a 'premature' recognition of Beijing, but did not pressure the British government to reverse their decision. In fact, before the outbreak of the Korean War and the advent of McCarthyism, the Truman administration was not entirely unsympathetic to the British government's policy of 'keeping a foot in the door' in China. As mentioned above, the Korean War which turned the Cold War into a hot war was a vital turning point: it not only intensified the conflict between East and West, but also deepened the antipathy between China and the US.

From mid-1950 onwards the American position against the People's Republic hardened, and they began to put more pressure on Britain over the China question. In November 1950, Britain's Foreign Secretary Ernest Bevin dropped a proposal to set up a de-militarized zone in North Korea when the American Secretary of State, Dean Acheson, ruled out a diplomatic solution to the war at that juncture. In early 1951 the British government joined the US in condemning China as an aggressor in Korea even though they believed that such a step would close the door for negotiations between Beijing and the West.

Over several other major issues, the British government inevitably backed down when Anglo-American relations were threatened by their differences over Far Eastern policies. The British government succumbed to American pressure over the question of Chinese representation in the UN and the CNAC and CATC affair, even though the Chinese government had made it very clear that these two questions were obstacles to the establishment of Anglo-Chinese diplomatic relations. Britain and the US had important policy differences over China, but the priority which British policy-makers attached to the importance of the Anglo-American alliance was paramount and has been demonstrated by this study. At least until 1954, Britain and the US disagreed over how to deal with problems in the Far East; their disagreement did not seriously threaten Anglo-American cooperation. The reason was that in their pursuit of an independent policy, British policy-makers were careful not to risk their friendly relationship with the US.

The British policy-makers' desire to develop an independent China policy while maintaining a close relationship with the US was to prove unrealistic; riding two horses at the same time was simply not practical. Their ambivalent attitude towards China has to be seen in the context of post-war British foreign policy thinking as Britain tried to adjust to a post-imperial role while struggling to maintain its status as a major world power. The Attlee and Churchill governments shared the broad foriegn objectives of maintaining a close relationship with the US, a common front with the Commwealth and a committment to Western Europe. In pursuing these three objectives all at the same time, as Christopher Hill suggested, Britain became engaged in some kind of eternal juggling act.[4] Britain's China policy as covered by this study was a good example of a juggling act which did not quite work out when British policy-makers failed to build a common front among their allies – the US, the Commonwealth and Western Europe. Britain was caught in between those who were more sympathetic to the People's Republic of China, and those who saw revolutionary China as a threat to international security.

Policy-implementation and Decision-Making

As stated at the outset, this study is not an attempt to construct a new theory of foreign policy decision-making. By looking at the formulation and evolution of Britain's China policy from late 1948 to 1954, it has examined the relation between policy formulation and implementation in detail. The importance of the implementation stage in foreign policy decision-making has been acknowledged by standard works on foreign policy decision-making such as G. T. Allison's *Essence of Decisions* and R. C. Snyder *et al.*, *Foreign Policy Decision Making*, but the number of detailed studies of the role of policy-implementation in the overall decision-making process is still limited.[5]

Part I has demonstrated that the British government's policy of 'keeping a foot in the door' in China, and the decision to recognize the new Chinese government was a product of both domestic and international factors. Britain's limited resources, the prevailing Cold War climate, policy-makers' suspicion of a Soviet expansionist design, the opinion of Britain's allies, the bureaucratic politics within Whitehall, Parliamentary party politics, the business lobby, and press opinion all played a part in policy-formulation.

The implementation of this policy ran into difficulty from the beginning when the People's Republic refused to establish diplomatic relations unless London agreed to certain terms. The first obstacle was Britain's policy of abstention over Chinese representation in the UN. British policy-makers were prepared to meet Beijing's demand for support in the UN, but the outbreak of the Korean War and subsequently China's military involvement in Korea presented new insuperable problems. As a result of the war Sino-American estrangement deepened, and the conflict between the East and West turned into open military confrontation. The hardening of American hostility against the Beijing regime and the changes in the international situation forced British policy-makers to revise their policy towards revolutionary China.

The difficulties that British policy-makers encountered in China when implementing their policy towards the People's Republic also contributed to the changes in British thinking on the China question. As argued in Part II, the Beijing government's adamant attitude, their uncompromising stance regarding Chinese representation in the UN, and the continued deterioration of the British business position in China were factors that London had not anticipated when Britain's China policy was being formulated at the end of 1948 and in 1949. As a result of these problems and the changes in the international environment, which occurred while a policy of 'keeping a foot in the door' in China was being implemented, the policy was reformulated to become 'keeping a toe in the door' by the British government.

The formulation and implementation of Britain's China policy between 1949 and 1954 was thus a continuing interrelated process rather than two distinctive and separate stages of policy decision-making and then its technical execution. This study confirms Michael Clarke's conclusion that decision-making in foreign policy is not a linear process.[6] The reformulation of Britain's policy towards China as analyzed in Part II, and the evolution of British policy-makers' attitudes towards the policy issues discussed in Part III, demonstrate that both the domestic context and the international environment in which policy implementation operate have a significant influence on policy decisions.

This study does not pretend to have adequately explored the problems concerning the relationship between policy-implementation and decision-making. But by tracing the policy changes arising from a single policy problem over a period of six years, it has highlighted how changing circumstances during the policy-implementation stage were important determinants of foreign policy decision-making. A better understanding of policy-implementation in the foreign policy decision-making process would require more detailed analysis on questions such as the interaction between the domestic and external environment during the process of policy implementation. Nonetheless, this book has provided a case study of the complex interaction between the formal (the office holders in the form of the Foreign Office) and informal (pressure groups in the form of the business lobby) processes of foreign policy-making both at the centre of decision-making in London, and in the field in China. In its turn the case study has been illuminated by its examination of the influence of bureaucratic politics and pressure group politics in Britain's China policy. Finally, the impact of the external environment was clearly demonstrated as British policy-makers kept revising their stances on several important issues in their relations with China in response to the international changes brought about by the Korean conflict.

Revolutionary China and International Society

A related question this study has sought to answer is whether or not the People's Republic in its formative years was revolutionary in the conduct of its foreign relations. One way of examining this problem is to use Hedley Bull's concepts of international system and international society. Bull has himself suggested in *The Anarchical Society* that the Marxist model provides a challenge to the existing states system. He also used China as an example of Marxist revolutionism which 'asserted the priority of just change over the preservation of the existing order'.[7]

Whether the People's Republic in its formative years attempted to challenge the fundamental rules and institutions of the existing society of states is thus a crucial question. Martin Wight once stated that, 'A revolutionary power, in the sense of one that wishes to alter the foundations of international society, will assume that other governments do not represent their peoples, and will try to manipulate or take advantage of the potential stratification of loyalties within other countries'. He also suggested that 'the first impulse of a revolutionary power is to abolish diplomacy altogether, even to abolish foreign policy'.[8]

Beijing's refusal to establish diplomatic relations with London unless the British government complied with their demands seemed on the surface to suggest that revolutionary China had no intention of playing the game by the existing code of diplomatic practice. The guiding principle for Beijing's early external relations as formulated in March 1949 and later confirmed in 'the Common Programme of the Chinese People's Political Consultative Conference' was that the new Chinese government, 'shall examine the treaties and agreements between the Kuomintang and foreign governments, and shall recognize, abrogate, revise, or re-negotiate them according to their respective contents'.[9]

It was quite clear that revolutionary China was determined to make a fresh start in its relations with other countries, and that it did not accept all the rules of international relations, but the conditions which they insisted the British government should meet before the establishment of diplomatic relations would not have appeared so unreasonable if the international situation had been different. In essence, the Beijing government demanded that they should be recognized as the sole legal government representing China abroad and in international organizations, and that their rights over Chinese properties overseas should be respected. Any newly formed government would have expected corresponding treatment by other governments which had accorded it diplomatic recognition.

The state of Anglo-Chinese relations in that early 1950s suggests that the People's Republic did not seek to challenge the conventional rules or common institutions of international society in a fundamental way. Revolutionary China certainly did not abolish diplomacy or foreign policy as Trotsky had attempted to do in 1917. The Beijing government did not recognize the diplomatic status of British representatives whose government had not established diplomatic relations with China, but diplomats from other countries with official relations with China enjoyed full diplomatic privileges. In fact British diplomats in China were granted semi-diplomatic status throughout the period when officially they were there only in the capacity of British representatives for negotiations on the establishment of diplomatic relations. The new Chinese government also accepted that the UN had an important role to play in international affairs and clearly wanted to represent China in that organization. In the initial stage of the Anglo-Chinese talks on the establishment of diplomatic relations the most important obstacle was in fact the British government's unwillingness to give full support to the Beijing's claim in the UN. The Chinese government also maintained economic relations and quasi-diplomatic relations with the British government despite the fact that Britain had been a symbol of Western domination and the fact that it sided militarily with the US in the Korean conflict.

Equally significant was Beijing's attitude towards the Malayan Communist Party. British officials did not find any evidence that the Chinese government were providing substantial material support to the Malayan Communists. China's official statements on the situation in Malaya were confined mainly to condemning the British authorities over the treatment of Chinese nationals, rather than an open attack on colonial rule in British territories in Southeast Asia. Although the Chinese Communists gave encouragement to the Malayan Communists, they neither overtly sought to export their revolution to Malaya nor officially denounced British colonial rule at the government level. In fact, they have accepted the continuation of British colonial rule in Hong Kong which is to last up to 1997, when the 'unequal treaties' which leased a large part of the colony to Britain are to expire.

The emergence of a revolutionary Chinese state was a significant event in the twentieth century with a great impact on international relations. Mao and his followers had no doubt as to where China would stand between the 'socialist' and 'capitalist' camps, while they were also determined to change the power relationship between China and former colonial countries. Moreover the People's Republic would provide a new model of revolution for many Afro-Asian peoples. But in 1949 the immediate task of China's revolutionary leaders was the reconstruction of China's economy and the implementation of their socialist programme at home. The new leadership also had to consolidate its power and authority. China had become embroiled in the Korean conflict, because the new Chinese leadership perceived a threat to their country's security. President Truman's decision to send the Seventh Fleet to the Taiwan Strait following the outbreak of war in Korea not only disrupted the Chinese Communist leaders' plan to occupy Taiwan, the last stronghold of their Kuomintang rival, but also marked America's participation in an unfinished civil war. Thus during the formative years of the People's Republic, revolutionary China's primary concern was with its survival and consolidation as a state, giving rise to a corresponding aspiration to register and confirm China's 'rightful' place in the world.

Part I of this study has suggested that Beijing's foreign policies were a result of an interplay of a revolutionary ideology, a strong sense of nationalism, and pragmatism. For the Chinese Communists, the 1949 revolution was not only a communist revolution to liberate the suppressed classes in China, but also a nationalist one to liberate China from Western domination, and so to establish China's position in the world.

This work has not solved the 'intrinsic logical conundrum', which as David Armstrong has observed, 'bedeviled attempts to weigh the influence of ideology in the foreign policies of Communist states'.[10] The fact that the Chinese revolution in 1949 was both communist and nationalist makes any such attempt to weigh the revolutionary element in the China's foreign policy more than difficult. Adam Watson, the co-editor with Hedley Bull of *The Expansion of International Society*, has argued that while Bull's distinction between international system and international society makes an important contribution to the theory of international relations, the complex situations of the 'real world' raise important problems about Bull's concepts. One such question raised by Watson was whether or not the People's Republic was a member of international society before it was admitted to the UN.[11] The interactions between China and Britain between 1949 and 1954 suggests that although the People's Republic was a revolutionary communist state which intended to revise the basis of its relationship with other states, it also wanted to be recognized in the established international society. The Chinese revolutionary leaders had attempted to repudiate those international regulations and treaties which they believed to be unjust and tried to eliminate the economic and political influences of a former imperial power in their country; but the Anglo-Chinese talks on diplomatic relations were centred upon Beijing's dissatisfaction at Britain's failure to recognize the full rights of the People's Government on behalf of China, rather than demands for a completely new set of international diplomatic conventions.

This work does not seek a full answer to whether or not the People's Republic in its infancy was truly revolutionary in international terms, but it has analyzed some of the problems involved. It concludes that in 1949 the Chinese Communists were seeking not only to establish a new revolutionary state, but also to be recognized as the legitimate rulers of their country and to secure a dignified position for the Chinese nation in the world. In that exercise, they were seeking entry to and not a repudiation of international society. That priority came into conflict with Britain's China policy which could not be detached from the paramount consideration of its relationship with the US. While Britain was prepared to accept revolutionary China into the established international society, its perceived interests in the special relationship with the US put the policy of recognition and dialogue under constant strain. But the number of contacts which remained between the two governments, even during the Korean War, suggests that the Peoples' Republic was from the beginning willing to be a member of 'international society', even if its entry into that society was to take rather longer.

Appendixes

APPENDIX 1   *The PRC's first appointments of diplomats abroad, 1949–54*

Country	Date	Rank
USSR	31.11.1949	Ambassador
Mongolia	10.7.1950	Ambassador
Poland	20.7.1950	Ambassador
N. Korea	13.8.1950	Ambassador
Indonesia	14.8.1950	Ambassador
Hungary	24.8.1950	Ambassador
Burma	5.9.1950	Ambassador
Bulgaria	8.9.1950	Ambassador
Czechoslovakia	13.9.1950	Ambassador
India	18.9.1950	Ambassador
Sweden	19.9.1950	Ambassador
E. Germany	12.10.1950	Ambassador
Denmark	8.11.1950	Minister
Switzerland	8.12.1950	Minister
Finland	31.3.1951	Minister
Pakistan	10.9.1951	Ambassador
UK	23.9.1954	Charge d'Affaires

SOURCE: *People's Handbook* (Beijing: Daigung Baoshe, 1955).

APPENDIX 3   *Value of Britain's Trade with China, 1946–55 (pounds ,000)*

Year	Import	Re-export	Export	Total
1946	2 697	29	7 827	10 553
1947	7 172	47	12 777	19 996
1948	8 201	67	8 650	16 918
1949	3 622	148	2 257	6 027
1950	10 324	4	3 587	13 915
1951	7 670	20	2 677	10 367
1952	3 011	40	4 541	7 592
1953	10 222	105	6 161	16 488
1954	8 959	93	6 826	15 878
1955	12 302	78	7 868	20 248

SOURCE: *The Trade of the U.K.* (London: HMSO).

APPENDIX 2   *China's major trade partners: 1950*
(in percentage share of total trade)

Country	Percentage
USSR	23.36
USA	23.00
Hong Kong	14.48
UK	7.10
Malaya	5.77
Japan	4.56
India	2.84
Holland	2.10
W. Germany	1.88
Pakistan	1.51
Other countries	13.40
TOTAL	100.00

SOURCE: *People's China*, April 1951.

Notes

Introduction

1. C. Hill and M. Light, 'Foreign Policy Analysis' in M. Light and A. J. R. Groom (eds), *International Relations, A Handbook of Current Theory* (London: Frances Pinter, 1985) p. 157. Hill and Light have provided a brief and useful survey of the current theories of foreign policy analysis, and their place in the study of international relations.

2. A. Shlaim, P. Jones and K. Sainsbury, *British Foreign Secretaries* (Newton Abbot: David and Charles, 1977) p. 14.

3. In addition to Light and Hill, *op. cit.*, two useful discussions of the different theoretical perspectives in the study of foreign policy decision-making are: J. E. Dougherty and R. L. Pfaltzgraff, Jr, *Contending Theories of International Relations: A comprehensive survey* (New York: Harper & Row, 1981), chapter 11, pp. 468–510; and B. P. White, 'Decision-making analysis' in T. Taylor (ed.), *Approaches and Theory in International Relations* (London: Longman, 1978) pp. 141–164.

4. For factors influencing foreign policy decision-making see for example, L. P. Bloomfield, *The Foreign Policy Process: A Modern Primer* (Englewood Cliffs, NJ: Prentice Hall, 1982); M. Clarke and B. White, *An Introduction to Foreign Policy Analysis: The Foreign Policy System* (Ormskirk and Northridge: G.W. & A. Hesketh, 1981); M. A. East, S. A. Salmore, C. F. Hermann, *Why Nations Act: Theoretical Perspectives for Comparative Foreign Policy Studies* (London: Sage, 1978); L. Jensen, *Explaining Foreign Policy* (Englewood Cliffs, NJ: Prentice Hall, 1982). A strong case for including policy implementation as a central part of foreign policy decision making has been made in M. Clarke, 'Foreign policy implementation: problems and approaches', *British Journal of International Studies*, Vol. 5, No. 2, 1979, pp. 112–128, and S. Smith and M. Clarke (eds), *Foreign Policy Implementation* (London: Allen & Unwin, 1985).

5. P. Calvert, *Revolution and International Politics* (London: Frances Pinter, 1984) p. 152.

6. See Martin Wight, *Power Politics* (Harmondsworth: Pelican Books, 1986) pp. 117–119.

7. A brief discussion of the views that the PRC was blatantly militant and aggressive can be found in N. Maxwell, 'The Threat From China', *International Affairs* (January 1971).

8. H. Bull, *The Anarchical Society: A Study of Order in World Politics* (London: Macmillan, 1977) pp. 9–10 and p. 13.

1 Actors and Stage

1. P. K. C. Tyan, foreword to Shih-fun Lin's *British Policies in China 1895–1905* (Canton: Wing Hing Printing Press, 1936) p. v.
2. P. Lowe, *Great Britain the Origins of the Pacific War: A Study of British Policy in East Asia, 1937–41* (Oxford: Clarendon Press, 1977) pp. 1–2. For a contemporary discussion of pre-war foreign economic domination of China see G. Clark, *Economic Rivalries in China* (New Haven: Yale University Press for the Carnegie Endowment for International Peace, 1932). The Department of Overseas Trade in London also published useful statistics.
3. Two studies which cover Britain's investments and economic influences in China prior to the outbreak of the 1937–45 Sino-Japanese War are: Chi-ming Hou, *Foreign Investment and Economic Development in China, 1840–1937* (Cambridge, Mass.: Harvard University Press, 1943); and E. M. Gull, *British Economic Interests in the Far East* (London: Oxford University Press, 1943). See also B. Dean, 'British Informal Empire: The case of China', *Journal of Commonwealth and Comparative Politics*, March 1976.
4. D. C. Watt, 'Britain and the Cold War in the Far East, 1945–58' in Yonosuke Nagai and Akira Iriye (eds), *The Origins of the Cold War in Asia* (New York: Columbia University Press; and Tokyo: University of Tokyo Press, 1977) p. 93.
5. R. Smith and J. Zametica, 'The Cold Warrior: Clement Attlee reconsidered, 1945–7', *International Affairs*, Spring (1985) pp. 237–252.
6. R. Smith and J. Zametica, *ibid.*, pp. 238–239.
7. Frank Roberts, 'Ernest Bevin as Foreign Secretary', in R. Ovendale (ed.), *The Foreign Policy of the British Labour Governments 1945–1951* (Leicester: Leicester University Press, 1984), p. 23. Roberts was Bevin's Private Secretary in the Foreign Office, 1947–49. Also see the chapter on Bevin in A. Shlaim, P. Jones and K. Sainsbury, *Foreign Secretaries* (Devon: Newton Abbot, 1977); and Kenneth Morgan, *Labour People: Leaders and Lieutenants, Hardie to Kinnock* (London: Methuen, 1987).
8. Quoted in A. Bullock, *Ernest Bevin: Foreign Secretary, 1945–1951* (London: Heinemann, 1983) pp. 3–4.
9. Diary entry 28 July 1945, *The Diaries of Sir Alexander Cadogan 1938–1945*, ed. by D. Dilks (London: Cassell, 1971) p. 776.
10. A. Adamthwaite 'Britain and the World, 1945–9: the view from the Foreign Office' *International Affairs*, Spring (1985), 224; A. Bullock, *op. cit.*, pp. 98–99, and F. Williams, *A Prime Minister Remembers* (London: Heinemann, 1961) p. 150; R. R. James, *Anthony Eden* (London: Weidenfeld & Nicolson, 1986) p. 319.
11. Sir Roderick Barclay. *Ernest Bevin and the Foreign Office 1932–1969* (published by the author, London, 1975), p. 83; Colin Crowe's letter to the writer 18 April 1986.

206 *Notes to pp. 11–16*

12. Dening's obituary in *The Times*, 31 January 1977; R. Barclay, *Ernest Bevin and Foreign Office 1932–1969*, *ibid.*, p. 83.; interviews and correspondence with Dening's former colleagues: letters from Ven. Michael Paton, 28 January 1986, Mr Andrew Franklin, 5 February 1986, Sir Colin Crowe, 18 April 1986, Mr Stanley Tomlinson, 22 April 1986, interviews with Mr Alec Adams, 28 June 1985, Sir Michael Wilford, and Sir Berkeley Gage, 9 July 1985.
13. For Dening's views on the PRC's foreign policy objectives see Dening to Strang 1 March 1951, FO371 93016 FZ1022/75G.
14. Younger, Diary 9 September 1951, a copy of the diaries in typescript is kept by Professor Geoffrey Warner at the Open University, UK.
15. Scott's obituary in *The Times*, 2 March 1982; letters from Sir Colin Crowe, and Mr Andrew Franklin; interviews with Mr Alex Adams, and Sir Berkeley Gage.
16. Minute by Rob Scott, 27 April 1951, FO371 93016 FZ1022/75G.
17. A. Eden, *The Memoirs of Sir Anthony Eden, Full Circle* (London: Cassell, 1960) p. 118.
18. Letter from Sir Denis Allen, 1 September 1986.
19. Interviews with Sir Michael Wilford, Mr Robin Edmonds and Mr Joe Ford.
20. See CAB134 FE(0)(51)33.
21. The proposal to set up the China and South East Asia Committee is in FO371 76013 F4286/10119/616; the records of meetings are in CAB134 669 and 670.
22. *Statistical Materials Presented during the Washington Negotiations 1945*, British Parliamentary Papers Cmd. 6707. See also R. Ovendale's introduction in R. Ovendale (ed.), *The Foreign Policy of the British Labour Governments, 1945–51* (Leicester: Leicester University Press, 1984) p. 3. A more detailed account of the economic problems of the Labour government is in A. Cairncross, *Years of Recovery: British Economic Policy, 1945–51* (London: Methuen, 1985).
23. Clement Attlee, *As it Happened* (London: Heinemann, 1954) pp. 150–151.
24. Cabinet paper 4 January 1948, CAB 129/23 CP(48)6; CAB 129/25CP(48) 72, 3 March 1948, the Cabinet paper's use of words is remarkably similar to Sir Halford Mackinder's famous dictum: 'Who rules East Europe commands the Heartland/Who rules the Heartland commands the World Island (Eurasia)/Who rules the World Island commands the World', H. Mackinder, *Democratic Ideals and Reality* (New York: Norton, 1962) p. 150; see also the Permanent Under Secretary Committee's British Policy Towards Soviet Communism, 28 July 1949 FO371 77622 N11007.
25. CAB 129/23 CP(48)6, 4 January 1948.
26. Minute by J. C. Sterndale-Bennett, 4 March 1945, FO371 46232 F1331/409/10.
27. Minute by Coulson, 6 March 1945; Minute by Hall-Patch, 10 March

1945; Minute by Victor Cavendish-Bentinck, 13 March 1945, FO371 46232 F1331/409/10.

28. A. Bullock, *Ernest Bevin: Foreign Secretary*, 1945–51, *op. cit.*

29. Memorandum on British foreign policy in the Far East prepared for the British Far East Representatives meeting in London by the Civil Planning Unit, FO371 54052 F6208/2129/G6.

30. Annual Report on China, 1946, 1 April 1947, FO371 63440 F4491/4491/10; see also A. Shai, *Britain and China, 1941–47: Imperial Momentum* (London: Macmillan, 1984 in association with St Antony's College, Oxford) pp. 134–135.

31. Memorandum by the Civil Planning Unit, 1946, *op. cit.*

32. Stock-taking memoranda by Esler Dening in early 1947, FO371 63549 F2612/2612/10; see also Shai, *op. cit.*, pp. 150–151.

33. FO371 63549 F2612/2612/10, *ibid.*

34. Board of Trade Minute 12 September 1946, BT60 83 C/42889; also see Shai, *ibid.*, p. 146.

35. H. O. Hooper to A. S. Gilbert, 8 September 1947, FO371 63308 F12378/37/10, BT60 83C/42889, also quoted in Shai, *ibid.*, pp. 151–152.

36. Ernest Bevin, 28 November 1945, HC Deb Vol. 416 Col 1306; see also E. Luard, *Britain and China* (London: Chattos & Windus, 1962) p. 64.

37. FO371 F399/34/10, FO371 F1546/159/10 quoted in C. Thorne, *Allies of A Kind: The United States, Britain, and the War against Japan, 1941–1945* (Oxford: Oxford University Press, 1978) p. 442.

38. Fuller discussions of the attitude of the British press towards the Chinese Communists in the mid forties can be found in Brian Porter, *Britain and the Rise of Communist China, A Study of British Attitudes 1945–54* (London: Oxford University Press) pp. 5–6; and E. Luard, *Britain and China, op. cit.*, p. 66.

39. Thorne, *Allies of a Kind, op. cit.*, Clark Kerr to Eden in early 1942, p. 184; Clark Kerr's reference to Molotov in FO371 F4114/3913/10; views of Hudson and Young in FO371 F2375, 1546 and 975/195/10, all quoted in Thorne p. 441.

40. The historian I. C. Y. Hsu, suggested that the thread of nationalistic-racial protest against foreign elements was a distinct theme of modern Chinese history. See his *The Rise of Modern China* (New York: Oxford University Press, 1990), p. 9.

41. The history of China during this period is well covered in J. Fairbank, E. Relschauer and A. Craig, *East Asia: The Modern Transformation* (Cambridge, Mass.: Harvard University Press, 1955). A specific study is W. L. Tung's *China and the Foreign Powers: The Impact of and Reaction to Unequal Treaties* (New York: Oceania, 1970).

42. L. Bianco, *Origins of the Chinese Revolution, 1915–1949* (Stanford: Stanford University Press, 1971) p. 59 and p. 87.

43. Two standard works on the Chinese Communist movement are: J.

Harrison, *The Long March to Power, A History of the Chinese Communist Party, 1921–72* (London: Macmillan, 1973); and B. Schwartz, *Chinese Communism and the Rise of Mao* (Cambridge, Mass.: Harvard University Press, 1951 and 1979).
44. Edgar Snow, *Red Star Over China* (Harmondsworth: Penguin, 1972) p. 161, p. 181.
45. Dick Wilson, *Chou: The Story of Zhou Enlai 1898–1976* (London: Hutchinson, 1984) p. 26; p. 61.
46. Quoted in B. Womack, *The Foundation of Mao Zedong's Political Thought, 1917–1935* (Honolulu: University of Hawaii Press, 1982) p. 28.
47. J. Harrison, *The Long March to Power, op. cit.*, p. 1.
48. Details of the CCP's Seventh National Congress can be found in *The Major Meetings of the CCP (Zhongguo Gongchandang Lici Zhongyao Huiyi)* (Vol. 1, Shanghai People's Publication, Shanghai, 1982) pp. 235–247.
49. The biographical analysis is compiled from *The Biographic Dictionary of Chinese Communism 1921–65*, by D. Klein and A. Clark (Cambridge, Mass.: Harvard University Press, 1971); and Union Research Institute's *Biography of Chinese Communists* (Hong Kong, 1965). The biographies of Dong Biwu and Lin Baiqu have been published in China: Hu Zhuanzhang and Ha Jianxiong, *A Biography of Dong Biwu (Dong Biwu Zhuanji)* (Hubei: Hubei People's Publication, 1985); and Writing Group on the Biography of Lin Baiqu, *A Biography of Lin Baiqu (Lin Baiqu Zhuan)* (Beijing: Hongqi Publication, 1986).
50. A useful discussion of the CCP's relations with the Soviet Union during the Second World War can be found in J. W. Garver, *Chinese-Soviet Relations, 1937–1945: The diplomacy of nationalism* (New York: Oxford University Press, 1988). For a Chinese perspective of the CCP's difficulties with the Soviet Union in the late 1940s see Yu Zhan and Zhang Guangyou, 'Whether Stalin had attempted to dissuade us from crossing the Yangtze River' [Guanyu Sidalin Zengfou Quanzu Wo Guo Zhangjiang De Tantao] in Pei Jianzhang *et al.* (eds), *New China's Diplomacy: Memoirs of China's Diplomats [Xin Zhongguo Waijiao Fengyun: Zhounguo Waijiaoguan Huiyilu]* (Beijing: Shijie Zhishi Chubanshe for the Foreign Ministry's Diplomatic History Office, 1990) pp. 15–21.
51. *Selected Works of Liu Shaoqi*, (Beijing: Foreign Languages Press, 1984), p. 424; first Chinese edition in 1981.
52. D. Wilson, *Chou: The Story of Zhou Enlai, 1898–1976, op. cit.*, pp. 298–299. Accounts of Zhou's influence and contribution to Chinese foreign policy from the Chinese perspective can be found in Part 3 of Lu Xingdou and Bai Yuntao, *Zhou Enlai and His Work [Zhou Enlai he Tade Shiye]* (Beijing: Zhonggong Dangshi Chubanshe, 1990) pp. 196–286.
53. R. C. Keith, *The Diplomacy of Zhou Enlai* (London: Macmillan, 1989) Chapter 2: Establishing the Foreign Ministry in the Cold

War, pp.33–58; D. Klein, 'The Management of Foreign Affairs in Communist China' in J. Lindbeck (ed.), *China: Management of a Revolutionary Society* (London: George and Allen, 1972); M. Yahuda, 'The Ministry of Foreign Affairs of the People's Republic of China', in Z. Steiner (ed.), *The Times Survey of Foreign Ministries of the World* (London: Times Books, 1982).

54.   D. Klein, 'The Management of Foreign Affairs in Communist China', in J. Linbeck (ed.), *China: Management of A Revolutionary Society, op. cit.* p. 308.

55.   Klein and Clark, *Biographical Dictionary of Chinese Communism 1921–65*, and Union Research Institute, *Biography of Chinese Communists, op. cit.*

56.   Zhou Gengsheng was author of a standard text on international law in Chinese, *International Law (Guo Ji Fa)*, the book was written in 1964, but it was published in 1976, five years after Zhou had died.

57.   See Wu's autobiography, *My Course, 1908–1949 [Wo de Lizheng]*, (Beijing: People's Liberation Army Publication, 1984).

58.   R. C. Keith, *The Diplomacy of Zhou Enlai, op. cit.*, p. 35.

59.   Alexander Eckstein, *China's Economic Revolution* (Cambridge: Cambridge University Press, 1977) p. 26.

60.   China Handbook Series: *Economy* (Beijing: Foreign Language Press, 1984) pp. 1–3.

61.   *Ibid.*, pp. 1–3, and pp. 34–35.

62.   Memorandum by the Chief of the Division of Chinese Affairs, John Carter Vincent, to the Acting Secretary of State Joseph Grew, 25 January 1945, *FRUS*, 1945, VII, p. 38; also Thorne, *Allies of a Kind, op. cit.*, p. 567; and Akira Iriye, *Across the Pacific: An Inner History of American-East Asian Relations, and Inner History of American-East Asian Relations* (New York: Harvest, 1967) pp. 240–243.

63.   Even though the Truman administration had became disillusioned and disenchanted with Chiang after General Marshall's mediation efforts failed in 1947 and had reduced its aid programme to the Kuomintang regime, it continued its support for the Kuomintang. See Tang Tsou, *America's Failure in China 1941–50*, Vol. 2 (Chicago: Chicago University Press, 1963) p. 475 and J. Gittings, *The World and China, 1922–1972* (London: Eyre Methuen, 1974) p. 137.

64.   Barbara W Tuchman, 'If Mao Had Come to Washington: An Essay in Alternative', *Foreign Affairs*, 51 (October 1972) 44–46.

65.   J. Reardon-Anderson, *Yenan and the Great Powers, the Origins of Communist Foreign Policy 1944–46* (New York: Columbia University Press, 1980) pp. 3–4, p. 161.

66.   For a general discussion of the sources of the PRC's foreign policy see the Introduction in M. Yahuda, *China's Role in World Affairs* (London: Croom Helm, 1978); Another relevant study is Wang Gung-wu, *China and the World since 1949: The Impact of Independence, Modernity and Revolution* (London: Macmillan, 1977).

67. For an official account of the second plenary session of the CCP's 7th Central Committee see *The CCP's Major Meetings (Zhongguo Gongchandang Lici Zhongyao Huiyi)* (1982) pp. 265–273. Other accounts of the meeting based on similar sources can be found in the numerous official histories of the CCP which have been published since the early 1980s such as: *Lectures on the History of the CCP (Zhongguo Gongchandang Lishi Jiangyi)* (Shandong People's Publication, 1980) pp. 405–410; *Lectures on An Outline History of the CCP (Zhongguo Gongchandang Jianshi Jiangyi)*, Vol. 1 (Guangdong People's Publication, 1981) pp. 257–260. The Common Programme was adopted by the Conference on 29 September 1949 in Beijing, 'The Common Program of the Chinese People's Political Consultative Conference', *The Important Documents of the First Plenary Session of the Chinese People's Political Consultative Conference* (Peking: Foreign Languages Press, 1949).

68. 'Report to the Second Plenary Session of Seventh Central Committee of the Communist Party of China, 5th March 1949', *Selected Work of Mao Tse-Tung*, Vol. IV (Beijing: Foreign Language Press, 1961) pp. 370–371.

69. R. C. Keith, *The Diplomacy of Zhou Enlai, op. cit.*, pp. 31–32; Zheng Weizhi, 'Independence is the Basic Canon', *Beijing Review* (7 January 1985) p. 16; See also Xue Mouhong and Pei Jianzhang, *Diplomacy of Contemporary China* (Hong Kong: New Horizon Press, 1990) p. 5. Compiled by Foreign Ministry officials, the original Chinese version of this book, *Dangdai Zhongguo Waijiao*, was first published by the China Social Science Academy in 1988.

70. 'Our foreign policy objective and responsibility', records of a talk given by Zhou Enlai to a group of Chinese diplomats, *The Selected Work of Zhou Enlai (Zhou Enlai Xuanji)* Vol. 2 (Beijing: People's Publication, 1984) pp. 85–86.

71. Zhou, *ibid.*, p. 87.

72. *Selected Work of Mao*, Vol. 4 (Beijing: Foreign Languages Press, 1961) p. 415.

73. Wu Xiuquan, a member of the PRC delegation to Moscow, suggested in his autobiography that Stalin was suspicious that the PRC was not firmly committed to the Soviet bloc. Wu Xiuquan, *Eight Years in the Foreign Ministry (Zai Waijiaobu Banian de Jingli)* (Beijing: World Culture Publication, 1983) p. 5; (English Edition: Beijing: New World Press, 1985) p. 10.

2 The Decision of Recognition

1. J. Melby, *The Mandate of Heaven* (Toronto: University of Toronto Press, 1968) p. 271. For an account of the Chinese civil war see Suzanne Pepper, *Civil War in China* (Berkeley: University of California Press,

1978).
2. Cabinet paper 9 December 1948, CP(48)299, Cab 129/31.
3. *Ibid.*
4. *Ibid.*
5. *Ibid.*
6. FO371 75810 F3305, Peter Scarlett, 17 February 1949.
7. *Ibid.*
8. The British government's traditional attitude of recognizing the facts, however should not be regarded as an absolute principle. See Malcolm Shaw, *International Law* (Kent: Hodder & Stoughton, 1977) p. 173. A general discussion of legal arguments concerning the recognition of states and governments can be found in I. Brown, *Principles of International Law* (Oxford: Oxford University Press, 1979), Chapter V, pp. 89–108. See also P. Calvert, *Revolution and International Politics* (London: Frances Pinter, 1984).
9. FO371 75810 F3305, Peter Scarlett, 17 February 1949 *op. cit.*
10. *Ibid.*, Bevin's minute undated; Bevin's approval in Scarlett's minute 23 February 1949.
11. See FO371 75810 F3305, F4351, F5099, and FO371 75816 F14878.
12. A detailed account of the incident can be found in Lawrence Earl, *Yangtze Incident: The Story of HMS Amethyst* (London: George Harrap, 1950). Reissued in 1980. An account from the Chinese perspective is Kang Moujiao, 'The Amethyst Incident' [*Yingjian Zishuijinghao Shijian*] in Pei Jianzhang *et al.* (eds) *op. cit.*, pp. 33–46.
13. See the summaries of these approaches in FO371 75816 F14878; the full text of the joint letter and Coates' minute in FO371 75810 F5972.
14. Noel Barber, *The Fall of Shanghai* (New York: Coward, McCann and Geoghegan, 1979) p. 164; private correspondence of Mr and Mrs Oakeshott, by kind permission of Mrs Jill Oakeshott.
15. CAB 29/36 CP(49)180, 23 August 1949.
16. FO371 75813 F10026 Jebb to Strang, 1 July 1949; Report by officials annex A to CP(49) 180, 23 August 1949. See also Chapter 5.
17. CAB134 288 FE(0)(49)63, Hong Kong to Colonial Office, 10 August 1949. The message was passed on to the governor from a former British Council representative in Beijing, Fitzgerald, who said that the message came from an Australian journalist, Michael Keon. But Fitzgerald also said two months earlier Zhou's private secretary had asked him to meet Zhou and he would only be allowed to refer to Zhou as a 'very high communist official'. The Americans also received a similar message. See also Nancy Tucker, *Patter in the Dust: Chinese-American Relations and the Controversy, 1949–50* (New York: Columbia University Press 1983) p. 48.
18. CAB134 288 FE(0)(49)63, Nanking to FO, 30 August 1949.
19. See also this chapter's section on the business lobby. Records of the interviews between British businessmen and senior Chinese officials in Shanghai on 29 August and 30 August 1949; Stevenson's meeting

with Zhang, FO371 75815 F14268.

20. G. T. Allison, *Essence of Decision: Explaining the Cuban Missile Crisis* (Boston: Little Brown, 1971); M. H. Halperin with the assistance of P. Clapp and A. Kantor, *Bureaucratic Politics and Foreign Policy* (Washington: The Brookings Institute, 1974).

21. FO371 75824 F17902/1023/10, letter to the Foreign Office from the Commonwealth Relations Office, 18 November 1949; F17906/1023/10, Ministry of Transport to the Foreign Office, 18 November 1949.

22. T236 1812, British Financial and Commercial Policy Towards a Communist Administration: OF/23/39/9A.

23. FO371 75864 F3041, B. Ganger-Taylor to Peter Scarlett, 17 February 1949.

24. T236 1814, and Ganger-Taylor's letter to Scarlett on 17 February 1949.

25. FO371 75825 F18316 1023/10, Board of Trade to the Foreign Office, 18 November 1949, also CRE 18133/49 Board of Trade, Commercial Relations and Export Department.

26. CAB 128 CM(49) 32nd meeting, 5 May 1949; CAB 134/669 SAC(49) 5th, 19 May 1949, China and South East Asia Committee meeting; DEFE 6/10 JP(49)97, chiefs of Staff Committee, report by the Joint Planning Staff, 14 September 1949.

27. FO371 75814 F13405/1023/10, MacDonald to Strang, 19 August 1949; Gimson to MacDonald, 15 August 1949.

28. FO371 75814 F13405/1023/10G, Strang to MacDonald, 2 September 1949, letter drafted by Dening.

29. FO371 75819 F15158, MacDonald to the Colonial Office, 6 October 1949; minute by Scarlett, 14 October 1949.

30. Alexander Grantham, *Via Ports from Hong Kong to Hong Kong* (Hong Kong: Hong Kong University Press, 1965) p. 139.

31. Minutes of the Bukit Serene Conference in CAB 134/288; MacDonald to Foreign Officer, 4 November 1949, FO371 75819 F16589.

32. Alan Sked and Chris Cook, *Post-War Britain: A Political History* (Brighton: Harvester, 1979) p. 15, p. 24.

33. Kenneth Morgan, *Labour in Power, 1945–1951* (Oxford: Oxford University Press, 1985) p. 46.

34. *Reports of Labour Party Annual Conference* for 1947, 1948 and 1949, the Labour Party. Dalton's remark is in the 1949 Report, p. 197 and Bevin's comments on China are on p. 187.

35. Morgan, *Labour in Power, op. cit.*, p. 59.

36. Herbert Morrison, *An Autobiography* (London: Odhams, 1960) p. 253; Kenneth Younger interview transcript, Nuffield College, Oxford, pp. 10–11, quoted in Morgan, *Labour in Power*, p. 61.

37. On 5 May 1949, R. A. Butler told Parliament that he had to give up a prepared speech on Far Eastern affairs because the Far East was left out in the specialized foreign affairs debates. *H.C. Debs*, 5th series, 1948–49, Vol. 1333. Details of the incident of the figures of British

casualties were reported to Parliament, *H.C. Debs*, 5th series 1948–49, Vol. 464, Col. 30.
38. *H.C. Debs*, Vol. 464, col. 1225.
39. Full text of Butler's summing up, *H.C. Debs*, 1948–49, Vol. 464, col. 1333–1341; Attlee, col. 1342.
40. *H.C. Debs*, Vol. 464, cols. 1248–1249; and 1251.
41. *Ibid.* 17 January 1948.
42. The two who spoke on China were Fitzroy Maclean and Lieut. Colonel Hamilton: 21 July 1949, *H.C. Debs*, Vol. 467, cols. 1655–1658, and cols. 1672–1673; opening speech by H. Macmillan, cols. 1570–1582.
43. *H.C. Debs*, Vol. 469 cols. 2225–6.
44. *Scotsman*, 17 January 1948.
45. *Manchester Guardian* and *News Chronicle*, 15 June 1948; *Scotsman*, 18 June 1948, *Observer* and *Sunday Chronicle*, 20 June 1948.
46. For discussions about the government's news machinery see M. Cockerell, P. Henessy, D. Walker, *Sources Close to the Prime Minister* (London: Macmillan, 1984) Chapter 4.
47. *Manchester Guardian*, 29 January 1949, 8 February 1949, 9 March 1949.
48. *The Times*, 20 January 1949; *Manchester Guardian*, 23 April 1949.
49. *Glasgow Herald*, 25 April 1949.
50. *Daily Telegraph*, 16 May 1949; *Glasgow Herald*, 16 May 1949; *Observer*, 15 May 1949; *Scotsman*, 26 May 1949.
51. *Manchester Guardian*, 26 May 1949; *The Times*, 23 June 1949.
52. *The Times* and *Scotsman*, 3 October 1949; *Manchester Guardian*, 4 October 1949, 15 October 1949.
53. K. Younger, 'Public Opinion and Foreign Policy', *British Journal of Sociology*, 6 (June, 1955), p. 169. Some studies of the role of public opinion in foreign policy are: B. C. Cohen, *The Public's Impact on Foreign Policy* (Boston: Little Brown, 1973); W. L. Lederer, *Nation of Sheep*, New York: W.W. Norton, 1961). A study of the British media and foreign affairs is P. Elliott and P. Golding 'The News Media and Foreign Affairs' in R. Boardman and A. J. R. Groom, *The Management of Britain's External Relations* (London: Macmillan, 1973) chapter 13.
54. For the role of the China lobby, see Ross Koen, *The China Lobby in American Politics* (New York: Harper & Row, 1974). An account of the China Association's history and its relations with the Foreign Office at the end of the 19th century is: N. A. Pelcovits, *Old China Hands and the Foreign Office* (New York: King's Crown, 1948).
55. Notes prepared by the China Association 12 January 1949, FO371 75846, F723/1153/10.
56. *Ibid.*, FO371 75846 F3972/1153/10.
57. Keith Oakeshott to his wife, 29 May, 1 June 1949, private correspondence between Mr and Mrs Oakeshott, kind permission by Mrs Oakeshott.

58. Quoted in N. Barber, *The Fall of Shanghai* (New York: Coward McCann and Geoghegan, 1979) p. 163 and p. 164.

59. Records of interviews in Shanghai on 29 August and 30 August, FO371 75867 F14852/1153/10; Tientsin to Nanking 14 September in Nanking to F.O. 29 September 1949, FO371 75867 F14767/1153/10 and F14768/1153/10.

60. Minutes by Peter Scarlett, 26 July 1949, FO371 75866 F11173/1153/10.

61. Record of the meeting, 29 July 1949, FO371 75866 F11173/1153/10.

62. Minutes by Strang, 29 July 1949, FO371 75866 F11497/1153/10.

63. China Association to FO, 14 October 1949, FO371 75617 F15516.

64. L. Jensen, *Explaining Foreign Office* (Englewood Cliffs, New Jersey: Prentice-Hall, 1982) p. 139.

65. Minutes by Dening, 17 February 1949, FO371 75810 F3305; R. Barclay to Dening on Bevin's views, 4 June 1949, FO371 75812 F8543.

66. See E. Barker, *The British Between the Superpowers, 1947–50* (London: Macmillan, 1983) p. 169.

67. Letter from F. W. Loudon, US representative of the British-American Tobacco company. This letter was passed on to the Foreign Office, FO371 75812 F12843.

68. FO371 75810 F4314, Stevenson to Foreign Office, 23 March 1949.

69. See Chapter 1.

70.. In his letter of transmittal to *The China White Paper* Acheson stated that, 'the ominous result of the civil war in China was beyond the control of the government of the United States'. He also wrote, 'It was the product of internal Chinese forces, forces which this country tried to influence but could not'. *The China White Paper* (Stanford University Press, 1967) p. XVII; Dean Acheson, *Present At the Creation* (London, 1960) p. 307.

71. Walter LaFaber, *America, Russia, and the Cold War, 1945–80*, 4th edn, (New York: John Wiley & Sons, 1980) pp. 50–59.

72. For a study of the US problems in China see Nancy Tucker, *Pattern in the Dust: Chinese-American Relations and the Recognition Controversy 1949–1950* (New York: Columbia University Press, 1983).

73. The Ambassador to the Secretary of State, Nanking, 3 May 1949, The Secretary of State to certain diplomatic and consular officers, Washington, 6 May 1949, *FRUS*, 1949, Vol. IX, p. 14 and p. 17; FO371 75810 F6875/1023/10.

74. The Ambassador in the United Kingdom to Secretary of State, London, 28 June 1949, The Secretary of State to the Ambassador of the UK, Washington, 20 July 1949, The Ambassador in the UK to the Secretary of State, London, 22 July 1949, *FRUS*, 1949, Vol. IX, pp. 47–48 and pp. 50–52.

75. FO371 75812 F8543, Roderick Barclay to Esler Dening, 4 June 1949; FO371 75812 F12843, Bevin to O. Franks on his meeting with Lewis Douglas, 26 August 1949.

76. Memorandum of Conversation by the Directory of the Office of Far

Eastern Affairs, Washington, 9 September 1949, *FRUS* 1949, Vol. IX, pp. 76–78.

77. Memorandum of Conversation by the Secretary of State, Washington, 13 September 1949, *FRUS*, 1949, Vol. IX, pp. 81–85. The British version in Bevin papers: FO800 462 FE49/21, Record of a meeting held at the State Department, Washington, 13 September 1949.

78. *Ibid.*

79. The document was transmitted to the State Department by the French Embassy on 6 October 1949, *FRUS*, 1949, Vol. IX, p. 103.

80. Details of the exchanges between the American Chargé in London and Foreign Office officials over this question is in The Chargé in the UK to the Secretary of State, London, 10 October 1949, Memorandum of Conversation, by the Acting Deputy Director of the Office of Chinese Affairs, Washington, 11 October 1949, *FRUS*, 1949, Vol. IX, p. 118 and pp. 120–121.

81. The Secretary of State to the Ambassador in the UK, 14 October 1949, Memorandum by the Secretary of State of a Conversation with President Truman, Washington, 17 October 1949, *ibid.*, p. 128.

82. The Ambassador in the UK to the Secretary of State, London, 18 October 1949; Memorandum by the First Secretary of Embassy in the UK, London, 21 October 1949, *FRUS*, 1949, Vol. IX, pp. 138–139.

83. Memorandum by Charlton Ogburn Jr. of the Bureau of Far Eastern Affairs: Decisions Reached by Consensus at the Meetings With the Secretary and the Consultants on the Far East, 2 November 1949; Memorandum by Troy L. Perkins, Office of Chinese Affairs, 5 November 1949, *FRUS*, 1949, Vol. IX, pp. 160–162; pp. 168–170. An account of American thinking on the recognition question is Nancy Tucker, *Pattern in the Dust, op. cit.*

84. Memorandum of Conversation by the Secretary of State, 8 December 1949, *FRUS*, 1949, Vol. IX, pp. 219–220; The British version of the meeting in Washington to FO, 8 December 1949, FO371 75826 F18481/1023/10.

85. The Secretary of State to Ambassador in the UK, Washington 23 December 1949, *FRUS*, 1949, Vol. IX, pp. 241–242.

86. Jawaharlal Nehru, *Toward Freedom: The Autobiography of Jawaharlal Nehru* (Boston: Beacon Press, 1958) p. 368.

87. For accounts of India's attitude towards the formation of the PRC see P. C. Chakravarti, *India's China Policy* (Bloomington: Indiana University Press, 1962). Nehru's remark to the Indian Parliament in N. Jetly, *India-China Relations, 1947–1977: A Study of Parliament's Role in the Making of Foreign Policy* (Atlantic Highlands, New Jersey: Humanities Press, 1979), p. 11. Mrs Pandit's remarks see V. L. Pandit, *The Scope of Happiness: a personal memoir* (London: Weidenfeld & Nicolson, 1979) p. 266.

88. FO371 75737 F943.

89. The Ambassador in India to Secretary of State, New Delhi 26 May

1949, p. 29; the Ambassador in India to Secretary of State, New Delhi, 21 June 1949, *FRUS*, 1949, Vol. IX, pp. 45–46.

90. Memorandum handed to Bevin on 21 November 1949, FO371 75822 F17248/1023/10.

91. Minutes by A. Franklin, 22 November 1949, FO371 75822 F17248/1023/10; FO371 75822 F17248/1023/10.

92. Records of the Commonwealth High Commissioners' meeting are in FO371 75822 F17330/1023/10. For a full discussion of the Canada's policy towards the PRC see Paul M. Evans and B. Michael Frolic (eds), *Reluctant Adversaries: Canada and the People's Republic of China, 1949–1970* (Toronto: University of Toronto Press, 1991), see especially Stephen Beecroft's chapter, 'Canadian Policy Towards China, 1949–1957: The Recognition Question'. On Australia's position see H. S. Albinski, *Australian Policies and Attitudes Toward China* (Princeton: Princeton University Press, 1965). A discussion of Pakistan's position is in J. P. Jain, *China Pakistan and Bangladesh* (New Delhi: Radiant, 1974). For Ceylon's position see L. M. Jacob, 'Sri Lanka-China Relations' in Ramakant (ed.), *China and South Asia*, New Delhi: Radiant, 1988), pp. 155–160.

93. FO371 75814 F13704; FE(0)(49)78, CAB134 288, Far Eastern (Official) Committee paper, 2 December 1949.

94. FE(0)(49)78, CAB134 288, Far Eastern (Official) Committee papers, 2 December 1949. The Dutch government's problems in Indonesia has been discussed in G. M. Kahin, *Nationalism and Revolution in Indonesia* (Ithaca: Cornell University Press, 1952).

95. French Aide Memoire, 2 February 1949, CAB134 287 F.E.(0)(49) 9, 24 February 1949. An account of the difficulties France faced in Indo-China can be found in D. Lancaster, *The Emancipation of French Indochina* (London: Oxford University Press for the Royal Institute of International Affairs, 1961).

96. FO371 75823 F17467/1023/10, French Aide Memoire, 12 November 1949. In fact the arrival of Chinese Communist forces at the Sino-Vietnamese border in December 1949 had an important impact on the Indochina War. See J. Taylor, *China and Southeast Asia: Peking Relations with Revolutionary Movements* (New York: Praeger, 1976) p. 4.

97. French Aide Memoire, 12 November 1949, *ibid.*

98. Minute by P. Scarlett, 30 November 1949, FO371 75823 F17467/1023/10; Dening to Strang, 9 December 1949.

99. M. Djilas, *Conversation with Stalin*, p. 141, quoted in John Gittings, *The World and China 1922–1972* (London: Eyre Methuen) p. 148; Similar remarks are also recorded by others, see Nancy Tucker, *Pattern in the Dust*, *op. cit.*, p. 222, n. 54.

100. John Melby, *Mandate of Heaven op.cit.*, p. 24.

101. John Gittings. *The World and China*, *op.cit.*, p. 151.

102. 'Revolutionary Forces of the World Unite', 30 November 1948, in *Selected Work of Mao Tse-tung*, Vol. IV (Beijing: Foreign Languages

Press) NCNA, North Shensi, 22 March 1949; Radio Beijing's report in *News Chronicle* and the *New York Times*, 4 April 1949; On the People's Democratic Dictatorship, *People's Daily*, 1 July 1949. Also in *Selected Work of Mao*, Vol. IV.

103. O. E. Clubb, *China and Russia: The 'Great Game'* (New York: Columbia University Press, 1971) p. 380.
104. CAB 128/13 CM80(48).
105. CAB 129/32, appendix to CP(49)39, 4th March 1949. Communist documents seized by the Hong Kong security authorities were presented by the Foreign Office to the Cabinet as evidence that the Chinese Communist Party was 'strictly orthodox, confident, mature, and at the highest level very well organized'. The Foreign Office also found that the documents did not provide any trace of Titoism.
106. CAB129/32 CP(49)180, 23 August 1949, Annex A. For a fuller discussion of Western expectation of Chinese 'Titoism' see B. Heuser, *Western 'Containment Policies in the Cold War: The Yugoslav Case, 1948–53* (London: Routledge, 1989) pp. 70–75.
107. CAB128/16 CM(49), 62nd Meeting, 27 October 1949.
108. Full text in CAB129/37 CP(49)214.
109. FO371 75816 F14782 1 October 1949; F15283, Stevenson to Foreign Office, 12 October 1949; 13 October 1949. Legally speaking the terminology of official communications or declaration of recognition can take different forms without using the term recognition. Ultimately it depends on the intention of the government concerned. I. Brown, *Principles of Public International Law* (Oxford: Oxford University Press, 1979) p. 93–4.
110. CAB134 286 FE(0)18th Meeting, 8 December 1949. The British Ambassador Ralph Stevenson, who had returned from China, was also present in this meeting.
111. CAB129/37 CP(49)248, 26 November 1949.
112. *Ibid.*
113. CAB128/16 CM(49)72, Cabinet meeting on 15 December 1949.

3   From Negotiations to Confrontation

1. The Chinese version as published in *CDER* did not mention this request for a representative to negotiate for the establishment of diplomatic relations in the case of Burma. The British government's version obtained from the Burmese had included a specific request for such. See FO371 75829 F19434/1023/10.
2. Nanking to FO, 30 December 1949, FO371 75830 F19521/1023/10.
3. FO to Nanking, 4 January 1950, *ibid.*
4. Nanking to FO, 7 January 1950, FO371 83280 FC1022/44.
5. Full text of Chinese reply in *CDER* 1949–50, p. 19; English translation in FO371 83295 FC1022/518.

6. NCNA: Peking, 9 January 1990.
7. FO to Nanking, 13 January 1950, FO371 83280 FC1022/58; FO to British Embassies, 19 January 1950, FO371 83280 FC1022/59.
8. Nanking to FO, 13 January 1950, FO371 838280 FC1022/94; Nanking to FO, 25 January 1950, FO371 83280 FC1022/142.
9. Nanking to FO, 29 January 1950, FO371 83283 FC1022/159; Nanking to FO, 30 January 1950, FO371 83283 FC1022/165; Bevin's approval in FO371 83283 FC1022/175.
10. Oslo to FO, 31 January 1950, FO371 83283 FC1022/173.
11. FO to Nanking, 1 February 1950, FO371 83283 FC1022/173.
12. NCNA: Peking, 13 February 1950.
13. Peking to FO, 17 February 1950, FO371 83285 FC1022/210; Peking to FO, 28 February 1950, FO371 83282 FC1022/221, minute by Franklin, 2 March 1950.
14. Instruction to Hutchison, FO to Nanking, 1 February 1950, FO371 83283 FC1022/159.
15. Chinese version in *CDER* 1949–50, p. 123; English version in FO371 83295 FC1022/518.
16. Peking to FO, 3 March 1950, FO371 83285 FC1022/228; a detailed account of the CNAC and CATC affair is in Chapter 7.
17. FO371 83285 FC1022/232, minutes by Franklin, 15 March 1950.
18. Delhi to CRO, 8 March 1950, minutes by Franklin, 10 March 1950, FO371 83285 FC1022/235.
19. Stockholm to FO, 16 March 1950, FO371 83286 FO1022/250.
20. Full text of Hutchison's oral communication to the Chinese in FO371 83295 FC1022/518.
21. Peking to FO, 17 March 1950, FO371 83286 FC1022/248.
22. FO371 88504 UP213/63.
23. FO371 83286 FC1022/254.
24. Memorandum of the Shanghai British Chamber of Commerce, 20 February 1950, FO371 83345 FC1106/40; Inter-departmental meeting on the position of British firms in China, 3 April 1950, FO371 83345 FC1106/45.
25. Records of Bevin's meeting with the China Association, 16 March 1950, FO371 83344 FC1106/30.
26. Air Commodore Harvey, *H.C. Deb*, Vol. 472, Col 215, 7 March 1950.
27. *H.C. Deb*, Vol. 474, Col 929, 24 March 1950.
28. *Ibid.* Col 598.
29. Sir Henry Gurney to CO, 28 March 1950, FO371 83549 FC1903/37; Gurney to CO, 7 May 1950, FO371 83551 FC1903/77.
30. Records of a bi-partite sub-committee meeting on 2 May 1959, FO371 83288 FC1022/314.
31. CAB 129/39 CP(50)73.
32. Full text in FO371 83295 FC1022/518.
33. Minutes by Franklin, 13 May 1950, FO371 83288 FC1022/319.

34. Peking to FO, 10 May 1950, FO317 83289 FC1022/325; Peking to FO, 11 May 1950, FC1022/334; Peking to FO 13 May 1950 and minutes by Franklin, FC1022/341.
35. Minutes by Dening with Bevin's approval, 9 May 1950, FO371 83288 FC1022/319.
36. Anthony Eden, *H.C. Deb.* Vol. 475, Col 2971, 24 May 1950; Ernest Bevin, *Ibid*, Col 2083.
37. *World Knowledge (Shejie zhishi)*, 19 May 1950; NCNA: Peking, 20 May 1950, 3 May 1950.
38. Minutes by A. Franklin, 26 May 1950, FO371 83290 FC1022/362.
39. The remark as appeared in *Hansard* was, 'It was an awkward decision to make' Ernest Bevin, *H.C. Deb*, Vol. 475, Col 2083, 24 May 1950. Apparently Bevin departed from the prepared speech when he spoke in the House and the Foreign Office had remedied the situation later by putting the official version on record. FO371 83291 FC1022/374.
40. *People's Daily*, 28 May 1950; *People's China*, 1 June 1950.
41. Minutes by Strang, 26 May 1950, FO371 83291 FC1022/381.
42. FO to Washington, 18 June 1950, FO371 81849 UP123/85.
43. Full text of the official communication in FO371 83295 FC1022/518; Instructions to Hutchison in FO to Peking, 6 June 1950, FO371 83291 FC1022/381; Meeting between Hutchison and Zhang in Peking to FO, 18 June 1950 in FC1022/401.
44. Note on British commercial enterprise in China, 24 May 1950, FO371 83350 FC1106/178; Reports on the business situation in China, Peking to FO, 14 July 1950, FO371 83350 FC1106/184, Shanghai to FO, 19 July 1950, FO371 83350 FC1106/187; British Chamber of Commerce, Shanghai: report for the year 1949–50, FO371 83350 FC1106/185.
45. Washington to London, 27 June 1950, *FRUS*, 1950, Vol. VII, Korea, pp. 186–187.
46. British Defence Co-ordination Committee, Far East to Ministry of Defence, 27 June 1950, see Prem 8 1405 Part I; minutes of Chiefs of Staff meeting 30 June 1950, DEFE CO(50) 100th meeting item 1.
47. Records of Cabinet meeting, 27 June, CAB 128/17 CM39(50).
48. Full text of Truman's statement in *Department of State Bulletin*, 3 July 1950. See also note 3 in *FRUS*, 1950, Vol. VII, Korea, p. 187.
49. See A. Whiting, *China Crosses the Yalu* (Stanford: Stanford University Press, 1960) p. 53; Stuart Schram, *Mao Tse-tung* (Harmondsworth: Penguin, 1967) p. 263.
50. NCNA: Peking, 9 June 1950.
51. Minutes by Franklin, 29 June 1950, FO371 83292 FC1022/414.
52. Younger Diary, 6 July 1950.
53. FO to Washington, 6 July 1950, FO371 84086 FK1022/112G.
54. FO371 84086 FK1022/111/G.
55. *Present At the Creation* (New York: Norton, 1969) p. 418.
56. Acheson's message to Bevin, 10 July 1950, *FRUS* 1950, Vol. VII, pp. 347–51, Acheson's instruction to Douglas, 10 July 1950, *FRUS*

1950, Vol. VII, pp. 351–2; also in FO371 84086 FK1022/111G.

57. Douglas's report to Acheson, 11 July 1950, *FRUS* 1950, Vol. VII, p. 351.

58. Douglas's report on 14 July of his meeting with Younger, Strang and Dening, *FRUS*, 1950, Vol. VII, pp. 380–385; The British version was provided by P. C. Holmes' minutes of the meeting in FO371 83293 FC1022/413G.

59. FO to Washington, 14 July 1950, FO371 84086 FK1022/111G.

60. CAB 128/18 CM 50 (50), 25 July 1950.

61. CAB 129/41 CP(50) 157.

62. FO371 83296 FC1023/6.

63. Peking to FO, 25 July 1950, FO371 83293 FC1022/439.

64. Minutes by Crowe, 29 July 1950; minute by a Foreign Office official whose signature I cannot read dated 19 August 1950, but the minutes indicated that the official had returned to London from Guangzhou, FO371 83293 FC1022/439.

65. FO to Washington, 1 August 1950, FO371 88422 UP123/103.

66. Chinese Foreign Ministry statement, 25 September 1950, *CDER*, 1949–50, p. 151.

67. *People's China*, 16 October 1950, p. 6.

68. Peking to FO, 5 October 1950, FO371 83294 FC1022/49.

69. FO371 83294 FC1022/495.

70. Memorandum on recent trading conditions in China, Commercial Section, British Consulate-General in Shanghai, 15 October 1950, FO371 92259 FC1103/2.

71. Minutes by Franklin, 30 August 1950, FO371 83295 FC1022/501.

72. For an account of Liu's visit see Michael Lindsay, *China and the Cold War* (Melbourne: Melbourne University Press, 1955) pp. 12–16.

73. Sir Michael Wilford was not aware of any plan to send Dening to China in 1950 when interviewed on 9 July 1985; Paton's letter to the writer, 28 January 1986.

74. Dening's itinerary in FO371 84519 FZ1026/1; Reports in *Evening News*, 11 October 1950, *Scotsman*, 17 October 1950.

75. See FO371 84519 FZ1026/4; Memorandum by Edwin Stanton, US Ambassador to Bangkok, *FRUS*, 1950, Vol. VI, p. 184. Details of the American approach in *FRUS*, 1950, Vol. VII, correspondence between Henderson and the State Department: p. 837, p. 875, p. 901, p. 921.

76. Younger to Strang, 12 June 1950, FO371 83327 FC1051/2.

77. FO to Peking, 6 October 1950, FO371 84519 FZ1026/1.

78. Dening to Strang, 17 October 1950, FO371 84519 FZ1026/12.

79. The final decision was made on 5 October 1950, according to Peng Dehuai, the Chinese military commander in Korea, see *Memoirs of a Chinese Marshall* (Beijing: Foreign Languages Press, 1984) pp. 472–74; see also Chapter 4.

80. Dening to Scott on the situation in Tibet, 30 October 1950, FO371 84519 FZ1026/20, Dening's proposal to tell the press about his China

visit, Hong Kong to FO, 30 October 1950, FO371 84519 FZ1026/22; Dening's personal letter to Hutchison, FO371 83295 FC1022/515.

81. The exchange and later Dening's affirmation that the objective was China are in FO371 84520 FZ1026/28 and FO371 84521 FZ1026/33.
82. FO371 83295 FC1022/513.
83. Peking to FO, 18 November 1950, FO371 83295 FC1022/514.

4 From Confrontation to the Establishment of Diplomatic Relations

1. A useful account of the Korean War with extensive references to British attitude is P. Lowe, *The Origins of the Korean War* (London: Longman, 1986).
2. DEFE 4/36: COS(50)142(8), COS(50)160(2), COS(50)161(1).
3. The British government's UN initiative is in Bevin to Attlee, 22 September 1950, CAB 129/42 CP(50)215; Bevin's personal message to Nehru, 28 September 1950, FO371 84109 FK/1023/11; Pannikar's reports on his meeting with Zhou, New Delhi to CRO, 3 October 1950, FO371 84109 FK1023/17G. The Chinese Foreign Ministry's own record of the meeting is in *Selected Work of Zhou Enlai on China Diplomacy* [*Zhou Enlai Waijiao Wenxuan*] (Beijing: Zhongyang Wenxian Chubanshe, 1990) pp. 25–27.
4. For an account of the Chinese internal debate on the question of intervention see *Memoirs of Nie Rongzhen (Nie Rogzhen Huiyilu)*, Vol. 3 (Beijing: People's Liberation Army Publication, 1984) pp. 733–739; *Memoirs of Chinese March: The Autobiographical Notes of Peng Dehuai (1898–1974)* (Beijing: Foreign Languages Press, 1984) pp. 472–474, Chinese edition: *Peng Dehuai Zusu* (Beijing: People's Publication, 1981) pp.257–258. Two studies of the Chinese motivation and decision to intervene are Allen Whiting's *China Crosses the Yalu*, (Stanford: Stanford University Press, 1960); and chapter two in Melvin Gurtov and Byong-Moo Hwang's *China under Threat* (Baltimore: Johns Hopkins University Press, 1980). Two more accounts published in China in recent years are: Du Peng, *At the Volunteers' Headquarters* [*Zai Zhiyuanjun Zongbu*] (Beijing: Jiefangjun Chubanshe, 1989) and Tan Jingqiao, *The War To Resist the US and Assist Korea* [*Kangmei Yuanzhao Zhanzheng*] (Beijing Zhongguo Shihui Kexueyuan Chubanshe, 1990).
5. FO to Washington, 17 November 1950, FO371 84114 FK1023/109G.
6. Washington to FO, 21 November 1950, FO371 84115 FK1023/110; Washington to London, 21 November 1950, *FRUS*, 1950, Vol. VII, pp. 1212–1213.
7. FO to Peking, 18 November 1950, FO371 84116 FK1023/138; Peking to FO, 23 November 1950, FO371 84117 FK1023/150.
8. *Department of State Bulletin*, 18 December 1950, p. 962; *Memoirs*

of Harry S. Truman Vol. II (London: Hodder & Stoughton, 1956) p. 403.

9. Washington to FO, 30 November 1950, FO371 84116 FK1023/197.

10. Minutes by Scott, 28 November 1950, FO371 84121 FK1023/224.

11. *H.C. Deb*, Vol. 481, Foreign Affairs Debate, 30 November 1950; Attlee's announcement in Col 1440; A record of Truman's press conference on 30 November 1950 in *Public Papers of the Presidents of the United States: Harry S. Truman, 1950* (Washington D.C.: 1965) pp. 724–28. R Jenkins, *Truman* (London: Collins, 1986) p. 178.

12. FO to Washington, 14 August 1950; Washington to FO, 16 August 1950; Washington to FO, 31 August 1950, Prem 8 1156. Dalton to Attlee, 30 November 1950, Dalton papers 9/9/108; Dalton diary 30 November 1950; Cabinet discussions CAB 128/18; also see Ben Pimlott's *Hugh Dalton*, (London: Jonathan Cape, 1985), p. 592; and Kenneth Morgan, *Labour in Power 1945–51* (Oxford: Oxford University Press, 1984) p. 427.

13. Attlee–Truman talks in Prem 8 1200; the American records of the meetings in *FRUS*, 1950, Vol. VII, pp. 1361–1374, pp. 1392–1408, pp. 1449–1475; Younger diary, 11 December 1950; Younger interview quoted in Morgan *op. cit.*, p. 429.

14. Acheson's description of the Attlee–Truman talks in *Present at the Creation* (New York: Norton, 1969) pp. 480–485; Acheson's summary of the first day meeting in *FRUS*, 1950, Vol. II, p. 1382.

15. Cabinet meeting, 22 December 1950, CAB 128/18 CM(50)85.

16. Peking to FO, 29 November 1950, FO371 92233 FC1027/1.

17. Cabinet meeting, 29 November 1950, CAB 128/18 CM(50)78.

18. Lester Pearson, the Canadian Secretary for External Affairs and member of the Cease-Fire Committee, provided a detailed account of the work of the Committee in his diary, *Lester Pearson Memoirs*, Vol. II (London: Victor Gollancz, 1974) Appendix 1, pp. 279–314.

19. *CDER*, 1951–53, pp. 3–4.

20. Cabinet meeting, 18 January 1951, Prem 8 1405, Part 4 T12/51; *Lester Pearson Memoirs*, Vol. II, *op. cit.*, pp. 168–169.

21. Attlee to Nehru, 18 January 1951, Prem 8, 1405, *ibid.*; *Lester Pearson Memoirs*, Vol. II, *ibid.*, pp. 168–169.

22. Cabinet discussion, 22 January 1951, CAB 128/19 CM(51)5.

23. Kenneth Younger diary, 7 January 1951.

24. Paris to FO, 20 January 1951, Prem 8, 1405, Part 4; *Lester Pearson Memoirs*, Vol. II, *op. cit.* p. 169.

25. Peking to FO, 22 January 1951, Prem 8, 1405, Part 4.

26. Peking to FO, 22 January 1951, *ibid.*

27. *The Times*, 23 January, 24 January 1951.

28. New York to FO, 22 January 1951, Prem 8, 1405, part 4.

29. Cabinet discussion, 23 January 1951, CAB 128/19 CM(51)6.

30. Cabinet discussions, 25 January 1951, CB 128/19 CM(51)7, CM(51)8.

31. Cabinet discussions on 26 January 1951 and 29 January 1951, CAB

128/19 CM(51)9; CM(51)10; See also Kenneth Younger diary 28 January 1951, 4 February 1951, Gladwyn Jebb, *Memoirs of Lord Gladwyn* (London, 1972) p. 247, and Hugh Gaitskell's diary on 2 February 1951, P. Williams (ed.), *The Diary of Hugh Gaitskell, 1945–55* (London: Jonathan Cape, 1983) p. 229–232.

32. Acheson, *Present at the Creation, op. cit.*, p. 513.
33. Meeting between Wrong and Rusk on 14 and 23 February 1951 in *Lester Pearson Memoirs*, Vol. II, *op. cit.*, pp. 175–179.
34. *The Times*, 24 January 1951, 1 February 1951; *Manchester Guardian*, 1 February 1951.
35. *CDER*, 1949–50, p. 194, also in FO371 92371 FC1821/3. See Chapter 7.
36. FO371 92378 FC1894/4.
37. Minute by G. G. Fitzmaurice, 9 January 1951, FO371 92378 FC1892/4; minute by A. Franklin, 10 January 1951, FO to Peking, 13 January 1951, FO371 92378 FC1892/6.
38. Humphrey Trevelyan to Colin Crowe, personal letter, 3 December 1953; minutes by P. Wilkinson and J. Addis on 30 December 1953, by Colin Crowe on 2 January 1954.
39. FO 371 92234 FC1027/48.
40. Minute by J. S. H. Shattock, 27 February 1951, FO371 92234 FC1027/48.
41. Personal letter from Scott to Jebb, 17 February 1951, FO371 92231 FC1027/34.
42. FO to Peking, 2 March 1951, FO371 92234 FC1027/33.
43. Minute by J. S. H. Shattock, 15 February 1951, FO371 92234 FC1027/33.
44. FO to Washington, 17 February 1951, FO371 92234 FC1027/33. Cabinet discussion, 5 April 1951, Cabinet Paper CP(51)100.
45. FO to New York, 7 April 1951, Fo371 922636 FC1027/81. *H.C. Deb*, series 5, Vol. 487, Attlee, 3 May 1951, Col 1427.
46. UN Doc. A/1799, 5th session General Assembly item 76, pp. 20–21, first committee meeting 443 and meeting 444; General Assembly 5th session Supplement no. 20A r.500(v) p. 2; *H.C. Deb*, series 5, Vol. 489, Shawcross, 19 June 1951, Cols. 245–52.
47. *CDER* 1951–53, p. 27, NCNA, 23 May 1951; *People's Daily*, 25 May 1951.
48. FO371 95597 UP122/114.
49. Lamb to Scott, 27 April 1951, FO371 92262 FC1103/65.
50. Reports about the North case: Peking to FO 27 April 1951, FO371 92380 FC1892/55, FC1892/62; other incidents in minute by K. R. Oakeshott, 8 May 1951, FO371 92380 FC1892/63.
51. General China Policy, 31 October 1951, FO371 92240 FC1027/242.
52. Shanghai to FO, 22 May 1951, FO371 92262 FC1103/65.
53. Anthony Eden, *The Memoirs of Sir Anthony Eden, Full Circle* (London: Cassell, 1960) p. 5.

54. John Colville, *The Fringes of Power, Downing Street Diaries, 1939–1955* (London: Hodder and Stoughton, 1985), p. 633. On Anglo-American special relations in this period see A. Seldon, *Churchill's Indian Summer: The Conservative Government, 1951–55* (London: Hodder & Stoughton, 1981), pp. 387–388.

55. Lord Reading had actually considered resigning over the recognition issue, A. Seldon, *ibid.*, p. 383. During mid 1952 the government had to persuade Lord Vansittert to withdraw a motion on suspending recognition in the House of Lords to avoid embarrassing Lord Salisbury because of his known views on the question of recognition which was in disagreement with the government's policy. Minutes by Lord Reading, 20 June 1952, and correspondence with Lord Vansittert in FO371 99260 FC1025/18.

56. Churchill to Jebb, Prem 11, 789, T115/53.

57. FO to Washington, 1 November 2952, FO371 95600 UP122/160.

58. Foreign Office Lists of 1949, 1950, 1951, 1952; Colin Crowe, letter to the writer, 18 April 1986.

59. According to Churchill's private secretary John Colville, it was Roger Makins who suggested these remarks on the spur of the moment when he went into the Prime Minister's room to tell him that they should be leaving for Capitol Hill. Churchill was putting the finishing touches to his speech and wrote the words down immediately, *The Fringes of Power, op. cit.*, pp. 639–70.

60. Leo Lamb to Robert Scott, 11 January 1952, FO371 99260 FC1025/9.

61. Minutes by J. M. Addis, 29 January 1952, FO371 99260 FC1025/9; minutes by J. O. Lloyd, 29 January 1952; C. H. Johnston, 30 January 1952, FO371 99260 FC1025/9.

62. R. H. Scott, 31 January 1952, FO371 99260 FC1025/7.

63. Background brief on China for the Foreign Secretary, R.H. Scott, 15 February 1952, FO371 99260 FC1025/7. See also Lloyd to Churchill, 21 June 1952; Prem 11, 301, PM/MS/52/98; Churchill to Lloyd, 23 August 1952; Eden to Churchill, 1 September 1952, and Churchill's reply, 3 September 1952, PM/52/108.

64. Minute by J. Addis, 17 August 1953, FO371 105225 FC1051/21.

65. Minute by John Addis, 17 August 1953; minute by Lord Reading, 18 August 1953, FO371 105225 FC1051/21.

66. FO to Peking, 10 August 1953, FO371 105225 FC1051/21.

67. Peking to FO, 25 August 1953, FO371 105225 FC1051/22.

68. Trevelyan to Scott, 27 August 1953, FO371 105225 FC1051/29.

69. Denis Allen to Trevelyan, 30 September 1953, FO371 105225 FC1051/29.

70. Cabinet paper: Policy in the Far East, 24 November 1953, CAB 129/64 C(53)330.

71. Statement in the House of Commons, Cmd papers 8639, 1952; *Manchester Guardian*, 20 May 1952; FO371 99287 FC1105/163.

72. Minute by J. W. Nicholls, 20 January 1953; J. M. Addis, 22 January

1953 FO371 105261 FC1151/19; W. D. Allen to Anthony Percival, 14 January 1954, FO371 105265 FC1151/66.

73. Sir W. Hayter to Denis Allen, 5 March 1954; Allen to Hayter, 13 March 1954, FO371 110245 FC1051/4.
74. Allen to Trevelyan, 24 February 1954, FO371 110245 FC1051/1.
75. *Ibid.*
76. Geneva Conference: Brief on UK's recognition and diplomatic relations with China since the setting up of the Central People's Government, undated, FO371 110245 FC1051/10.
77. Peking to FO, 26 March 1954 and 5 April 1954, FO371 110245 FC1051/7.
78. Minutes by C. T. Crowe, 6 April 1954, FO371 110245 FC1051/7; J. F. Ford, 23 April 1954, FO371 110245 FC1051/9.
79. Minute by Colin Crowe, 24 May 1954, FO371 110245 FC1051/10.
80. H. Trevelyan, *Worlds Apart: China, 1953–55 USSR, 1962–65* (London: Macmillan, 1971) p. 82.; minute by Colin Crowe, 24 May 1954, FO371 110245 FC1051/10.
81. A study of the Conference by a participant is James Cable, *The Geneva Conference of 1954 on Indochina* (London: Macmillan, 1986). Eden's first meeting with Zhou was recorded in E. Shuckburgh, *Descent to Suez: Diaries 1951–56* (London: Weidenfeld & Nicolson, 1986) pp. 183–4. Eden's own account of the dinner meeting is in Anthony Eden, *The Memoirs of Sir Anthony Eden: Full Circle* (London: Cassel, 1960) p. 123.
82. Letter from Sir Denis Allen, 1 September 1986; interview with Mr Joe Ford.
83. US delegation to the Department of State Geneva, 2 June 1954, *FRUS*, 1952–54, Vol. XVI, The Geneva Conference, pp. 1010–1011; letter from Sir Denis Allen, 1 September 1986.
84. Geneva to FO, 4 June 1954, FO371 110245 FC1051/17.
85. Cabinet discussion, 5 June 1954, CAB 128/27, Part I, CC(54)39.
86. Geneva to FO, 11 June 1954, FO371 110245 FC1051/22.
87. Geneva to FO, 14 June 1954, FO371 110245 FC1051/23.
88. Record of Cabinet discussion, 15 June 1954, CAB 128/27, Part I, CC(54)40.
89. Peking to FO, 7 July 1954, FO371 110246 FC1051/35; FO to Peking, 20 July 1954, FO371 110246 FC1051/34,
90. Report on the Work of the Government delivered at the First Session of the First National People's Congress on 23 September 1954, *People's China*, No. 20, October 1954.
91. For an account of Attlee's visit and others by British businessmen see Humphrey Trevelyan, *Worlds Apart: China 1953–55, USSR 1962–65, op. cit.*, pp. 118–120.

5   Chinese Representation in the United Nations

1. Cadogan diaries, Cadogan papers, ACDA 1950 1/21, Churchill College, Cambridge.
2. See Chapter 3.
3. FO to UK Delegation to United Nations, 23 December 1949, FO371 75831 F19277/1025/10.
4. FO to Nanking, 2 February 1950, FO371 83283 FC1022/175.
5. NCNA: Peking, 89 January 1950.
6. Oslo to FO, 31 January 1950, FO371 83283 FC1022/173.
7. Minute by Hector McNeil, 30 January 1950; New York to FO, 26 January 1950, FO371 88503 UP213/25.
8. FO to New York, 1 February 1950, FO371 88503 UP213/25.
9. Minute by Parrott, 3 February 1950; Nanking to FO 3 February 1950, FO371 88503 UP213/30.
10. Minute by Gladwyn Jebb, 4 February 1950, FO371 88503 UP213/25.
11. Washington to FO, 6 February 1950, FO371 88503 UP213/36; Minute by G. Jebb to Secretary of State, 8 February 1950, FO371 88503 UP213/39.
12. FO 371 88504 UP213/63.
13. FO to Peking, 24 March 1950, FO371 88415 UP123/9.
14. Evan Luard, *A History of the United Nations*, Vol. I (London: Macmillan, 1982) p. 315.
15. Minute by Jebb to Dening and Strang, 8 March 1950, FO to Cairo, FO371 UP213/63.
16. Conversation between Bevin and Schuman, 7 March 1950, FO371 88504 UP213/55G; Conversation between O Franks and US officials, 10 March 1950, FO371 88504 UP213/60. Cairo to FO, 6 April 1950, FO371 88415 UP123/10; Quito to FO, 15 April 1950, UP123/15.
17. FO371 88416 UP123/24.
18. FO371 88416 UP123/29.
19. FO to Peking, 9 May 1950, FO371 88416 UP123/36.
20. Kenneth Younger Diary, 14 May 1950.
21. Minute by Younger, 11 May 1950, FO371 88419 UP123/83.
22. FO371 88417 UP123/48.
23. Peking to FO, 31 May 1950, FO371 88418 UP123/63.
24. Minute by Dening, 30 May 1950; Minute by Strang, 31 May 1950, FO371 88419 UP123/83.
25. Meeting of Strang, Dixon, Scott, Shattock and Parrott, 14 June 1950, on a response to the Soviet approach, FO371 81849 UP123/85.
26. FO371 88419 UP123/79C PM/50/KY/22.
27. Paris to FO, 17 June 1950; FO371 88419 UP123/81.
28. Washington to FO, 17 June 1950; FO371 88419.
29. FO to Washington, 18 June 1950, FO371 88419 UP123/82; FO371 88420 UP123/103.
30. Washington to FO, 26 June 1950, FI371 818420 UP123/106.

31. FO371 818420 UP123/107.
32. Minute by Dening, 1 August 1950, FO to Washington, 1 August 1950, FO371 88422 UP123/133; Jebb, New York to FO, 2 August 1950, Bevin to Younger, 4 August 1950, UP123/142, FO to Washington, UP123/143.
33. 000"Dean Acheson, *Present at the Creation* (New York: Norton, 1969) p. 148.
34. WAshington to FO, Minute by P. C. Holmer, 17 August 1950; C. Crowe, 21 August 1950, FO371 88423 UP123/154.
35. Delhi to CRO, 8 September 1950, FO371 88424 UP123/177.
36. FO to New York, 12 September 1950, FO371 88424 UP123/177; FO371 88424 UP123/181.
37. Delhi to CRO, 23 September 1950, FO371 88425 UP123/211.
38. *CDER*, 1949–1950, p. 151.
39. Andrew Franklin minute, 2 October 1950, FO371 88425 UP123/211, P. C. Holmer minute, 28 September 1950, FO371 88425 UP123/212.
40. R. Scott minute, 7 November 1950, FO371 88426 UP123/229.
41. FO371 95592 UP122/5.
42. FO371 95592 UP122/14; UP122/29.
43. FO371 95593 UP122/35.
44. FO371 95594 Up122/47.
45. Minutes by J. S. H. Shattock, 22 May 1951, P. C. Holmer, 18 May 1951, FO371 95598 UP122/111; K. Younger, FO371 95598 UP122/113.
46. New York to FO, 21 May 1951, FO371 95598 UP122/112.
47. FO371 95598 UP122/114.
48. FO371 95596 UP122/89.
49. FO371 95597 UP122/105.
50. *Manchester Guardian* and *The Times*, 25 June 1951.
51. FO to Washington, 1 November 1951, FO371 95600 UP122/160.
52. Entry to Eden's private secretary Sir E. Shuckburgh's diary on 30 April 1954. *Descent to Suez: Diaries 1951–56* (London: Weidenfeld & Nicholson, 1986) pp. 183–84.
53. For example *People's Daily*, 10 January 1951.
54. Samuel Kim, *China, the United Nations and World Order* (Princeton, N.J.: Princeton University Press, 1979) pp. 92–93. For an account of the evolution of the PRC's attitude towards the UN see B. S. Weng, 'Communist China's Changing Attitude Towards the UN', *International Organization*, XX, 4 August 1966.
55. For an account of Dong's activity during his trip to the US, see Hu and Ha, *Biography of Dong Biwu*, [*Dong Biwu Zhuangji*] (Hubie: People's Publication, 1985) pp. 200–3.
56. *Selected Work or Mao Tse-tung*, Vol. III, Beijing, 1961, 1965, pp. 306–307, also quoted in Samuel S. Kim *China, the United Nations and World Order, op. cit.*, p. 100.
57. Zhou Gengseng, *International Law*, [*Gou Ji Fa.*], Vol. 2 (Beijing: Commerce Press, 1981) p. 726.

58. *People's China*, No. 14, 16 July 1955.
59. *000"CDER*, 1949–50, pp. 86–87 and pp. 90–92; NCNA: Peking, 1950 No. 100–104, 111, 116, 121, 124, 133, 138–139, 145, 159 and 166.
60. James C. Hsiung, *Law and Policy in China's Foreign Relations* (New York: Columbia University Press, 1972) pp. 89–90.
61. Wu Xiu-quan, *Eight Years in the Foreign Ministry [Zai waijiaobu bainian de jingli]* (Beijing: World Knowledge Press, 1983), p. 38, p. 52.
62. Peking to FO, 14 March 1951, FO371 95593, UP122/46.
63. See Chapter 3; for a specific study of the experience of the Dutch see Ko Swan Sik's 'The Establishment of Diplomatic Relations and the Scope of Diplomatic Immunity: The Dutch Experience with China' in J. A. Cohen (ed.), *China's Practice of International Law: Some Case Studies* (Cambridge, Mass.: Harvard University Press, 1972).
64. B. S. J. Weng, *Peking's UN Policy: Continuity and Change* (New York: Praeger, 1972) p. 225.

6 British Commercial Interests in China

1. Records of an interview with the Foreign Office on 2 February, China Association papers, CA: minutes and circulars 1950, 50/G/10, 6 February 1950.
2. *Ibid.*; record of an interview with Mr Bevin, CA: minutes and circular 1950, 50/G/25, 17 March 1950; see also FO371 83344 FC116/30.
3. CA: 1950, 50/G/26, 17 March 1950.
4. FO371 83345 FC1106/39, record of a meeting held in the Foreign Office on 30 March 1950.
5. *Ibid.*
6. *Ibid.*, and also FO371 83345 FC1106/45.
7. CA: 1950, 50/G/29.
8. CA: 1950, 50/G.29, 50/G/33.
9. See Chapter 3 on the Anglo-Chinese negotiations, and Chapter 7 on the CNAC/CATC affair.
10. FO371 83350 FC1106/178; FC1106/184.
11. CA: 1950, 50/M/6.
12. K. G. Lieberthal, *Revolution and Tradition in Tientsin, 1949–1952* (Stanford, California: Stanford University Press, 1980) pp. 82–88.
13. CA: 1950, 50/M/8.
14. CA: 1950, 50/G/53, 50/G/60, 50/G/67.
15. FO371 83350 FC1106/187; FC1106/192.
16. FO371 83351 FC1106/194.
17. FO371 83352 FC1106/210.
18. Dening's meeting with China Association representatives on 23 August 1950, FO371 83351 FC1106/206.
19. FO371 83352 FC1106/214; FC1106/215.

20. Peking to FO 21 August 1950, FO371 83352 FC1106/225.
21. See Chapter 4 on the political consequences of the Korean War on Anglo-Chinese relations.
22. FO371 92262 FC1103/45; FC1103/68.
23. FO371 92263 FC1103/93.
24. FO371 92264 FC1103/103.
25. FO371 92263 FC1103/98; FO371 92264 FC1103/104; 138; 148; 171.
26. FO371 99282 FC1105/3.
27. T. G. Rawski, *China's Transition to Industrialization: Producer Goods and Economic Development in the Twentieth Century* (Ann Arbor: University of Michigan Press, 1986) p. 30; W. Brugger, *Democracy and Organization in the Chinese Industrial Enterprise, 1948–1953* (Cambridge: Cambridge University Press, 1976) p. 67
28. *Ibid.*
29. Board of Trade to FO, 21 February 1952, FO371 99282 FC1105/3.
30. See *British American Company's enterprise in China: A collection of source material [Yingmeigongsi zai Hua Qiye]*, edited by Economics Research institute, Shanghai Social Science Academy, in four volumes (Beijing: China Publisher, 1983).
31. FO371 99283 FC1105/59; 99285 FC1105/114.
32. FO371 99284 FC1105/82.
33. FO371 99284 FC1105/130.
34. See reports in the *Manchester Guardian*, the *Financial Times*, and *The Times*.
35. FO371 99286 FC1105/130. Mitchell to Addis, 9 September 1952.
36. CA: Monthly Bulletin No. 77, 20 October 1952.
37. *Reuter* despatch: the *Manchester Guardian* and *The Times*, 20 May 1952.
38. 'Common Programme of the Political Consultative Conference': article 37 and 56, *The Important Documents of the First Plenary Session of the Peoples Political Consultative Conference* (Beijing: Foreign Language Press, 1949).
39. Ye Jichuang, Speech at the second Session of the First national People's Congress, *People's Daily*, 30 July 1955, quoted in Feng-Hwa Mah, *The Foreign Trade of Mainland China* (Edinburgh: Edinburgh University Press, 1972) p. 2.
40. 'Sino-British Trade and its Future' [Zhongying Maoyi], *New Construction [Xin Jianshe]*, 29 January 1950, Vol. 1, No. 11.
41. See Gene T. Hsiao, *The Foreign Trade of China: Policy, Law and Practice* (Berkeley: University of California Press, 1977) p. 10.
42. *World Knowledge [Shijie Zhishi]*, 29 March 1952, No. 12.
43. FO371 99318 FC1152/8.
44. FO371 99318 FC1152/6.
45. FO371 99318 FC1152/15.
46. FO371 99318 FC1152/27.
47. FO371 99318 FC1152/14.

48. The British and Chinese governments' exchanges were published in *Correspondence Between the Government of the United Kingdom of Great Britain and Northern Ireland and the Central People's Government of China on British Trade in China*, Parliamentary Command Paper presented in August 1952, Cmd 8639.
49. *The Times*, 22 July 1952.
50. Board of Trade to the Foreign Office, 30 August 1952, FO371 99320 FC1152/91.
51. Minute by Johnston, 4 September 1952, FO371 99320 FC1152/91.
52. FO371 99320 FC1151/91.
53. F. S. Tomlinson to Johnston, letter, 22 October 1952, FO371 99321 FC1152/102.
54. FO371 99321 FC1152/103.
55. CAB 129/59, Memorandum by the President of the Board of Trade C(53)81. For a discussion of the problems of economic sanctions see M. Doxey, *Economic Sanctions and International Enforcement* (London: Macmillan for the Royal Institute of International Affairs, 1980).
56. CAB 129/59 C(53)81.
57. FO371 105261 FC1151/19.
58. See Chapter 4.
59. McCarthy's allegations in FO371 105248B FC1121/53, 105249, 105250 FC1121/92; the Foreign Office's notice to British firms concerning the Peking conference, FO371 105261 FC1151/19.
60. CA: 1953, Bulletins 53/M/8 20 June 1953; NCNA: Peking, 6 July 1953; FO371 105265 FC1151/127.
61. FO371 105266 FC1151/136; 110287 FC1151/60; FO371 110287 FC1151/34.
62. FO371 110288 FC1151/45.
63. FO371 110288 FC1151/46.
64. Record of meeting at Geneva on 7 May 1954, FO371 110288 FC1151/50A.
65. Record of meeting at Geneva on 7 May 1954, FO371 110288 FC1151/50A.
66. FO371 110288 FC1151/50.
67. FO371 1102890 FC1151/86; FC1151/87B, FC1151/88, FC1151/89.
68. FO371 110290 FC1151/94, FC1151/98, FC1151/110, FC1151/111, FC1151/113; *The Times, Financial Times*, 14 July 1954; *World Knowledge [Shijie Zhishi]*, 1954 No. 16, No. 17,
69. Peking to FO, 7 December 1954, FO371 110292 FC1151/171; *Financial Times*, 24 December 1954.
70. Robert Boardman, *Britain and The People's Republic of China 1949–74* (London: Macmillan, 1976) p. 88.

7 **British Colonial Interests in Southeast Asia**

1. Memorandum prepared for British Far East representatives meeting in London in 1946 by the civil planning unit, FO371 54052 F6208/2129/G6, see Chapter 1; see also 76386 5572/3/500G PUSC(32); also see Alan Bullock, *Ernest Bevin, Foreign Secretary 1945–51* (London: Heinemann, 1983) pp. 743–750.
2. Economic Intelligence Department, 13 April 1949, FO371 76049 F5704/1114/61.
3. For an account of the policy of the Malayan authorities towards Kuomintang activities see, V. Purcell, *The Chinese in Southeast Asia*, 2nd edn (London: Oxford University for the Royal Institute of International Affairs, 1965) pp. 213–301.
4. Gurney to CO, 3 January 1950, FO371 83548 FC1903/1.
5. Gurney to CO, MacDonald to CO, 5 and 7 January 1950, *ibid.*
6. Minute by Coates, FO371 83548 FC1903; Hutchison to FO, 10 January 1950.
7. FO371 83548 FC1903/8.
8. FO371 83548 FC1903/14, FC1903/19, FC1903/21,83549 FC1903/26.
9. Gurney to CO, 28 March 1950, FO371 83549 FC1903/37.
10. *Ibid.*
11. MacDonald and Gimson to CO, 1 April 1950, FO371 83549 FC1903/43; FC1903/42. A. Short, *The Communist Insurrection in Malaya*, 1948–60 (London: Frederick Muller, 1975) p. 215.
12. Hutchison to FO, 31 March 1950, FO371 83549 FC1903/40.
13. FO371 83549 FC1903/37.
14. FO to MacDonald, 10 April 1950, FO371 83550 FC1903/46.
15. MacDonald to FO, 10 April 1950, FO371 83550 FC1903/50.
16. MacDonald to FO, 10 April 1950, *ibid* and FC1903/51; Gurney to CO, 10 April 1950, FO371 83550, FC1903/53.
17. CAB 129/39 CP(50)75; CM(50) 24th meeting.
18. Hutchison to FO, 19 April 1950, FO371 83550 FC1903/60.
19. Malaya Committee meeting, 21 April 1950, CAB134 497, MALC(50)6; also Prem 8 1406.
20. Gurney to CO, 7 May 1950, FO371 83351 FC1903/97; Gimson to CO, 10 May 1950, FC1903/78.
21. Dening to Paskin, FO371 83551 FC1903/80.
22. Dening to Foreign Secretary, 13 May 1950, FO371 83551 FC1903/83. Dening attributed part of the Malayan problem to the fact that the colonial authorities had neglected the Chinese problem before and since the war.
23. *Ibid.*
24. Paper submitted to the Far Eastern (Official) Committee, CAB 134290 FE(0)(50)30, the paper was examined on 12 May 1950, CAB134 289 FE(0)(50)4; MoD to FO, 16 May 1950 COS 599/17/5/50, FO371 83290 FC1022/360G; Treasury to FO, 8 May 1950, FO371 83289

FC1022/347.
25.	J. D. Murray to Dening, FO371 83551 FC1903/84; Dening's note to the Foreign Secretary, FC1903/82; letter from the private secretary of the Colonial Secretary to the private secretary of the Foreign Secretary, FO371 83553 FC1903/116.
26.	W. Wallace, *The Foreign Policy Process in Britain* (London: The Royal Institute of International Affairs, 1975) p. 77; the consensual style of Cabinet decision-making has been demonstrated by C. Hill's *The Decision-Making Process in Relation to British Foreign Policy, 1938–1941* (D.Phil. thesis, 1978, Oxford University) p. 230. See also C. J. Hill, *Cabinet Decisions on Foreign Policy, The British Experience, October 1938–June 1941* (Cambridge: Cambridge University Press, 1991).
27.	FO371 83552 FC1903/91.
28.	FO371 83552 FC1903/91, FC1903/92. For an account of Wang Renshu's (Wang Yen-shu) activities as the PRC's ambassador to Indonesia see D. Mozingo, *Chinese Policy Towards Indonesia* (Ithaca: Cornell University Press, 1976) pp. 90–98.
29.	FO371 83552 FC1903/98.
30.	Peking to FO, 27 July 1950, 28 July 1950, FO371 83552 FC1903/110, FC1903/106; Minutes by Colin Crowe FO371 83553 FC1903/110.
31.	FO to CO, 1 August 1950, FO371 83553 FC1903/110.
32.	CO's agreement to grant transit visas in FO371 83553 FC1903/112; MacDonald to FO, 10 August 1950, in FC1903/118.
33.	A brief official account of the deportation of suspected communists and their dependents to China by the Malayan authorities can be found in FO371 92371 FC1821/122A.
34.	CRO to UK High Commissioner, Australia, 8 January 1951, FO371 92371 FC1821/12.
35.	NCNA: Peking, 29 December 1950.
36.	Hutchison to FO, 1 January 1951, FO371 92371 FC1821/2.
37.	See Chapter 4.
38.	Peking to FO, 28 April 1951, FO371 92373 FC1821/93; 30 April 1951, FC1281/94.
39.	For an account of the MCP armed struggle against the colonial authorities see A. Short, *The Communist Insurrection in Malaya, 1948–60 op. cit.*
40.	See Chapter 4.
41.	Gurney to CO, 6 October 1949; Dening to Paskin, 28 October 1949, FO371 76021 F15689/10140/619.
42.	JIC reports quoted in John Hingham to Gurney 20 March 1950, FO371 184479 FZ1018/5G.
43.	A. Short, *The Communist Insurrection in Malaya: 1948–60, op. cit.*, p. 502.
44.	Note of the meeting between the Foreign Secretary and the Commonwealth Ambassadors in Washington, 16 September 1949, FO371 76024

F14 305/1024/61G.

45. The draft version in CAB134 287 FE(0)(49)25; revised and presented as Cabinet paper on 23 May 1949, CAB 129/35 CP(49)120.

46. See Chapter 2 for the Amethyst incident's effect on Britain's China policy.

47. Memorandum by the Minister of Defence on his visit to Hong Kong, 17 June 1949, CAB 129/35 CP(49)184.

48. Cabinet meeting, 26 May 1949, CAB 128/65 CM38(49).

49. Memorandum jointly presented by the Foreign and Colonial Secretaries on 19 August (CP(49)177), which stated that the British government could not negotiate with a Chinese government which was unfriendly, undemocratic, and not united and stable is closed in the PRO, but a copy is available in the Arthur Creech-Jones papers, Hong Kong, Box 57 File 1, Rhodes House Library, Oxford. Cabinet meeting, 29 August 1949, CAB 128/16 CM54(49).

50. A colonial official told the Governor of Hong Kong that 'what actuated the government was the thought that if Hong Kong were lost it would rebound to the government's disadvantage at the next election'. This, the Governor thought, was 'perhaps unduly cynical', Sir Alexander Grantham, *Via Ports: From Hong Kong to Hong Kong* (Hong Kong: Hong Kong University Press, 1965) p. 143.

51. S. Y. S. Tsang, *Democracy Shelved: Great Britain, China, and Attempts at Constitutional Reform in Hong Kong, 1945–1952* (Hong Kong: Oxford University Press, 1988) p. 130.

52. Hong Kong Record: HKRS D&S; minute of conversation with Hong Kong's Colonial Secretary, 8 February 1947, FO371 63387 F3337/376/10; J. Nicoll to J. Griffiths, 21 July 1950, FO371 83263 FC10112/80; Grantham to Griffiths (enclosure) 6 July 1949, FO371 75782 F10882/1016/10G.

53. Bough's confidential memorandum, Heathcote-Smith to Lamb (enclosure), 2 December 1948, FO371 75779 F124/1016/10, see also S. Y. S. Tsang, *Democracy Shelved*, op. cit., pp. 86–87.

54. Colonial Political Intelligence Service, March 1951, CO371 4789.

55. See Chapter 3 for an account of the negotiations.

56. The Chinese Foreign Ministry's official statement in *CDER*, 1949–50, p. 116; A Grantham to CO, 10 January 1952, FO371 99243 FC10111/7; Hong Kong Colonial Secretariat to FO, FO371 99245 FC10111/74.

57. Foreign Office circular telegram to British representatives abroad, 21 March 1950, Annex A to Cabinet paper CP(50)61, 3 April 1950; for a pro-Beijing account see 'The CNAC and CATC Affair' in *Hong Kong and China: A collection of historical material* [*Xianggang yo Zhongquo*] (Hong Kong: Wide Angle, 1981) pp. 14–22.

58. *Ibid.*

59. Grantham recalled that during his interview with Donovan, the general also threatened to 'make it hot' for the governor if he did not hand the planes to CAT., Grantham, *op. cit.*, 1965, p. 162.

60. Memorandum by the Colonial Secretary and the Minister of State at the Foreign Office, 3 April 1950, CAB 129/39 CP(50)61.
61. *Ibid.*
62. Cabinet meeting 6 April, CM(50)19th meeting; Cabinet paper and annex, 21 April 1950, CAB 129/39, CP(50)74; Cabinet meeting 24 April 1950, CM(50)24th meeting.
63. Kenneth Younger dairy, 8 April 1950.
64. Grantham, *op. cit.*, 1965, p. 163.
65. See Chapter 3.
66. See Peter Wesley-Smith, *Unequal Treaty, 1898–1997; China, Great Britain and Hong Kong's New Territories* (Hong Kong: Oxford University Press, 1983); see also David Bonavia, *Hong Kong 1997: The final settlement* (Bromley: Columbus Books, 1985); and Ian Scott, *Political Change and the Crisis of Legitimacy in Hong Kong* (Hong Kong: Oxford University Press, 1989).

Conclusion

1. Robin Edmonds briefly mentioned Dening's secret mission on information supplied by me in his book, *Setting The Mould: the US and Britain, 1945–50* (Oxford: Oxford University Press, 1986) p. 148, pp. 304–5n. On the Malayan authorities' response to the possible appointment of Chinese Communist consuls see Anthony Short, *The Communist Insurrection in Malaya, 1948–60* (London: Frederick Muller, 1975) pp. 213–216.
2. See E. Lauterpacht (ed.), *International Law, Being the Collected papers of Hersch Lauterpacht*, Vol. 3: *The Law of Peace*, Parts II–VI (Cambridge: Cambridge University Press, 1977) p. 115.
3. H. G. Nicholas, *The United States and Britain* (Chicago: The University of Chicago Press, 1975) pp. 133–137; John Baylis, *Anglo-American Defence Relations, 1939–84: The Special Relationship* (London: Macmillan, 1984) p. 61.
4. C. Hill, 'The Historical Background: Past and Present in British Foreign Policy', in Smith, M. Smith, S., White, B. (eds), *British Foreign Policy: Tradition, Change and Transformation* (London: Unwin Hyman, 1988) p. 44.
5. G. T. Allison, *Essence of Decision* (Boston: Little Brown, 1971); R. C. Snyder *et al.*, *Foreign Policy Decision Making*, (New York: Free Press, 1962). The appearance of S. Smith and M. Clarke (eds), *Foreign Policy Implementation* (London and Winchester: Allen & Unwin) has remedied the situation to a degree, but most of the existing literature on foreign-policy analysis has little to say on this question.
6. M. Clarke, 'Foreign Policy implementation: problems and approaches', *British Journal of International Studies* (Vol. 5 No. 2, 1979) pp. 112–128.

7. H. Bull, *The Anarchical Society* (London: Macmillan, 1977) pp. 311–312.
8. Martin Wright, *Power Politics* (2nd edn) (Harmondsworth: Penguin, 1986) p. 88 and p. 117.
9. 'The Common Program of the Chinese People's Political Consultative Conference', in *The Documents of the First Plenary Session of the Chinese Political Consultative Conference* (Peking: Foreign Language Press, 1949) p. 20.
10. J. D. Armstrong, *Revolutionary Diplomacy: Chinese Foreign Policy and the United Front Doctrine* (Berkeley: University of California Press, 1977) p. vii.
11. H. Bull and A. Watson (eds), *The Expansion of International Society* (Oxford: Oxford University Press, 1984); A. Watson, 'Hedley Bull, state systems and international societies' in *Review of International Studies* (1987, No. 13) pp. 147–153.

Bibliography

I PRIMARY SOURCES: *UNPUBLISHED MATERIAL*

British Government Records, Public Record Office at Kew

(a) Board of Trade

BT 60 Files concerning China, 1946.

(b) Cabinet Office

CAB 128 Cabinet Minutes and Conclusions, 1948–54.
CAB 129 Cabinet Memoranda, 1948–54.
CAB 134 Far Eastern (Official) Committee; China and South East Asia
   Committee; Malayan Committee.

(c) Colonial Office

CO 371 and 537, selected files.

(d) Ministry of Defence

DEFE 4 Chiefs of Staff Minutes, 1949–51.
DEFE 5 Chiefs of Staff Memoranda, 1949–51.
DEFE 6 Reports of the Joint Planning Staff, 1949–51.

(e) Foreign Office

FO 371 Political Correspondence:
Records on China 1947–54.
Records on Korea 1950–51.
Records on the United Nations 1949–51.

(f) The Foreign Secretary's working files

FO 800 Bevin Papers.

(g) Prime Minister's Office

PREM 8 Clement Attlee.
PREM 11 Winston Churchill.

(h) Treasury

T236 Files concerning China 1948–9.

Private Collections

(a) British Library of Political and Economic Science, LSE

Hugh Dalton papers and diaries.

(b) Churchill College, Cambridge

A. V. Alexander papers.
Clement Attlee papers.
Ernest Bevin papers.
Alexander Cadogan papers.
Chandos papers.
Patrick Gordon Walker papers.
Philip John Noel-Baker papers.
William Strang papers.

(c) Rhodes House Library, Oxford

Arthur Creech-Jones papers.
Fabian Colonial Bureau papers.

(d) School of Oriental and African Studies, London

China Association papers.

(e) Papers in Private Hands

Private Correspondence between Mr and Mrs Keith Oakeshott (Mrs Oakeshott's possession).
Kenneth Younger Diaries.
(Lady Younger; a typed transcription is now kept by Professor Geoffrey Warner at the Open University).

Interviews/Correspondences

Mr Alec Adams.
Sir Denis Allen.
Mr Patrick Coates.
Sir Colin Crowe.
Mr Robin Edmonds.
Mr Joe Ford.

Mr and Mrs Andrew Franklin.
Sir Berkeley Gage.
Mrs Jill Oakeshott.
Ven Michael Paton.
Mr Brian Steward.
Sir Stanley Tomlinson.
Sir Nigel Trench.
Sir Michael Wilford.

PRIMARY SOURCES: *PUBLISHED MATERIAL*

British Parliamentary Papers

(a) Hansard, 5th Series House of Commons Debates

(b) Command Papers

Cmd 6703 *Statistical materials presented during the Washington Negotiations (1945)*.
Cmd 8078 *The Korean War: Summary of Events, 1950*.
Cmd 8110 *The Prime Minister's Visit to the United States, 1950*.
Cmd 8159 *UN Resolution on Chinese Intervention, 1951*.
Cmd 8366 *The Korean War: Further Summary of Events, October 1950 – May 1952, 1952*.
Cmd 8596 *Armistice Negotiations and Prisoners of War Camps, June 1951–May 1952, 1952*.
Cmd 8639 *Correspondence between the British and Chinese Governments on British Trade in China, 1952*.
Cmd 8716 *The Indian Proposal for Resolving the Prisoners of War Problem, 1952*.
Cmd 8793 *The Korean War: Further Developments to January 1953, 1953*.
Cmd 8938 *Armistice Agreement at Panmunjom, 1953*.
Cmd 9186 & 9239 *The Geneva Conference (Documents), 1954*.

United States Government Documents: Washington D.C.

Foreign Relations of the United States:

1949, Vols VIII and IX.
1950, Vols VI and VII.
1951, Vols II.
1952–1954, Vols III and XVI.
Department of State Bulletin, selected issues.
United States Relations with China with Special Reference to the Period 1944–1949, 1949.

Published Documentary Source Material In Chinese

Collected Documents on the External Relations of the People's Republic of China (Zhonghua Renmin Gongheguo Duiwaiguanxi Wenjianji), 4 Vols, 1949–1958 (Beijing: World Knowledge Publications, 1957).
The Chinese Communist Party's Major Meetings (Zhongguo Gongchandang Lici Zhongyao Huiyi), Vol. 1 (Research and Teaching Group of the CCP Central College of the Party, Shanghai: People's Publication, 1982).
British American Company's Enterprise in China: A Collection of Documents (Yingmei Gongsi Zai Hua Qiye), 4 Vols., Economic Institute at the Shanghai Social Science Academy (ed.) (Beijing: China Publisher, 1983).
Hong Kong and China: A Collection of Historical Material (Xianggang yu Zhongguo) (Hong Kong: Wide Angle, 1981).

Newspapers and Public Media Materials

(a) In English

Chatham House Press Cuttings, 1946–54, British Newspaper Library, Colindale.
The Manchester Guardian, 1948–54, Manchester, selected issues.
The Times, 1948–54, London, selected issues.
China Reconstruct, 1950–54, Beijing, selected issues.
New China News Agency Reports, 1949–54, selected issues.

(b) In Chinese

Union Research Institute Newspaper Collection, 1949–54, Baptist College, Hong Kong.
People's Daily (Renmin Ribao), 1949–54, selected issues.
World Knowledge (Shijie Zhishi), 1950–54, selected issues.

Reference Works

(a) In English

Biography of Chinese Communists (Hong Kong: Union Research Institute, 1965).
The Biographical Dictionary of Chinese Communism, 1921–65, compiled by D. Klein and A. Clark (Cambridge, Mass.: Harvard University Press, 1971).
China Handbook Series: *Economy* (Beijing; Foreign Languages Press, 1977) Foreign Office Lists: 1946–1955.
Statistic Year Book of China, 1981, Statistic Bureau, PRC (Hong Kong: Economic Information and Agency, 1981).
Survey of International Affairs, 1949–55 (Royal Institute of International

Affairs).

The Times Survey of Foreign Ministries of the World, edited by Z. Steiner
(London: Times Books, 1982).

(b) In Chinese

People's Hand Book (*Renmin Shouche*) 1950–55 (Beijing: Daigung
Baoshe).

Memoirs, Published Diaries and Contemporary Writings

(a) In English

Acheson, D., *Present at the Creation: My Years in the State Department*, (New
York: Norton, 1969).

Attlee, C. R., *As it Happened* (London: Heinemann, 1954).

——, 'Britain and America: Common Aims, Different Opinions', *Foreign
Affairs*, 32 (2 January 1954).

Barclay, R., *Ernest Bevin and the Foreign Office, 1932–1969* (published by
the author, London, 1975).

Barnett, A. D., *China on the Eve of Communist Takeover* (New York: Praeger,
1963).

Collar, J. J., 'British Commercial Relations with China', *International Affairs*,
Vol. 29, No. 4 (October 1953).

Colville, J., *The Fringes of Power, Downing Street Diaries 1939–1955*,
(London: Hodder & Stoughton, 1985).

Dilks, D., *The Diaries of Sir Alexander Cadogan, 1938–1945* (London:
Cassell, 1971).

Eden, A., *The Memoirs of Sir Anthony Eden, Full Circle* (London: Cassell,
1960).

Eisenhower, D. D., *The White House Years: Mandate for Change 1953–1956*
(New York: Doubleday, 1963).

Gladwyn, J., *Memoirs of Lord Gladwyn* (London: 1972).

Hu Chiao-mu, *Thirty Years of the Communist Party of China* (Peking: Foreign
Languages Press, 1952).

Hudson, G. F., 'Will Britain and America split in Asia?', *Foreign Affairs*, 31
(4 July 1953).

Lie, T., *In the Cause of Peace: Seven Years with the United Nations* (London:
Macmillan, 1954).

Liu Shaoqi, *Selected Work of Liu Shaoqi* (Beijing: Foreign Languages Press,
1984).

Macmillan, H., *Tides of Fortune, 1945–1955* (London: Macmillan, 1969).

Mao Zedong, *Selected Work of Mao Tse-Tung* (Beijing: Foreign Languages
Press, Vol. I, 1967, Vol. II and III, 1965, Vol. IV, 1961 and Vol. V,
1977).

Melby, J. F., *The Mandate of Heaven: Record of a Civil War, China 1945–49*
(Toronto: University of Toronto Press, 1968).

Moran, Lord, *Winston Churchill: The Struggle for Survival, 1940–65* (London: Sphere, 1966).

Morrison, H., *Herbert Morrison: an Autobiography* (London: Odam, 1960).

Nehru, J., *Toward Freedom: The Autobiography of Jawaharlal Nehru* (Boston: Beacon Press, 1958).

Pandit, V. L., *The Scope of Happiness: a personal memoir* (London: Weidenfeld & Nicolson, 1979).

Pannikkar, K. M., *In Two Chinas: Memoirs of a Diplomat* (London: George Allen, 1955).

Peng Dehuai, *Memoirs of a Chinese Marshall – The autobiographical notes of Peng Dehuai (1898–1974)*, translated by Zeng Longpu and edited by S. Grimes (Beijing: Foreign Languages Press, 1984) (also Chinese edition).

Shuckburgh, E., *Descent to Suez, Diaries, 1951–56* (London: Weidenfeld & Nicolson, 1986).

Snow, E., *Red Star over China* (New edition, Harmondsworth: Penguin, 1972).

Strang, Lord, *Home and Abroad* (London: Andre Deutsch, 1956).

Talbott, S., *Khrushchev Remembers* (London: Book Club Associates, 1971).

Trevelyan, H., *Worlds Apart, China 1953–55, USSR 1962–65* (London: Macmillan, 1971).

Truman, H. S., *The Truman Memoirs, Vol II: Years of Trial and Hope, 1946–1953* (London: Hodder & Stoughton, 1956).

Williams, P. M., *The Diary of Hugh Gaitskell, 1945–55* (London: Jonathan Cape, 1983).

Wu Xiuquan, *Eight Years in the Ministry of Foreign Affairs: (January 1950–October 1958) – Memoirs of a Diplomat* (Beijing: New World Press, 1985) (also Chinese edition).

Zhou Enlai, *Selected Work of Zhou Enlai*, Vol. I (Beijing: Foreign Languages Press, 1980)

(b) In Chinese

Chen Yun, *Selected Work of Chen Yun, 1926–1949* [*Chen Yun Xuanji, 1926–1949*] (Beijing: People's Publication, 1984).

Nie Rongzhen, *Memoirs of Nie Rongzhen* [*Nie Rongzhen Huiyilu*], Vols 1–3 (Beijing: Peoples's Liberation Army Publication, 1984).

Peng Dehuai (see English edition above) [*Peng Dehuai Zisu*] (Beijing: People's Publication, 1981).

Wu Xiuquan (see English edition above) [*Zai Waijiaobu Bainian de Jingli*] (Beijing, World Knowledge, 1983).

Zhou Enlai, *Selected Work of Zhou Enlai*, Vol. II [*Zhou Enlai Xuanji*] (Beijing: People's Publication, 1984).

Zhou Enlai, *Selected Work of Zhou Enlai on China's Diplomacy* [*Zhou Enlai Waijiao Wenxuan*] (Beijing: Zhonggong Zhongyang Wenxian Chubanshe, 1990).

Zhu De, *Selected Work of Zhu De* [*Zhu De Xuanji*] (Beijing: People's Publication, 1983)

II SECONDARY WORKS: *BOOKS*

(a) In English

Albinski, H. S., *Australian Policies and Attitudes Toward China* (Princeton: Princeton University Press, 1965).

Allison, G. T., *Essence of Decision* (Boston: Little Brown, 1971).

Armstrong, J. D., *Revolutionary Diplomacy, Chinese Foreign Policy and the United Front Doctrine* (Berkeley: University of California Press, 1977).

Barber, J., *Who Makes British Foreign Policy?* (Milton Keynes: The Open University Press, 1976).

——, and Smith, M. (eds), *The Nature of Foreign Policy: A Reader*, (Edinburgh: Homes McDougall in association with the Open University Press).

Barber, N., *The Fall of Shanghai* (New York: Coward, McCann and Geoghehan, 1979).

Barker, E., *The British Between the Super Powers, 1945–50* (London: Macmillan, 1983).

Bianco, L., *Origins of the Chinese Revolution, 1915–1949* (Stanford: Stanford University Press, 1971).

Bloomfield, L. P., *The Foreign Policy Process: A Modern Primer* (Englewood Cliffs, New Jersey: Prentice Hall, 1982).

Blum, R. M., *Drawing the Line: The Origins of the American Containment Policy in East Asia* (New York: Norton, 1982).

Boardman, R., *Britain and the People's Republic of China 1949–74* (London: Macmillan, 1976).

Boardman, R. and Groom, A. J. R., *The Management of Britain's External Relations* (London: Macmillan, 1973).

Bonavia, D., *Hong Kong 1997: the final settlement* (Bromley: Columbus, 1985).

Borg, D. and Heinrich, W., *Uncertain Years: Chinese-American Relations 1947–50* (New York: Columbia University Press, 1980).

Brownlie, I., *Principles of Public International Law* (Oxford: Clarendon Press, 1979) Brugger, W., *Democracy and Organization in the Chinese Enterprise (1948–1953)* (Cambridge: Cambridge University Press, 1976).

Bull, H., *The Anarchical Society: A Study of Order In World Politics* (London: Macmillan, 1977).

——, and Watson, A., *The Expansion of International Society* (Oxford: Clarendon Press, 1984).

Bullock, A., *Ernest Bevin, Foreign Secretary 1945–51* (London: Heinemann, 1983).

Cable, J., *The Geneva Conference of 1954 on Indochina* (London: Macmillan, 1986).

Cairncross, A., *Years of Recovery: British Economic Policy, 1945–51* (London: Methuen, 1985).

Carlton, D., *Anthony Eden: A Biography* (London: Allen Lane, 1981).

Chakravarti, P. C., *India's China Policy* (Bloomington: Indiana University Press, 1962).

Chan, G., *China and International Organizations: Participation in Non-Governmental Organizations Since 1971* (Hong Kong: Oxford University Press, 1989).

Chan Lau Kit-ching, *China, Britain and Hong Kong, 1989–1945* (Hong Kong: The Chinese University Press, 1990).

Ch'en, J., *China and the West: Society and Culture 1815–1937* (London: Hutchison, 1979).

Clark, G., *Economic Rivalries in China* (New Haven: Yale University Press, 1932).

Clarke, M. and White, B., *An Introduction to Foreign Policy Analysis: The Foreign Policy System* (Ormskirk and Northedge: G.W. & A. Hesketh, 1981).

Clubb, O.E., *China and Russia: The 'Great Game'* (New York: Columbia University Press, 1971).

Cohen, B. C., *The Public's Impact on Foreign Policy* (Boston: Little Brown, 1973).

Cohen, W. I., *America's Response to China: An Interpretative History of Sino-American Relations* (New York: John Wiley & Sons, 1971).

——, *Dean Rusk* (Totowa, New Jersey: Cooper Square, 1980).

Cole, G. D. E., *The Post-War Condition of Britain* (London: Routledge & Kegan Paul, 1956).

Cockerell, M., Hennessy, P. and Walker, D., *Sources Close to the Prime Minister: Inside the hidden world of the new manipulators* (London: Macmillan, 1984).

Costin, W. C., *Great Britain and China, 1833–1860* (Oxford: Oxford University Press, 1937).

Darby, P., *British Defence Policy East of Suez, 1947–1968*, (London: Oxford University Press for the Royal Institute of International Affairs, 1973).

Deighton, A. (ed.) *Britain and the First Cold War* (London: Macmillan, 1990).

Dilks, D. (ed.), *Retreat from Power: Studies in Britain's Foreign Policy of the Twentieth Century*, Vols I & II (London: Macmillan, 1981).

Donnithorne, A., *China's Economic System* (London: Allen & Unwin, 1967).

Donoughue, B. and Jones, G., *Herbert Morrison: Portrait of a Politician*, (London: Weidenfeld & Nicolson, 1973).

Doxey, M. P., *Economic Sanctions and International Enforcement* (London: Macmillan for the Royal Institution of International Affairs, 1984).

Earl, L., *Yangtse Incident* (London: Harrap, 1950, 1980).

East, M. A., *et al.*, *Why Nations Act: Theoretical Perspectives for Comparative Foreign Policy Studies* (Beverly Hills, CA and London: Sage, 1978).

Eatwell, R., *The 1945–1951 Labour Governments* (London: Batsford Academic 1979).

Edmonds, R., *Setting the Mould: The US and Britain, 1945–50* (Oxford: Oxford University Press, 1986).

Endacott, G. B., *A History of Hong Kong* (Hong Kong: Oxford University Press, 1964).

Etzold, T. H. (ed.) *Aspects of Sino-American Relations Since 1784* (New York: New viewpoints, 1978).

Evans, P. M., and Frolic, B. M. (eds), *Canada and the People's Republic of China, 1949–1970* (Toronto: University of Toronto Press, 1991).

Fairbank, J., Reischauer, E. and Craig, A., *East Asia: The Modern Transformation* (Cambridge, Mass.: Harvard University Press, 1955).

Fang, P. J. and L. G. J., *Zhou Enlai – A Profile* (Beijing: Foreign Languages Press, 1986).

Ficher, W. R., *The End of Extraterritoriality in China* (Berkeley: University of California Press, 1962).

Foot, R., *The Wrong War: American Policy and the Dimensions of the Korean Conflict 1950–53* (Ithaca: Cornell University Press, 1986).

Frankel, J., *British Foreign Policy 1945–73* (London: Oxford University Press for the Royal Institute of International Affairs, 1975).

——, *The Making of Foreign Policy* (London: Oxford University Press, 1963).

Gaddis, J. L., *The United States and the Origins of the Cold War, 1941–1947* (New York: Columbia University Press, 1972).

Garver, J. W., *Chinese-Soviet Relations, 1937–1945: The Diplomacy of Chinese Nationalism* (New York: Oxford University Press, 1988) .

Gittings, J., *The World and China, 1922–72* (London: Eyre Methuen, 1974).

Goldsworthy, D., *Colonial Issues in British Politics 1945–1961: From 'Colonial Development' to 'Wind of Change'* (London: Oxford University Press, 1971).

Gurtov, M. and Hwang, B. M., *China Under Threat, the Politics of Strategy and Diplomacy* (Baltimore: Johns Hopkins University Press, 1980).

Gull, E. M., *British Economic Interests in the Far East* (London: Oxford University Press, published under the auspices of the Royal Institute of International Affairs, 1943).

Harrison, J. P., *The Long March to Power: A History of the Chinese Communist Party 1921–72* (London: Macmillan, 1972).

Heuser, B., *Western 'Containment' Policies in the Cold War: The Yugoslav Case* (London: Routledge, 1989).

Hill, C. J., *The Decision-Making Process in Relation to British Foreign Policy, 1938–1941* (D.Phil thesis, University of Oxford, 1978).

Hill, C. J. *Cabinet Decisions on Foreign Policy: The British Experience, October 1938–June 1941* (Cambridge: Cambridge University Press, 1991).

Hooper, B., *China Stands Up: Ending the Western Presence, 1948–1950*, (Sydney: Allen & Unwin (Australia), 1986).

Hou, C., *Foreign Investment and Economic Development in China, 1840–1937* (Cambridge, Mass.: Harvard University Press, 1965).

Howe, C., *China's Economy: A Basic Guide* (London: Granada, 1978).

Hsiao, G. T., *The Foreign Trade of China: Policy, Law and Practice*, (Berkeley: University of California Press, 1977).

Hsiung, J. C., *Law and Policy in China's Foreign Relations: A Study of Attitudes and Practice* (New York: Columbia University Press, 1972).

Hsu, I. C. Y., *The Rise of Modern China* (New York: Oxford University Press, 1990).

Hu, S., *Imperialism and Chinese Politics* (Beijing: Foreign Language Press, 1981).

Hudson, G. F., *Questions of East and West* (London: Odhams, 1953).

Iriye, A., *Across the Pacific, an Inner History of American East Asian Relations* (New York: Harvest/HBJ, 1967).

——, *The Cold War in Asia: A Historical Introduction* (Englewood Cliffs, New Jersey: Prentice-Hall, 1974).

Jain, J, P., *China in World Politics* (New Delhi: Radiant Press, 1976).

——, *China, Pakistan and Bangladesh* (New Delhi: Radiant, 1974).

James, R. P., *Anthony Eden* (London: Weidenfeld & Nicolson, 1986).

Jenkins, R., *Truman* (London: Collins, 1986).

Jensen, L., *Explaining Foreign Policy* (Englewood Cliffs, New Jersey: Prentice Hall, 1982).

Jetly, N., *India-China Relations, 1947–1977: A Study of Parliament's Role in the Making of Foreign Policy* (Atlantic Highlands, New Jersey: Humanities Press, 1979) .

Kahin, G. M., *Nationalism and Revolution in Indonesia* (Ithaca: Cornell University Press, 1952).

Kalicki, J. H., *The Pattern of Sino-American Crises: Political-Military Interactions in the 1950s* (London: Cambridge University Press, 1975).

Kennedy, P., *The Realities Behind Diplomacy, Background Influences on British External Policy, 1865–1980* (London: Fontana, 1981).

Keith, R. C., *The Diplomacy of Zhou Enlai* (London: Macmillan, 1989).

Kim, S. S., *China, The United Nations, and World Order* (Princeton: Princeton University Press, 1979).

LaFeber, W., *America, Russia, and the Cold War, 1945–1980* (4th edition) (New York: John Wiley & Sons, 1976).

Lancaster, D., *The Emancipation of French Indochina* (London: Oxford University Press for the Royal Institute of International Affairs, 1961) .

Lauterpacht, H., *Recognition in International Law* (London: Cambridge University Press, 1947).

Leifer, M., *The Foreign Relations of the New States* (Camberwell: Longman, 1974).

——, (ed.), *Constraints and Adjustments in British Foreign Policy* (London: Allen & Unwin, 1972).

Leuchtenburg W. E. *et al.*, *Britain and the United States: Four Views to Mark the Silver Jubilee* (London: Heineman, 1979).

Liao, K. S., *Anti-foreignism and Modernization in China, 1860–1980: Linkage Between Politics and Foreign Policy* (Hong Kong: Chinese University Press, 1984).

Lieberthal, K. G., *Revolution and Tradition in Tientsin, 1949–1952*, (Stanford: Stanford University Press, 1980).

Light, M. and Groom, A. J. R., *International Relations: A Handbook of Current Theory* (London: Frances Pinter, 1985).

Lindbeck, J. M. H. (ed.), *China: Management of a Revolutionary Society* (London: Allen & Unwin, 1972).

Lindsay, M., *China and the Cold War* (Melbourne: Melbourne University Press, 1955).

Lowe, P., *Great Britain and the Origins of the Pacific War: A Study of British Policy in East Asia, 1937–41* (Oxford: Clarendon Press, 1977).

——, *Britain in the Far East: a survey from 1819 to the present* (London: Longman, 1981).

——, *The Origins of the Korean War* (London: Longman, 1986).

Luard, E., *Britain and China* (London: Chatto & Windus, 1962).

——, *a History of the United Nations*, Vol. 1: *The Years of Western domination 1945–1955* (London: Macmillan, 1982).

MacDonald, C. A., *Korea: the War Before Vietnam* (London: Macmillan, 1986).

Mitchell, J., *Crisis in Britain 1951* (London: Secker & Warburg, 1963).

Morgan, K. O., *Labour in Power, 1945–1951* (Oxford: Oxford University Press, 1984).

——, *Labour People: Leaders and Lieutenants, Hardie to Kinnock* (Oxford University Press, 1987).

Mozingo, D., *Chinese Policy towards Indonesia* (Ithaca: Cornell University Press, 1976).

Murfett, M., *Hostages on the Yangtze* (Annapolis: US Naval Press, 1991).

Newman, R. P., *Recognition of Communist China? A Study in Argument* (London: Macmillan, 1961).

Nicholas, H. G., *The United States and Britain* (Chicago: The University of Chicago Press, 1975).

Northedge, F. S., *Descent from Power: British Foreign Policy, 1945–73*, (London: Allen & Unwin, 1974).

Ovendale, R., *The English-Speaking Alliance: Britain, the US, the Dominions and the Cold War, 1945–51* (London: Allen & Unwin, 1985).

——, *The Foreign Policy of the British Labour Governments, 1945–1951* (Leicester: Leicester University Press, 1984).

Pelcorits, N. A., *Old China Hands and the Foreign Office* (New York: King's Crown Press, 1948 under the auspices of American Institute of Pacific Relations).

Pelling, H., *The Labour Governments, 1945–51* (London: Macmillan, 1984).

Pepper, S., *Civil War in China: The Political Struggle, 1945–1949*, (Berkeley; University of California Press, 1978).

Pimlott, B., *Hugh Dalton* (London: Jonathan Cape, 1985).

Pollack, J, D., *Security Strategy and the Logic of Chinese Foreign Policy* (Berkeley: California Institute of East Asian Studies, University of California, 1981).

Porter, B., *Britain and the Rise of Communist China, a study of British attitudes 1945–1954* (London: Oxford University Press, 1967).

Pratt, J. T., *China and Britain* (London: Collins, 1946).

Purcell, V., *The Chinese in Southeast Asia* (2nd edn) (London: Oxford University Press for the Royal Institute of International Affairs, 1965).

Quested, R. K. I., *Sino-Russian Relations: A Short History* (Sydney: Allen & Unwin, 1984).

Ramakant (ed.), *China and South Asia* (New Delhi: South Asian Publisher, 1988).

Reardon-Anderson, J., *Yenan and the Great Powers: the origin of Chinese Communist foreign policy, 1944–46* (New York: Columbia University Press, 1979).

Rosenau, J, N., *The Scientific Study of Foreign Policy* (New York: The Free Press, 1971).

Rothwell, V. H., *Britain and the Cold War 1941–1947* (London: Cape, 1982).

Schram, S., *Mao Tse-Tung* (Harmondsworth: Penguin, 1967).

Schwartz, B. I., *Chinese Communism and the Rise of Mao* (Cambridge, Mass.: Harvard University Press, 1979).

Shai, A., *Britain and China, 1941–47* (London: Macmillan, 1984).

Shaw, M., *International Law* (London: Hodder & Stoughton, 1977).

Shlaim, A., Jones, P. and Sainsbury, K., *British Foreign Secretaries Since 1945* (Newton Abbot; David and Charles, 1977).

Short, A., *The Communist Insurrection in Malaya, 1948–60* (London: Frederick Muller, 1975).

Sked, A. and Cook, C., *Post-War Britain, a political history* (Brighton, Sussex: Harvester, 1979).

Smith, M. *et al.* (eds), *British Foreign Policy, Traditional Change and Transformation* (London: Unwin Hyman, 1988).

Smith, S. and Clarke, M. (eds), *Foreign Policy Implementation* (London & Winchester, MA: Allen & Unwin, 1985).

Solinger, D. J., *Chinese Business Under Socialism: The Politics of Domestic Commerce, 1949–1980* (Berkeley: University of California Press, 1984).

Snyder, R. C. *et al.*, *Foreign Policy Decision Making* (New York: Free Press, 1962).

Taylor, J., *China and Southeast Asia: Peking's relations with revolutionary movements* (New York: Praeger, 1976).

Thompson, T. N., *China's Nationalisation of Foreign Firms: the politics of hostage capitalism 1949–1957* (Baltimore: University of Maryland School of Law, 1979).

Taylor, T. (ed.), *Approaches and Theory in International Relations* (London: Longman, 1978).

Thorne, C., *Allies of a Kind: The United States, Britain, and the War Against Japan, 1941–45* (London: Oxford University Press, 1978).

——, *The Far Eastern War: States and Societies, 1941–45* (London: Unwin, 1985).

Trotter, A., *Britain and East Asia, 1933–37* (London: Cambridge University Press, 1975).

Tsang, S. Y. S., *Democracy Shelved: Great Britain, China and Attempts at Constitutional Reform in Hong Kong, 1945–52* (Hong Kong: Oxford University Press, 1988).

Tsou, T., *America's Failure in China 1941–50*, Vols 1 & 2. (Chicago: University of Chicago Press, 1963).

Tucker, N. B., *Pattern in the Dust: Chinese-American Relations and the Recognition Controversy, 1949–1950* (New York: Columbia University Press, 1983).

Tung, W. L., *China and the Foreign Powers: The Impact of and Reaction to Unequal Treaties* (New York: Oceania, 1970).

Van ness, P., *Revolution and Chinese Foreign Policy, Peking's Support for Wars of National Liberation* (Berkeley: University of California Press, 1971).

Vital, D., *The Making of British Foreign Policy* (London: Allen & Unwin, 1968).

Wallace, W., *The Foreign Policy Process in Britain* (London: Allen & Unwin for the Royal Institution of International Affairs, 1975).

Wang, G., *China and the World since 1949: The Impact of Independence, Modernity, and Revolution* (London: Macmillan, 1977).

Weng, B. S. J., *Peking's UN Policy: Continuity and Change* (New York: Praeger, 1972).

Wesley-Smith, P., *Unequal Treaties 1898–1977, China, Great Britain and Hong Kong* (Hong Kong: Oxford University Press, 1980).

Whiting, A. S., *China Crosses the Yalu, the decision to enter the Korean War* (Stanford: Stanford University Press, 1960).

Wight, M., *Power Politics* (2nd edition, Harmondsworth: Penguin for Royal Institution of International Affairs, 1980).

Williams, F., *A Prime Minister Remembers: The War and Post-War Memoirs of the Rt Hon Earl Attlee* (London: Heinemann, 1961).

Williams, P. M., *Hugh Gaitskell* (Oxford: Oxford University Press, 1982).

Wilson, D. (ed.), *Mao Tse-tung in the Scale of History* (London: Cambridge University Press, 1977).

Woodhouse, C. M., *British Foreign Policy since Second World War* (London: Hutchison, 1961).

Xue Mouhong and Pei Jianzhang (*et al.*) *Contemporay Diplomacy of China* (Hong Kong: New Horizon, 1991). This is a translated and up-dated version of *Dangdai Zhongguo Waijiao*, an official diplomatic history first published in Beijing in 1988.

Yahuda, M. B., *China's Role in World Affairs* (London: Croom Helm, 1978).

(b) In Chinese

(Works written by collective groups such as a research group or a writing group are listed under their title)

A Biography of Lin Baiqu [Lin Baiqu Zhuan] (Beijing: Hongqi Chubanshe, 1986).

Du Peng, *At the Volunteers' Headquarters* [*Zai Zhiyuanjun Zongbu*] (Beijing: Jiefangjun Chubanshe, 1989).

Guo Tingyi, *An Outline History of Modern Chinese History* [*Jindal Zhongguo Shigang*], 2 Vols (Hong Kong: Chinese University of Hong Kong Press, 1980).

Hu Sheng, *Imperialism and Chinese Politics* [*Diguozhuyi yu Zhongguo Zhengzhi*] (New Edition, Beijing: Renmin Chubanshe, 1977).

Hu Zhuanzhang and Ha Jianxiong, *A Biography of Dong Biwu* [*Dong Biwu Zhuanji*] (Hubei: Hubei Renmin Chubanshe, 1985).

Lectures on an Outline History of the CCP [*Zhongguo Gongchandang Jianshi Jiangyi*] (Guangzhou: Guangdong Renmin Chubanshe, 1981).

Lectures on the History of the CCP [*Zhongguo Gongchandang Lishi Jiangyi*] (Shangdong: Renmin Chubanshe, 1980).

Lu Xingdou and Bai Yun Tao, *Zhou Enlai and His Work* [*Zhou Enlai he Tade Shiye*] (Beijing: Zhonggong Dangshi Chubanshe, 1990).

Pei Jianzhang *et al.* (eds) *New China's Diplomacy: Memoirs of China's diplomats* [*Xin Zhongguo Waijiao Fengyun: Zhonguo Waijiaoguan Huiyilu*] (Beijing: Shijie Zhishi Chubanshe for the Foreign Ministry's Diplomatic History Office, 1990).

Tan Jingqiao, *The War To Resist the US and Assist Korea* [*Kangmei Yuanzhao Zhanzheng*] (Beijing Zhongguo Shihui Kexueyuan Chubanshe, 1990).

Wu Dongzhi (ed.), *A Diplomatic History of China: The Period of the Republic of China 1911–1949* [*Zhongguo Waijiaoshi: Zhonghuaminguo Shiqi, 1911–1949*] (Henan: Henan Remin Chubanshe, 1988).

Xue Mouhong and Pei Jianzhang, *Contemporay Diplomacy of China* [*Dangdai Zhongguo Waijiao*], (Beijing: Zhongguo Shihuikexueyuan, 1988).

SECONDARY WORKS: *ARTICLES*

Adamthwaite, A., 'Britain and the World, 1945–9: the view from the Foreign Office', *International Affairs*, Vol. 61, No. 2 (Spring 1985).

Baylis, J., 'Britain, the Brussels Pact and the Continental Commitment', *International Affairs*, Vol. 50, No. 4 (August 1984).

——, 'The Anglo-American relationship and Alliance Theory', *International Affairs*, Vol. 62, No. 4 (1985).

Bell, C., 'China and the International Order', in H. Bull and A. Watson (eds), *The Expansion of International Society* (Oxford: Oxford University Press, 1984).

Clarke, M., 'Foreign Policy implementation: problems and approaches', *British Journal of International Studies*, No. 5 (1979).

Dockrill, M., 'The Foreign Office, Anglo-American Relations and the Korean War, June 1950–June 1951', *International Affairs*, Vol. 62, No. 3 (Summer 1986).

Farrar, P. N., 'Britain's Proposal for a Buffer Zone South of the Yalu in November 1950: Was it a Neglected Opportunity to end the Fighting in Korea?', *Journal of Contemporary History*, Vol. 18, No. 2 (April 1983).

Gong, G. W., 'China's Entry into International Society', in H. Bull and A. Watson (eds), *The Expansion of International Society* (Oxford: Oxford University Press, 1984).

Hill, C. and Light, M., 'Foreign Policy Analysis', in M. Light and A. J. R. Groom (eds) *International Relations: A Handbook of Current Theory* (London: Frances Pinter, 1985).

Holland, R. F., 'The Imperial Factor in British Strategies from Attlee to Macmillan, 1945–63', *Journal of Imperial and Commonwealth History*, Vol. XII, No. 2 (January 1984).

Hosoya, C., 'Japan, China, the United States and the United Kingdom, 1951–2: the case of the "Yoshida Letter"', *International Affairs*, Vol. 60, No. 2 (Spring 1984).

Klein, D. W., 'Peking's Evolving Ministry of Foreign Affairs', *China Quarterly*, No. 4 (October to December 1960).

Louis, W. R., 'The Special Relationship and British Decolonization', *International Affairs*, Vol. 61, No. 3 (Summer 1985).

Murthy, N. V. K., 'Recognition of Communist China under International Law, with special reference to the policies of Great Britain, the United States, and India', *Indian Journal of Political Science*, 20, 2 (April–June, 1959).

Newton, S., 'Britain, the Sterling Area and European Integration, 1945–50', *The Journal of Imperial and Commonwealth History*, Vol. XIII, No. 3 (May 1985).

Osterhammel, J., 'Imperialism in Transition: British Business and the Chinese Authorities, 1931–37', *China Quarterly*, No. 98 (June 1984).

Ovendale, 'Britain, the United States, and the Cold War in Southeast Asia, 1949–1950', *International Affairs*, Vol. 48, No. 3 (Summer 1982).

——, 'Britain, the United States, and the Recognition of Communist China', *The Historical Journal*, Vol. 26. No. 1 (1983).

Reynolds, D., 'A "special relationship"? American, Britain and the international order since the Second World War', *International Affairs*, Vol. 62, No. 1 (Winter 1985).

Shao, Kuo-kang, 'Zhou Enlai's Diplomacy and the Neutralization of Indo-China, 1954–55', *China Quarterly* (September 1986).

Smith, R. and Zametica, J., 'The Cold War Warrior: Clement Attlee reconsidered, 1945–7', *International Affairs*, Vol. 61, No. 2 (Spring 1985).

Stockwell, A. J., 'British Imperial Policy and Decolonization in Malaya, 1942–52', *The Journal of Imperial and Commonwealth History*, Vol. XIII, No. 1 (October 1984).

Tuchman, B. W., 'If Mao had Come to Washington: an Essay in Alternative', *Foreign Affairs*, 51 (October 1972).

Watson, A., 'Hedley Bull, states systems and international societies', *Review of International Studies*, No. 2 (April 1987).

Watt, C. C., 'Britain and the Cold War in the Far East, 1945– 58', in Yonosuke Nagai and Akira Iriye (eds), *The Origins of the Cold War in Asia* (New York and Tokyo: Columbia University Press in association with Tokyo University Press, 1977).

Weng, B. S., 'Communist China's Changing Attitude towards the United Nations', *International Organisation*, XX, 4 (Autumn 1966).

Wolf, D. C., '"To Secure a Convenience": Britain Recognizes China – 1950', *Journal of Contemporary History*, Vol. 18, No. 2 (April 1983).

Zheng Weizhi, 'Independence is the Basic Canon', *Beijing Review* (7 January 1985).

Index

Acheson, Dean, 81, 136, 137, 142, 184, 195
  Acheson-Bevin Washington meeting (1949), 55–56
  attitude towards the Chinese civil war, 54
  on Anglo-American relations, 88
  on Britain's recognition of Communist China, 55–6, 57–8, 67
  on China's intervention in the Korean War, 99, 100
  on Chinese representation in UN, 88, 137, 140
  on the establishment of the PRC, 54–55
  on the Korean War, 87–88
  on the Korean War peace negotiations, 106
  on Sino-Soviet relations, 56
Addis, J., 224 n61 n64 n65
Alexander, A.V. 44, 184
Alien Affairs Departments (PRC), Tianjin, Shanghai
  see under Chinese government (PRC)
Allen, Denis, 11, 116, 118, 121
  on Britain's China policy, 119
  on recognizing a communist Chinese government, 12
  relationship with Antony Eden, 12
Allison, G. T., 37, 196
America see United State
Amethyst Incident, 35–36, 43–44, 47, 68, 184
Anglo-American relations
  and British trade with China (PRC), 163–164
  and British foreign policy, 1, 9, 14, 15, 196, 201
  and Chinese representation in the UN, 82–83, 85, 135–136, 140, 142–143
  and disagreement over China and

the Far East, 53–54, 79–80, 87–89, 106, 141, 194–196
  Churchill's attitude towards, 112–113
  impact of Korean War on, 99–104, 105–107
  see also Lend-Lease
Anglo-Chinese relations
  breakthrough in Geneva, 120–124
  negotiations on establishing diplomatic relations, 72–84, 80–84
  new phase in 1951, 107–109
  see also under Britain, and under China (PRC)
Armstrong, D., 200
Attlee, C. R. 42, 44, 123–124, 136
  Attlee-Turman meeting (1950), 100–101
  on Anglo-American relations, 9, 52, 106
  on British foreign policy, 9, 44, 196
  on China's intervention in Korea, 101, 103
  on Korean War, 87, 100–101
  on United Nations Organization, 9
  relationship with Ernest Bevin, 10, 22
Austin, Warren, 105
Australia, 92
  attitude towards recognition of Communist China, 59–60

Bajpal, Girja Shankar, 59
Bangkok, 92, 133
Barclay, Sir Roderick E, 205 n11, 214 n65 n75
Baylis, John, 194
Bedell Smith, Gen W., 122–123
Beijing economic conference (1953), 163–165
Belgium, attitude towards recognition of Communist China, 61
Berlin blockade, 14, 45

Bevin, Ernest, 8, 9–10, 22, 35, 42, 53, 65, 87, 140, 142, 149, 184
and Esler Dening's secret mission to China, 93
on Anglo-American relation, 15, 55, 87–88
on British foreign policy objectives, 14–15
on China's intervention in Korean War 98–99, 103: proposal to establish a de-militarised zone, 99, 195
on Chinese civil war, 17
on Chinese Communist consul controversy, 178
on Chinese representation in UN, 82, 87–88, 134–137
on recognition of Communist China, 78, 80, 82
on Soviet threat, 14–15
relationship with Clement Attlee, 10
relationship with Anthony Eden, 10
relationship with Foreign Office officials *see under* Allen, D.; Dening, E; and R. Scott
Bianco, Lucien, 19
Board of Trade, British *see under* British government (ministries and departments)
Bolshevik Revolution, 3, 19
Borneo, 40
Bough, H. C., 186
Boyce, Sir Leslie, 17
Boyd-Orr, Lord, 159–160
Bradley, Omar, 101
Braun, Otto, 24
Britain
China policy: changes between 1949 and 1954, 192–196; Chinese communism, 18–9; Chinese representation in the UN, 36, 75–76 130–143, 194 *see also under* United Nations; establishment of official diplomatic relations, 120–124; impact of Korea War, 107–109, 114–115, 115–117; policy after the Second World War, 15–18; policy of 'keeping a foot in

the door' in China, 32–42; policy of 'keeping a toe in the door' in China, 117–118; policy formulation (bureacratic politics, 37, 38–42, 67, 79, 178–179, 190, 196; business lobby, 49–52; 148, 168–169; foreign policy makers, 8–10; party politics, 42–45; the press, 45–48)
colonial interest in Southeast Asia, 170–191
commercial interest in China, 3, 7, 18, 78, 117–118, 148–169: end of British commercial empire in China, 156–157; Korean War and British business in China, 152–156; recognition and its aftermath, 148–152; trade missions to China, 165–167; *see also* Sino-British trade
post-World War II conditions, 13–15: economic situation 14
relations with United States, *see under* Anglo-American relations; *see also under* British government *and*, British Parliament
British-American Tobacco Company, 49, 156
British business lobby and the question of recognition, 49–52
British Chamber of Commerce, Shanghai, 50, 51–52, 111–112, 149, 157
British Council for the Promotion of International Trade, 118, 163–164, 167
British commercial interest in China *see under* Britain
British Defence Co-ordination Committee, *see under* British government (committees)
British government (Conservative), 12
China policy, 112–115
British government (Labour), 1, 8–10
China policy, 31, 65–66, 71–72, 95, 113

British government (ministries and
  departments)
  Board of Trade, 12–3, 17, 38–39,
    67, 91, 110, 118, 149, 153,
    155, 159–160, 162, 163, 164:
    Commercial Relations and
    Export Department, 212 n25
  Central Information Office, 73
  Chiefs of Staff, 9, 12–13, 39, 177:
    and Korean War, 85; and the
    Chinese Communist consul
    controversy, 177–178
  Colonial Office, 12–3, 38, 40,
    67, 79, 190: and the Chinese
    Communist consul controversy,
    172, 173, 176–79; on transit
    visas for Chinese diplomats,
    179–180; and the MCP,
    183; attitude towards Hong
    Kong's position, 184; attitude
    towards the CNAC and CATA
    affair, 188
  Commonwealth Relations Office, 38
  Foreign Office: and Britain's China
    Policy, 10–13; and Chinese
    representation in the UN,
    130–131; and the Communist
    consul controversy, 172–179;
    and transit visas for Chinese
    diplomats, 179–180; and the
    Malayan Communist Party,
    183; and the CNAC and
    CATC affair, 188; China and
    Korea Department, 161; Civil
    Planning Unit, 16; Economic
    Intelligence Unit, 171; Eco-
    nomic Relations Department,
    15; Far Eastern Department,
    10, 15, 31, 34, 57, 77, 80, 93,
    95, 135, 165; Southeast Asian
    Department, 12, 173, 180
  Ministry of Defence, 37, 39–40,
    67, 190: attitude towards the
    Chinese Communist consul
    controversy, 176–177
  Joint Planning Staff, 39–40
  Ministry of Transport, 38
  Treasury, 12, 13, 38–39
    67, 149, 153: Overseas
    Financial Division,
    13
British government (committees)
  British Defence Co-ordination
    Committee, 184
  China and South East Asia
    Committee, 13, 193
  Far Eastern (Official) Committee,
    13, 38
  Joint Intelligence Committee
    (JIC), 183
  Malaya Committee, 231 n19
British Information Service
  see under British government
    (ministries and departments)
British Industrial Fair, 165
British Parliament, 68, 78, 81, 110
  and Opposition politics, 42–45, 110
  debate on the policy of recognition,
    78–79, 81
  reaction to the possible use of
    atomic bomb, 100
British Press, and the recognition of
  Communist China, 45–48
  see also under Britain, China policy,
    policy formulation
Bull, Hedley, 4, 198, 200
Bukit Serone Conference, Singapore,
  41, 65, 172
Burdett, S. L., 50
Burgess, Guy, 12
Burma, 96, 143, 179
  recognition of Communist
    China, 72–73
bureacratic politics and foreign policy,
  37, 179
  see also under, Britain, China
    policy, policy formulation
business lobby, British, 169
  see also under, Britain, China
    policy, policy formulation
Butler, R. A., 43–44, 212 n37

Cabot, John, 50
Cabinet Paper CP(48)299, 32–34,
  64
Cadogan, Six Alexander, 8, 10,
  129, 132
Calvert, Peter, 3

Index

255

Canada, 103, 104, 138
  attitude towards recognition of
    Communist China, 59–60
Canton, *see* Guangzhou
CAT, 187–188
  see also CNAC and CATC
    aircraft affair
CATC, *see* CNAC and CATC
    aircraft affair
Cavendish-Bentinck, Victor, 15
Central Air Transport Corporation,
  see CATC
Central Intelligence Agency, US, *see*
  under United States
Ceylon, attitude towards recognition of
  Communist China, 59–60
Chen Jiakang, 23, 144
Chen Yun, 21, 22
Chennault, General Claire, 187
Chiang Kai-shek, 8, 17–18, 20, 21, 26,
  27, 54, 63, 145
  see also Kuomintang, Taiwan
Chiefs of Staff, British
  see under British government
    (ministries and departments)
China Lobby, U.S., 49, 54
China (PRC)
  and international society, 198–201
  attitude towards Britain, 28–30; 73,
    74–76, 80, 107–09
  attitude towards repatriation of
    overseas Chinese in Malaya,
    107–108
  attitude towards UN's role as an
    international organization,
    143–146
  attitude towards UN membership,
    74, 80–1, 102–103, 104, 196
  Chinese People's Relief Administra-
    tion, *see under* Malaya
  Chinese People's Relief Committee
    for the Overseas Chinese
    Refugees of Malaya, the, *see*
    under Malaya
  conditions in 1949, 25–26
  economic conditions, 25–26
    (industrial readjustment, 155)
  foreign policy makers, 8–10
  foreign policy principles, 27–29

revolutionary diplomacy, 3–4,
  198–201 *see also under*
  Chinese Communist Party,
  Chinese government (PRC)
China and Korea Department, British
  see under British government
    (ministries and departments),
    Foreign Office
China and South East Asia Committee,
  British
  see under British government
    (committees)
China Association, 49, 51–2, 78,
  148–152, 154, 156, 160, 164–165
China National Import and Export
  Corporation (CNIEC), 160, 161
China White Paper, The (August
  1949), 54
  letter of transmittal, 214 n70
Chinese Advisory Committee, Malaya
  see under Malaya
Chinese civil war
  see under China (PRC)
Chinese Communist consuls in
  Malaya, 172–179
Chinese Communist Party, 19, 21–22,
  23, 24, 26, 27, 144, 169
  Alien Affairs Bureaus/Departments,
    24
  and the Chinese civil war, 17, 21,
    25, 27, 32, 34, 35, 36, 49,
    71, 200
  Central Committee, 21, 25: 2nd
    plenary session of the seventh
    Central Committee (March
    1949), 27–28
  industrial policy, 155
  politburo, 21, 22, 25
  post Second World War relations
    with the West, 26–27
  relations with the Malayan
    Communist Party, 182–183
  see also China (PRC), Chinese
    government (PRC)
Chinese government (PRC)
  Foreign Affairs Bureau, 36
  Government Administration
    Council, 25
  Ministry of Foreign Affairs, 22,

23–25, 107: Treaty Committee
24; Western Europe and
African Division, 74
Ministry of Foreign Trade, 165
People's Association for Friendship
with Foreign Countries, 23
Public-Private Relation Mediation
Committee, Tianjin, 151
see also under China (PRC) *and*,
Chinese Communist Party
Chinese National Aviation Corporation
see CNAC
Chinese National People's Congress:
September 1950, 90; September
1954, 123
Chinese People's Political Consultative
Conference, 158
Common Programme of, 28, 198
Chinese People's Relief Administra-
tion, (PRC)
see under Malaya
Chinese People's Relief Committee for
the Overseas Chinese Refugees of
Malaya, the, (PRC)
see under Malaya
Chinese representation in the United
Nations, 129–147
Chinese People's Liberation Army, *see*
Red Army
Chongqing, 22, 23, 27, 111
Chungking, *see* Chongqing
Churchill, Winston, 9, 42, 115
on British foreign policy, 112–113
on China's intervention in Korean
War, 114
on the Kuomintang government in
Taiwan, 113
on the recognition of Communist
China, 45, 113
Civil Air Transport, *see* CAT
Civil Planning Unit, British
see under British government
(ministries and departments),
Foreign Office
Clark Kerr, Sir Archibald, 18
Clarke, Michael, 197
CNAC, *see* CNAC and CATC
aircraft affair
CNAC and CATC aircraft affair,

76, 90, 151, 187–191,
195
Coates, P. D., 36
Cold War, 1, 7, 18–19, 26, 30, 34, 35,
45–6, 53, 54, 67, 131, 147, 164,
178, 182, 195, 196
and Korean War, 84–85, 91
effect on Sino-British relation, 84
Colonial Office
see under British government
(ministries and departments)
colonialism, 183
colonial power, 4
Comintern, 22, 24
Commercial Relations and Export
Department, British
see under British government
(ministries and departments),
Board of Trade
Commonwealth, 15, 31, 52, 53, 196
Commonwealth Countries' attitudes
towards recognition of
Communist China, 58–60
Commonwealth High Commis-
sioners' meeting 15 November
1949, 59
Commonwealth Relations Office,
British
see under British government
(ministries and departments)
Conservative Party, 42–45, 113
see also British government
(Conservative)
Coulson, J. E., 15
Creech-Jones, A., 176
Crimea Conference, 144
Crowe, Colin, 10, 90, 113–114,
120, 165
Cuba, 133
Cultural Revolution, 124, 190
Czechoslovakia, 145

Dalton, Huge, 42, 101
Daily Telegraph, 47
decision-making approach in foreign
policy studies, 2–3
see also under Britain, China policy,
policy formulation
de-colonization, 61

Democratic Party, U.S., 54
Defence, Ministry of, British
  see under British government
    (ministries and departments)
Dening, E., 12, 13, 35, 38, 57, 62, 96,
    137, 139, 175
  as Assistant Under-Secretary of
    State, 11
  as designated ambassador to
    China, 93
  as chairman of Far Eastern (Official)
    Committee, 13, 38
  attitude towards Chinese representa-
    tion in UN, 135
  attitude towards the establishment of
    People's Republic of China, 11,
    41, 53, 55, 206 n13
  disagreement with the Colonial
    Office: on Chinese Communist
    consuls in Malaya, 175,
    177–178; on recognition of
    Communist China, 41
  on Anglo-Chinese relation, 16–7
  recognition of Communist China,
    41, 55, 65
  relationship with Ernest Bevin, 11,
    55
  secret mission to China, 92–5, 140
Denmark, 142
  diplomatic relation with PRC, 77
Dong Biwu, 21, 144, 145
Donovan, General, 188
Douglas, Lewis, 55, 57, 88
Dumbarton Oaks Conference, 144
Dumouriez, 3
Dutch, 179
  in Indonesia, 61

East Berlin, 161
East Germany, 145
Eckstein, Alexander, 25
Economics Intelligence Unit, British
  see under British government
    (ministries and departments),
    Foreign Office
Economics Relations Department,
    British
  see under British govern-
    ment (ministries and

departments), Foreign
  Office
Ecuador, 133
Eden, Anthony, 8, 18, 166
  and the Conservative government's
    China policy, 112
  and the establishment of official
    diplomatic relations with the
    PRC, 120–124
  dinner meeting with Zhou Enlai in
    Geneva (1954), 121
  on Chinese representation in the UN,
    113, 142
  on recognition of Communist China,
    81, 143
  on total embargo against China, 115
  relationship with Ernest Bevin, 10
Egypt, 133
Extra-Territoriality in China, 7

Far Eastern Department, British
    Foreign Office
  see under British government,
    (ministries and departments),
    Foreign Office
Far Eastern (Official) Committee,
    British government
  see under British government
    (committees)
Federation of British Industries (FBI),
    164, 165, 166
Fitzmaurice, G. G., 223 n37
Financial Times, 167
Ford, Joe, 113–114, 120, 121, 166
Foreign Affairs, Ministry of, PRC
  see under Chinese Government
    (PRC)
foreign policy policy formulation and
    implementation, 196–198
  see also interest groups, business
    lobby, party politics, public
    opinion
  see also under Britain, China policy,
    policy formulation
France 32, 53, 60
  and Chinese representative in UN,
    77, 133–134, 136
  attitudes towards the recognition of
    Communist China, 61–2

Franklin, Andrew, 80–81, 219 n51
Franks, Sir Oliver, 57, 99–100, 137
French Revolution, 3

Gaitskell, Hugh, 106
Ganger-Taylor, B, 212 n24
Gao Gang, 21
general election (1950), British, 75
George VI, King, 1
Geneva, 24, 118, 143
Geneva Conference, 98
    and Anglo-Chinese relations,
        117–124, 165–166
Germany
    see also East Germany, 21, 24, 45
Gillett, Michael, 113
Gimson, Sir Frankly, 40, 174, 177,
    179–180
Gittings, John, 63
Glasgow Herald, 47
Graham, Walter, 73, 109
Grantham, Sir Alexander, 35, 41, 189
Griffiths, James, 176
Grew, Joseph, 209 n62
Guangzhou 32, 63, 90
Guilin, 23
Gurney, Sir Henry, 172–174, 176,
    177, 183

Hall-Patch, Edmund, 15
Halmilton, Lieut. Colonel, 213 n42
Halperin, Morton, 37
Harding, John, 174, 176
Harvey, Air Commodore, 78
Hayter, W. Sir, 225 n73
Henderson, Loy, 92
Hickerson, John, 132
Hill, Christopoher J., 2, 196
Ho Chi Minh, 175
Holmer, P. C., 140–141
Hong Kong, 16, 23, 32, 39–40, 41, 44,
    81, 82, 85, 86, 92, 93, 94, 160,
    161, 180, 190–191
    and the Korean War, 89, 170, 176
    Colonial Secretary of Hong Kong,
        185–186
    in Anglo-Chinese relations: Britain's
        position in 1949, 184–185;
        Chinese Communist attitude
    towards, 185–186; the CNAC
        and CATC affair in, 187–190
Hong Kong and Shanghai Banking
    Corporation, 49
House of Commons, British
    see under British Parliament
Huan Xiang, 24, 74, 75, 120, 121–122
Huangpu Military Academy, 22
Hungary, 145
Hurley, Patrick, 26
Hutchison, John, 73–75, 77, 78,
    80–81, 83, 89–91, 93, 94,
    99–100, 104, 108–109, 113,
    131–132, 134–35, 150, 151, 154,
    173, 175, 179, 181
Hudson, G. F., 18

imperialism, 4, 7, 8, 183
India, 53, 88, 92, 96, 133, 137, 143,
    179, 180
    attitude towards recognition of Com-
        munist China, 58–60, 72–73
    mediation in the Korean War,
        103–104
Indochina, 33, 61, 62, 86, 100, 118,
    133, 175
Indonesia, 179
industrial readjustment in China
    see under China (PRC), economic
        conditions
industrialisation in China
    see under China (PRC), economic
        conditions, industrial
        adjustment
interest groups and foreign policy, 52,
    148, 168–169
international system and international
    society, 4, 198, 200–201
Italy, 142
    attitude towards recognition of
        Communist China, 61
Iverchapel, Lord, 49

Japan, 13, 14, 21, 24, 27, 92, 94
Japanese Peace Treaty, 11, 154
Jardine, Matheson and Company, 49,
    50, 152, 157–158, 160
    see also under Keswick, W.,
        J., and T.

Jebb, G., 36, 105, 106, 137, 141
Jenkins, Roy, 100
Johnson, Charles, 161–162
Joint Chiefs of Staff, British
  see under British government
    (ministries and department)
Joint Intelligence Committee
  (JIG), British
  see under British government
    (committees)
Joint Planning Staff, British
  see under British government
    (ministries and departments),
    Ministry of Defence

Kaesong, 112
Kailan Mining Administration, 50
Kang Sheng, 21
Kang Youwei, 20
Keswick, W., 49
  see also Jardine Matheson
Keswick, J., 49, 149, 152, 157–158,
  160
  see also Jardine Matheson
Keswick, T., 160
  see also Jardine Matheson
Kim, Samuel, 143
Korean War, 72, 84–117
  additional measure against China,
    109–112
  and Anglo-American disagreement
    in the Far East, 87–89
  Anglo-Chinese relations after its
    outbreak, 89–91
  armistice 112–117
  branding of China as an aggressor,
    102–112
  Britain's buffer zone proposal,
    99–100
  Britain's initial reaction, 85–86
  British dilemma in the Korean War,
    101–02
  China's initial reaction, 86–87
  China's intervention, 98–102:
    impact on Anglo-Chinese
    relations, 115–117; initial
    British reaction, 98–100
  Israeli Resolution, 106
  peace negotiation: efforts for a

negotiated peace in Korea,
  102–5; peace initiative aborted,
  105–107
UN Cease-Fire Committee, 102, 106
UN embargo against China, 110,
  148, 154–156, 159, 163
US reaction 85–87, 100, 103,
  106–107
Kunming, 111
Kuomintang, 19, 25, 29, 49, 144, 145,
  185, 198
  activities in British Malaya, 171
  and Britian's relations with the PRC,
    73, 77, 186, 187–188
  British attitude towards, 17–18, 113
  organizations in Hong Kong,
    77, 186
  relations with the Soviet Union, 63
  relations with the US, 54
  representation in UN, 37, 75–77,
    80–81, 90, 129–143
  rivalry with the Chinese Commun-
    ists, 7, 8, 20, 21, 23, 26, 27, 32,
    35, 61, 86, 200
  Shanghai blockade, 36
  see also Chiang Kai-shek, Taiwan

Lamb, Leo, 109, 111, 113, 114, 116,
  156, 160–161, 164
Lanzhou Eighth Route Army
  Office, 24
Labour Party, British, 9, 42–45, 75
  see also under British government
    (Labour), *and also* British
    government (Conservative)
Lahore, 140
Lauterpacht, Sir Hersch, 193–194
League of Nations, 143
Leninism, *see* Marxist-Leninism
Lei Renmin, 120, 166–167
Lend-Lease Agreement, 14
Li Kenong, 23
Liang Qichao, 20, 21, 22
Liao Chengzhi, 23
Lin Baiqu, 21
Liu Ningyi, 91
Liu Shaoqi, 21, 22
Lloyd, Selwyn, 123
London Chamber of Commerce, 165

London Export Corporation, 161, 163
London School of Economics and
    Political Science, 24
Lowe, Peter, 7
Luxembourg, attitude towards recogni-
    tion of Communist China, 61

MacArthur, D., 97, 99, 100
Mackinder, H. Sir, 206 n24
Macmillan, Harold, 43
MacDonald, Malcolm, 40, 41, 173,
    174, 175–176, 180
Maclean, Fitzroy, 213 n42
Makins, Roger, 224 n59
Malaya, 32, 39–40, 41, 45, 82, 86,
    190–191
    and Britain's China policy 171–190
    and the Korean War, 89
    Chinese Advisory Committee,
        Malaya, 174
    Chinese Communist counsuls
        controversy, 172–179
    Chinese People's Relief Administra-
        tion, China (PRC), 182
    Chinese People's Relief Committee
        for the Overseas Chinese
        Refugees of Malaya, China,
        (PRC), 182
    importance to Britain, 171
    question of transit visas for Chinese
        Diplomats, 179–180
    repatriation of Chinese from, 107,
        181–182
    relation with PRC 171–183
    see also under Singapore and,
        Southeast Asia
Malaya Committee, British
    see under British government
        (committees)
Malayan Communist Party (MCP), 33,
    40, 170, 199
    relations with CCP, 182–184
Malik, Jacob, 112
Manchester Guardian, 18, 45, 46, 47,
    107, 142
Manchuria, 21, 32, 62, 63
Mao Tse-tung, *see* Mao Zedong
Mao Zedong, 18, 21, 22, 31, 75, 124
    conversion into Marxism, 20

on China's foreign policy, 27–29
on NATO, 63
on policy of 'leaning to one side',
    63, 200
on the United Nations Organization,
    144
on world order, 143
Marshall, General, 54
Marshall Plan (Aid), 45, 188
Marxism, 20
    see also Marxist-Leninism
Marxist-Leninism, 19, 29, 183
Medan, 179
Menon, Krishna, 59
McCarthy, 164
McCarthyism, 164, 195
McNeil, Hector, 51, 132
Mediterranean, 9
Middleditch, David, 50
Middle East, 9, 13, 14, 15, 142
Ministry of Defence, British
    see under British government
        (ministries and departments)
Ministry of Foreign Affairs, PRC
    see under Chinese government
        (PRC)
Ministry of Transport, British
    see under British government
        (ministries and departments)
Military Assistance Programme,
    US, 188
Morrison, Herbert, 43, 110, 111, 142
Moscow Economic Conference (1952),
    159–162
Mountbatten, Lord, 11
Mukden, *see* Shenyang

Nanjing, 32, 34, 35, 43, 63, 73,
    111, 113
National People's Congress (Septem-
    ber 1954), PRC
    see under Chinese government
        (PRC)
NATO, 45, 63, 164
Nehru, Jawaharlal, 59
    attitude towards Communist
        China, 58
    attitude towards China's
        conditions for peace

negotiation in the Korean
War, 103
attitude towards Chinese representa-
tion in UN, 137–138
Netherlands, 60
see also Dutch
New China News Agency, Xinhua
(NCNA), 63, 73, 74, 81, 91, 131,
182, 186
New York, 94, 99, 132, 138, 141
New Zealand, attitude towards recogni-
tion of Communist China, 59–60
News Chronicle, the, 45
Nicholas H. G., 194
Nie Rongzhen, 98
North Atlantic Alliance, *see* NATO
North Atlantic Pact, *see* NATO
North Atlantic Treaty Organization,
see NATO
Norway, 74, 133
nuclear weapons, 100–101

Oakeshott, Keith, 36, 50, 223 n50
Observer, 47
O'Donovan, Patrick, 47
Ogburn, Carlton, 215 n83
Opposition in British Parliament, *see*
British Parliament
Oversaes Chinese in Southeast Asia,
40, 170
see also under Malaya, Singapore,
Southeast Asia
Overseas Financial Division, British
see under British government
(ministries and departments),
Treasury

Pakistan, attitude towards recognition
of Communist China, 59–60
Pan American Airways, 187
Pandit, Vijaya Lakshmi, 58–59
Panmunjom, 112
Pannikar, K. M., 98, 138, 154
Paton, Michael, 92
Pearson, Lester, 103, 105
Peng Dehuai, 21
Peng Zhen, 21, 99, 186
People's Association for Friendship
with Foreign Countries, (PRC)

see under Chinese government
(PRC)
People's China, 82, 182
People's Daily, 63, 82, 110, 114
Perkins, Troy L., 215 n83
Pingshan, Chinese Communist Party
Central Committee meeting, 28
Portugal, attitude towards recognition
of Communist China, 61
Platts-Mills, John, 43
Public-Private Relation Mediation
Committee, Tianjin
see under Chinese government
(PRC)
pressure groups *see* interest groups
public opinion and foreign policy, 48
see also British press

Qiao Guanhua, *also* Qiao Mu, 23,
24, 186
Qinghua University, 23, 24

Rau, B. N., 105
Radio Beijing, 63
Reading, Lord, 116
Red Army (Chinese People's
Liberation Army), 21, 93
Red Cross Society of China, 182
Red Sea, 9
Ren Bishi, 21
Republican Party, U.S., 54
Reuter, 186
revolutions and international relations,
1–2, 3–4, 198–201
see also under China (PRC),
revolutionary diplomacy
Roosevelt, F., 26
Rothwell, Victor, 193
Rusk, Dean, 107, 136
Russia, see Soviet Union

Salisbury, Marquess of, 113
San Franciso, 144, 145
San Franciso Conference (1945), 21,
24, 144
Sargent, Orme, 8
Schuman Robert, 61
Scandinanvian countries, 60–61
see also Demark, Norway, Sweden

Scarlett, Peter, 34–35, 41, 51, 62
Scotsman, 45
Scott, Robert, 12, 116
  on Anglo-American relations and the China question, 100
  on British policy of recognition and negotiations, 114–115
  on China policy, 12, 109
  on Esler Dening's secret mission to China, 94
  on Korean War and Chinese representation in the UN, 139, 141, 173
  relationship with Ernest Bevin, 12
Second World War, 1, 7, 21, 26, 33, 38, 54
Seventh Fleet, US, 85, 86, 200
Seymour, Sir Horace, 17, 49
Shanghai, 35–36, 37, 49, 50, 51, 52, 83, 91, 108, 111, 121, 149–151, 152–153, 155, 160, 161
Shanghai Chamber of Commerce, British
  see British Chamber of Commerce, Shanghai
Shanghai, Kuomintang blockade, 36, 50, 51, 78–79, 149
Shantou, 181
Shattock, John T. H., 77
Shawcross, Hartley, 189
Shenyang, 32, 34, 108
Shenyang School, 20
Shijie Zhishi, 81–82, 159
Shinwell, E., 177
Shlaim, Jones, 2
Shone, T., 137
Short, Anthony, 183
Siam, 33
  see also Thailand
Simon Commission on India, 9
Singapore
  British colonial interests in, 170–172
  British Ministry of Information (Singapore branch), 11
  Bukit Serene Conference, 65
  Chinese in Singapore, 40
  transit visas for Chinese diplomats, 179–180, 190

  see also under Malaya, Southeast Asia
Sino-Afghan Treaty of Friendship and Non-Aggression, 145
Sino-British trade, 17, 157–168
  the Moscow Economic Conference, 159–162
  dilemma of Britain's China trade policy, 163–165
  turning point in Sino-British trade relations, 165–168
  see also under Britain, British commercial interest in China
Sino-British Trade Committee, 167
Sino-Soviet Treaty of Friendship, Alliance and Mutal Assistance, 145
Slessor, Marshal Sir John, 98
Snow, Edgar, 20
Snyder, R. C., 196
Southeast Asia, 32–33, 39–40, 45, 119, 133
  British Colonial Interest in
  see under Britain
  see also under Indo-china, Indonesia, Malaya, Singapore, Vietnam
South-East Asia Commissioner-General, 174
  see also Malcolm MacDonald
Southeast Asian Department, British
  see under British government (ministries and departments), Foreign Office
Soviet Communist Party, 26
Soviet Union, 9, 12, 14–15, 17, 18, 21, 22, 24, 29, 32, 37, 46, 54, 137, 138, 141, 193
  and Chinese representation in UN, 129, 133, 135, 140
  relation with Communist China, 62–4, 75–76
  trade relation with China (People's Republic), 159, 169
Stalin, J., 21, 29, 63
Stanton, Edwin, 220 n75
State Department, United States
  see under United States
Sterndale-Bennett, J. C., 15
Stevenson, Sir Ralph, 16, 35, 54, 65

Strang, Sir William, 8, 10, 36, 40, 51, 82, 85, 92, 93, 135
Stuart, Leighton, 55
Sumatra, 179
Sun Yat-sen University, the Soviet Union, 21, 62
Sweden, diplomatic relation with PRC, 77

Taiwan, 26, 73, 76, 86, 87, 88, 89, 99, 101, 105, 107, 113, 145, 152, 200
see also Kuomintang, Taiwan
Taiwan Strait, 85, 86, 200
Tamsui, 73
Tenant, Peter, 166
Thailand, 140
see also Siam
Thorne, C., 17
Tianjin, 32, 34, 35, 50, 151
Tibet, 26, 93, 100
Times, 18, 46, 47–48, 105, 107, 142, 161, 193
'Titoism' in China, 29, 217 n105
Tihwa, 108
Tokyo, 94
Transport, Ministry of, British
see under British government (ministries and departments)
Treasury, British
see under British government (ministries and departments)
Trevelyan, Humphery, 116, 119–120, 121–122, 123, 166–67
Tribune, 91
Trotsky, Leon, 3, 199
Truman, Harry S., 55, 87, 136, 200
on the recognition of Communist China, 56–77
on Korean War, 85
Truman-Attlee talks, 100–101
Trevelyan, Humphrey, 116–117
Tsang, Steve Yui-sang, 185
Tubingen University, 24

United Nations
United Nations Conference on International Organization in San Fransisco, *see* San Fransisco Conference
and the Korea War: branding of China as an aggressor, 106–107; embargo against China, 109–110; United Nations Additional Measures Committee, 110; United Nations Cease-Fire Committee, 102–103, 106; United Nations Good Offices Committee, 110, 141; United Nations Political Committee, 102, 105; United Nations Security Council 85–86
Chinese representation in: United Nations International Children Fund, 82–3, 85, 133, 135–136, 140; United Nations Economic Commission for Asia and the Far East (ECAFE), 133, 140; United Nations Economic and Social Council (ECOSOC), 83, 135, 136–137, 139, 142; United Nations Food and Agricultural Organization (FAO), 140; United Nations General Assembly, 37, 57, 59, 76, 90, 96, 102, 113, 138, 139, 140, 145, 162, 194; United Nations Security Council, 36, 37, 74, 75–76, 83, 88, 131–134, 137, 138, 142; United Nations Trusteeship Council, 140, 142
United States:
army observer section in Yan'an, 26
attitude towards Chinese civil war 54
attitude towards Chinese representation in UN, 77, 132, 136
attitude towards Britain's recognition of Communist China, 55–58
Central Intelligence Agency, 98
China policy and domestic politics, 54
on recognition of the Chinese Communist government, 53–8
relations with Britain, *see* Anglo-American relations

State Department, 27, 55–56, 57, 136–137, 142, 188
Urumuqi *see* Tihwa
Urquhart, Sir Robert, 152
USSR *see* Soviet Union

Vansittart, Lord, 224 n55
Vietminh, 119
Vietnam, 618
Vincent, John Carter, 209 n62

Wallace, William, 178
Wang Bingnan, 23
Wang Ming, 21
Wang Renshu, also Wong Yan-seok, 179–180
Wang Jiaxiang, 23
Waseda University, 24
Watson, Adam, 200
Watt, D. C., 7
Western Europe, and the recognition of Communist China, 60–62
   see also under Beligium, Denmark, France, Luxembourg, the Netherlands, Norway, Sweden
Whitehall, 38–42, 45, 171
   see also under British government (ministries and departments)
Wilford, Michael, 92
Willauer, Whiting, 187
Wilson, Dick, 22
Wong yan-seok, *see* Wang Renshu
World War II *see* Second World War
Wrong, Hume, 107
Wu Xiuquan, 24, 145, 210 n73

Xiamen, 111
Xinhua *see* New China News Agency
Xin Jianshe, 158
Xinjiang, 108

Yan'an, 18, 24, 26, 27
Yalta Agreement, 63
Yalu River, 94, 99, 100, 114, 139
Yangtze Incident, see Amethyst Incident
Yangtze River, 16, 43, 63
Yao Chongming, *see* Yao Zhongming
Yao Zhongming, 180
Ye Jichuang, 158
Yee Tsoong Tobacco
   see also British-American Tobacco, 156
Younger, Kenneth, 11, 43, 48, 78–79, 85, 87, 88, 92–3, 101, 134, 141, 135, 140, 176, 189
Youth, 20
Yugoslavia, 64, 133

Zhang Hanfu, 23–24, 75, 77, 99, 104, 108, 109, 116, 119–120, 144
Zhang Wentian, 21
Zhangsha Normal School, 20
Zhou Gengseng, 24, 144, 209 n56
Zhou Enlai, 21–22, 27, 28, 56, 59, 75, 94, 95, 143
   and the Geneva Conference (1954), 120–121, 124
   as Foreign Minister, 20–23, 25
   mid-night meeting with K. M. Pannikar, 98
   on China's relations with Western countries, 28, 37, 86
   on Chinese representation in UN, 90, 102–103, 138–139
   on foreign nationals in China, 154
   on Korean War peace negotiations, 102–103
   on US Seventh Fleet's stationing in the Taiwan Strait, 86
Zhu De, 21, 22
Zilliacus, Konni, 43